Jac the Clown

Hjalmar Bergman

Jac the Clown

Translated by
Hanna Kalter Weiss

CAMDEN HOUSE

Published by Camden House, Inc.
Drawer 2025
Columbia, SC 29202 USA

Printed on acid-free paper.
Binding materials are chosen for strength and
durability.

ISBN: 1–57113–041–1

Library of Congress Cataloging-in-Publication Data

Bergman, Hjalmar, 1883–1931.
  [Clownen Jac. English]
  Jac the Clown / Hjalmar Bergman ; translated by Hanna Kalter Weiss.
      p.   cm. -- (Studies in Scandinavian literature and culture)
  ISBN 1–57113–041–1 (alk. paper)
  I. Weiss, Hanna Kalter, 1922--   . II. Title. III. Series:
Studies in Scandinavian literature and culture (Unnumbered)
PT9875.B53C5813 1996
839.73'72 -- dc20   95–43117
                                                          CIP

Contents

Acknowledgments

The idea to translate Hjalmar Bergman's *Clownen Jac* first occurred to me during one of the several interviews I conducted in 1989 with Lars Ahlin, whose novel *Kanelbiten* I was then translating under a Fulbright Grant. Lars Ahlin told me how much the work of Hjalmar Bergman had influenced him in his own writings. I gathered a great deal of information on Hjalmar Bergman at the time, but had to wait for a second research trip granted by The Swedish Institute in 1992 to complete this research.

I wish to thank Marna Feldt of The Swedish Information Service in the United States and Gunilla Forsén and Helen Sigeland of The Swedish Institute in Stockholm for their dedicated support and invaluable advice throughout this project. They enabled me write the introduction to this translation and to bring this project to a successful conclusion.

I also want to express my appreciation to all the people at the Royal Library in Stockholm for their kind help and to Albert Bonniers AB for letting me use the necessary manuscripts in their Archives during the summer of 1992.

Last but not least, an appreciative thank you to Professor Robert E. Bjorck who patiently read my manuscript as editor for Camden House's Scandinavian series and suggested the unavoidable improvements.

This list would not be complete without mentioning gratefully the Writer's Union in Stockholm for providing a congenial home away from home during my stay in Stockholm.

Hanna Kalter Weiss
September 1995

Introduction:
The Prodigal Son Who Couldn't
Go Home Again.

HERE FOR THE first time in English translation is the scandalous, explosive story of Jac the Clown, alias Hjalmar Bergman, the towering figure in Swedish literature and one of the most influential, prolific playwrights and authors of the twentieth century in Sweden and beyond. As the title indicates, the novel tells the story of Jac, an early representative of this century's great social outsiders in literature. Unable to make contact with his fellow humans, Jac feels doomed to be their lackey, a clown serving a world of clowns. He has become famous and fabulously wealthy entertaining a public he considers childish, intellectually immature, extremely shallow, volatile, and easily goaded to mob violence by crooked, selfish, money-hungry business leaders. Earning his living with slapstick that exposes his personal terror, Jac is at odds with himself. He feels contempt for his audience and disgust with himself for catering to cheap common taste. At the same time, he is extremely proud of his art, thinking that his unique talent is never properly recognized under the hype of the mass media, much less appreciated for what he considers the right reasons. Underneath all this angry cynicism he hides his great character flaw: he loathes himself. He cannot love either himself, or those close to him. His personal relationships fail. Torn between love and hate, he remains aloof, alone — a clown.

An early "psychological" novel with a prophetic message, *Jac the Clown* baffled most literary critics at a time when writers were mainly preoccupied with the socioeconomic concerns between the two world wars. Written in 1929, the novel reflects, but does not mention the economic rumblings of a worldwide depression and the dictatorships forming on the European continent with their wild, threatening noises of hate and war. The setting of many scenes in the novel is often strange, bizarre, surreal, almost like the mythical "magic realism" of a much later time. Bergman stunned his readers, preoccupied with their local politics, with his story comparing two worlds — the peaceful, landed economy of an ideal, strongly religious, agrarian past with the hateful, money-oriented business economy of a world in the making. Nostalgically he remembered an idealized rural farm life in Sweden while decrying the self-serving corporate executives in the United States. He sounded like a preacher lashing out at the world with his "clown catechism," which he himself declared to be the crucial part of the novel. Recognition of the novel's greatness, of what it had to say and its prophetic vision, came only slowly. Today it is a classic in Scandinavian literature.

Novelist, playwright and short story writer Hjalmar Elgérus Bergman was born September 19, 1883 in Örebro, a busy lumbering and mining town in central Sweden. His father Claes Bergman, a wealthy local banker, expected his only son to follow him in the banking business. Much to his dismay, the young Hjalmar never showed any interest for the business world. There developed considerable friction between the domineering father and his son. Claes considered the obese, rather clumsy, introverted boy mentally deficient and was not above ridiculing him, often in public.[1] An authoritarian school environment compounded Hjalmar's emotional distress, and taunting peers did not make things easier. Bergman grew up shy and extremely self-conscious. Permanently scarred, he never overcame his feelings of inferiority, his basic distrust of others, and his fear of the unpredictability of human existence. It can be argued that Bergman's traumatic childhood experiences contributed to, perhaps even caused, his ambivalent sexual identity. Whatever the underlying reasons, his complex feelings in an openly critical society which only accepted what it considered the norm must be considered in analyzing and evaluating his writings.

Claes Bergman liked to take his son along on business trips through the countryside. His motives were obvious. He wanted Hjalmar to learn "the business." But his plan backfired. What the young Bergman learned was to love the folklore and the legends of his native Bergslagen and make them his own. He later proved to have been a keen, highly perceptive observer of the people he met. They live on in his stories against the background of his native province of Bergslagen. They became the vivid characters in his plots, whose subject matter dealt with their life style, their everyday affairs, their loves and their hates, their likes and dislikes, their idiosyncrasies and their hypocrisies. Though speaking to local concerns, Bergman presented his motley humanity with brutal honesty. The universal veracity of his characters made Hjalmar Bergman the great writer he came to be.

A loner already as a young student, he consciously isolated himself to protect his integrity.[2] Privately tutored at home, Bergman matriculated by special exam in 1900. He enrolled subsequently at Uppsala University. Apparently he never intended to finish his formal studies. He wanted to become a writer. After a year he left Uppsala to begin a life of constant travel all over Europe. In 1908 he married Stina, the daughter of actor and theater producer August Lindberg. A complicated and unhappy union, the marriage heightened rather than lessened Bergman's anxieties. Stina became his love-hate object in his rebellion against authority while he grappled with his homosexuality. His love of young boys and his long, open relationship to

Werner Fütterer, a 14-year old German schoolboy when they first met in 1922, did nothing to improve this marriage.

Childless, the couple continued their travels, partly to escape the harsh northern winters, partly because Bergman had something of the vagabond in him. They visited Austria, France and Switzerland, but preferred Germany and outright loved Italy. Florence became Bergman's declared favorite city and they spent many winters there. In 1917 they bought their estate Segelholmen in the Stockholm archipelago where they spent the summer months from then on. It provided some kind of fixed resting point in their unsteady lives. It also brought him closer to his fellow writers and literary critics in Sweden.

Following a recommendation of Bergman's friend Victor Sjöberg, Goldwyn engaged Bergman as a script writer to Hollywood in 1923. Bergman accepted with high hopes. The couple spent Christmas of 1923 and the winter months of 1924 in the United States. They rented a bungalow in Santa Monica, bought a car and went on sightseeing trips in the colorful California countryside.

The move was a culture shock. It did not take long for Hjalmar Bergman to develop an overriding dislike for the United States. The vast, vibrant country in the West, its climate and most of all its multinational, multiracial people and their emerging culture appalled him. The tradition bound, cultured European from provincial central Sweden found their habits, their opinions, their food and above all their business practices unfamiliar, strange, outright deceptive and loathsome. He longed for Italy, a country that he knew and loved. In a letter from California dated December 22 [1923?] Stina confessed to Tor Bonnier, "We have come such a long way, but gained nothing. Hjalmar dislikes it here something terrible and would like to return immediately . . . . It's real summer during the day, but cold at night. Divinely beautiful, but banal."[3]

Bergman's disappointment came to a head when Metro and Mayer bought into the Goldwyn company and changed their contract. The couple returned to Europe after only three months. His retrospective novel *Clownen Jac* (1930) became a biting testimony to Bergman's negative feelings on the United States, its people and their habits.

Written in 1929 as a radio series, *Clownen Jac* was the last work Hjalmar Bergman produced. Six weeks after its publication he was dead. Erik Hjalmar Linder described the tragic details.

Bergman's euphoria after having finished the novel did not last long. His dissolution, brought on primarily by his uncontrollable addiction to alcohol, worsened steadily. He appeared drunk in public. His speech became slurry, unclear. Consequently, his decision to read the last two chapters himself at their radio premiere shocked everyone who knew him. Per Lindberg and others tried hard to dissuade him. But Bergman stubbornly insisted, because " . . . they are the book's most important chapters. The audience needs to hear and understand it [the clown's catechism]."[4]

To everyone's surprise, Bergman pulled himself together for the performance. That night behind the microphone he was the great clown once again. Even Stina called afterward to congratulate him. Then reaction set in and his health went downhill.

It was an open secret that Hjalmar Bergman was an alcoholic. Stina Bergman fought a lifelong, hard but losing battle against his addiction. By the time of the reading they were living separately because Bergman had decided to travel again. Stina refused to come along. In the end he literally drank himself to death. He died, alone, on a stopover in Berlin on his way to Italy, of a ruptured aneurysm (blodstockning i hjärnan, varigenom en åder sprängdes)[5] on January 1, 1931. He was 47 years old.

Hjalmar Bergman began his writing career when he was still a young boy and he never stopped writing until his untimely death in 1931. In writing he found detachment, solitude and perhaps even some kind of awkward inner peace because it offered him a ready outlet for his suppressed feelings of humiliation and his inner turmoil. Writing gave meaning to his life, a sense of private importance that helped him to survive. It provided a longed-for catharsis, however temporary. Unfortunately, it could not reverse his self-destructive behavior, above all his addiction to alcohol.

No one ever questioned the greatness of Hjalmar Bergman, the writer, although opinions about him vary. He has often been labeled a Realist with a preference for *fin de siècle* themes of decadence; others saw him as a Freudian; a Symbolist; even a fundamental Expressionist. In fact he may have drawn from all these movements in the course of his writing career. But in the final analysis, he relied on his own intuition. His idea of the writer's task was to synthesize the writer's own experiences in the characters he created and the world who shaped them. He believed that the readers "interpret and conquer what the artist has offered them in his work, the atmosphere that shaped it."[6] He was his own person who developed his singular characters. Brutally honest in the process, he endowed them with universal dimensions. Then he presented them with his distinctly "Bergmanian irony," a black humor obviously designed to shock the reader into recognizing his and his societies incongruities.

Bergman focused on the psychological hang-ups of his characters — especially the tensions arising from their moral, mostly puritanical upbringing as opposed to their secret, suppressed longings. With the objectivity of the disinterested, aloof outsider, he recorded the individual's inward struggle with himself, his society, his God, his Fate. Adding to his greatness as a writer was his ability to present the most disturbing topics with an ironic twist, a ridiculing sarcasm that often exceeds the limits of the amiable. According to Frederick Böök, "there is a strange atmosphere of coldness [in his work]. His drastic humor is hard, almost heartless, his high spirits have a touch of cruelty."[7] Never good-natured, Bergman was irritatingly, even brutishly honest in his stubborn pursuit of psychological truth, exposing ruthlessness, pretense, hypocrisy, idiosyncrasy and sexual deviations. In short, he ran the gamut of human shortcomings, including his own. In personal relationships as well as in business affairs he was without regard for public reaction. Like his clown, he "doesn't care what they think."[8]

Bergman admired Dostoyevsky whose work admittedly influenced him greatly. Like the great Russian novelist, he was preoccupied with man's two-faceted soul. Like him, Bergman questioned his society's religious world view without really abandoning it. It may be just a coincidence that, like Dostoyevsky, Bergman himself provided a good case study of morbid pathology.

There is a striking parallel to William Faulkner as well. Both writers described a stagnant, close-minded, naively fundamentalist wealthy upper middle class. Trying to preserve the status quo, it held stubbornly on to inherited mores because it rightly feared the sociopolitical changes rumbling underneath the outer pastoral calm of their world, a transformation that would eventually disinherit them both. Both Oxford in Mississippi and Örebro in Bergslagen were rural places in the early stages of industrial development at the turn of this century. Jefferson in Yoknapatawpha and Wadköping in Bergslagen, the Sartorises and the Snopeses, the Markurells and the Borck clan are all of a kind. Culturally, however, these two writers confronted different issues. Faulkner faced the race problem in a stagnant, backward society while Bergman took issue with the old statare system, which paid the farmhand in kind, and an ancient aristocracy unwilling to give up inherited privileges and come to terms with a changing everyday reality.

On a different level, Bergman's battle against an outdated authoritarian system may be compared to the rebellion of his contemporary Franz Kafka. He may never have met the Jew from Prague, nor is it likely that he read his German writings, most of which were published after their deaths. But there is a strange similarity between these two great European "bourgeois outsiders." Both had problems with their patriarchal, domineering fathers. Both were trying to make sense of a society not of their making, but of which they were, reluctantly and resentfully, a part. Kafka metamorphosed his Gregor Samsa into a disgusting insect that needed to be swept out with the garbage. Bergman featured a bizarre clown with many masks trying to cope with the same hostile, selfish, absurd society.

Bergman's greatest plays are still part of today's repertoire, especially in Scandinavia. Many have been made into movies over the years. Much of his work has been translated into English. *Markurells i Wadköping* (1919), translated as *God's Orchid* (1923), describes a ruthless financier consumed with love for a son he learns is not his child. *Herr von Hancken* (1920) is a farcical pastiche of a vainglorious aging hero, eventually stripped of his pretensions. *Farmor och vår herre* (1921), translated as *Thy Rod and Thy Staff* (1937) is about a domineering matriarch forced to review her behavior, her outlook and her actions in the course of which she learns humility. *Chefen fru Ingeborg* (1924), translated as *The Head of the Firm* (1936), deals with a young man's infatuation with his future mother-in-law who destroys him in the end. *Swedenhielms* (1925, The Swedenhielm Family) is a biting comedy about a fictitious Swedish Nobel Prize winner and his family. *Patrasket* (1928, The Rabble) is a tragicomedy, strangely pre-Holocaust, about a Jewish family fleeing the pogroms in Eastern Europe and trying to build a new life with the help of embarrassed relatives in Germany. His last work was *Clownen Jac* (1930). The novel focuses on a man, a loner, driven by fears he cannot control and an inability to give or receive love. Introduced as a radio series with the participation of the author, it is considered Bergman's "most modern novel."[9] It is certainly his most Kafkaesque and surreal work, both in setting and theme.[10]

Per Lindberg, Erik Hjalmar Linder and many other commentators have at length discussed the background and setting that led to the creation of Jac The Clown. According to Per Lindberg, Jonathan Borck "was born along with *Farmor och vår Herre* (Grandma And Our Lord) in the fall of 1921," and he [Bergman] decided to let the "problem child" return as the servant's son in his novel.[11] Hans Levander traced the clown to the sad hotel guest Borck, a man unable to laugh in private life, in the short story "Den andre" (The Other) in 1928.[12] Erik Hjalmar Linder pointed to Bergman's great interest in early films by Charlie Chaplin, Buster Keaton and Harold Lloyd as another inspiration. Like these clowning artists, Bergman's clown Jac Tracbac was a circus and movie artist featuring comically disastrous experiences in an absurd world, often using terror to make people laugh. There were striking parallels between scenes in Charlie Chaplin's movie *Circus* (1928) and scenes in Bergman's novel, such as the terror-stricken clown's reactions to the apes and their antics, to the disastrous trapeze acts and to the noisy banality of fireworks.[13] Bergman was known to have seen all the Chaplin movies. The physical description of the small, slim, nervous Borck/Tracbac was an exact description of the famous movie clown in Hollywood.

Yet another clown contributed to the shaping of Jac Tracbac. Bergman dedicated the novel to Gösta Ekman, who portrayed many of Bergman's characters on stage. Ekman played the lead in the Danish film *Klovnen* (The

Clown) in 1926 and Bergman visited him in the Copenhagen studio during the production.

Bergman had planned to write a biographical novel for several years. But the real impetus for *Clownen Jac* came from Sven Jerring during a walk with Bergman through Hagaparken in Stockholm in 1929. Jerring suggested a radio series of 24 chapters, each 45 minutes long, about the clown.[14]

The idea of the clown as the entertainer with the bleeding heart was hardly a novel idea. Universally recognized as the symbol of the double-faced man, the clown can be traced back to the early Middle Ages with their wayfaring entertainers who became the forerunners of both circus and opera artists. These clowns' most famous descendants still appear on stage as barbers in Rossini's and Mozart's operas. Traveling on the European continent at the turn of the century, Bergman may have seen them in Picasso's series of Harlequins, or in modern versions as the masked men in James Ensor's painting "Intrigue," or in Munch's "Skriket" ("The Scream"). The idea of the human mask-masked human permeated all the arts at the turn of the century and thereafter. Expressionists like Emil Nolde, Oskar Kokoschka, Max Beckmann, George Grosz and many others were fascinated with man's double-faced nature and he returns time and again in their paintings and caricatures. Their contemporary Bergman's clown was a child of the time. In Bergman's case, he is the Puritan Nathan Borck hiding under the mask of clown Jac Tracbac. Bergman himself hid under the mask of both.

The clown figure as a two-faced man had preoccupied Bergman all along. He used the harlequin in *Arlecchino's Dream* and *Death's Harlequin*.[15] Returning to him in *Clownen Jac*, he mentioned Leoncavallo's clown, obviously as a model for his own. Like the Surrealists after the First World War, Bergman transposed his personal rebellion against authority to his protagonist. Like his creator, the clown remained very much the bourgeois in outlook and behavior. Sverker Ek saw Bergman as a slave to his own fantasy, " . . . a witch doctor who conjures up an entire phantasmagoria . . . as if he had no control over his own creatures," a practice "showing his personal deficiency."[16] In an undated letter to Tor Bonnier, Bergman himself explained his double nature, " . . . the boy [Werner Fütterer?] is soon going to leave, presumably for a month. I'm not worried. On the contrary. The entire business is but one step toward absolute loneliness. If I ever can be lonely. I am two. And, Tor, let me tell you that I am never as happy as when I enter an empty apartment, or walk on an empty street, or 'have a dialogue.' Just the two of us. After all, there's no one else who understands what we are mumbling [about]."[17] It is significant to note that before his death Bergman left a manuscript on Per Lindberg's desk. It was for a new radio comedy. Its title: "Bakom masker" (Behind Masks).[18] It can safely be argued that, trying to come to grips with the meaning of life in general and his own in particular, Bergman consciously used Nathan Borck/Jac Tracbac, the man with the mask, as the representative of his own dichotomy.

From the beginning Bergman's work was confessional in nature, and his last novel must be seen as a recapitulation of his own life. As early as May 16, 1925, five years before his death, Bergman wrote to Tor Bonnier, " . . . I have started a new department in my literary production. I count on about ten more years (I might be wrong here) and I intend to use these to find out and describe what is important in life."[19] *Clownen Jac* became his final showdown with his upbringing, with his family, with Wadköping/Örebro, with the world around him, but above all with himself. *Clownen Jac* is "Clownen Jag," which translates to, "I, the Clown." Likewise, 'Tracbac" means "tracing back." The clown is backtracking his life. He is raised by his grandmother on the Swedish estate Sanna, meaning "true" or "truth." Throughout the novel Bergman puns with the words *sann* (true), *sanning* (truth), and *sannerligen* (indeed). That the estate is later bought by Jac's cousin Lillemor and her Pietist husband, who farms on Sanna, gives rise to various interesting interpretations, as does naming the "illicit" daughter between Nathan/Jac and Lillemor Sanna Sanna, and the complications arising from the layered discoveries of the truth about the clown. Born in Sweden as Jonathan Borck, the clown becomes Tracbac, the famous clown in the United States. Tracbac alias Nathan Borck alias Hjalmar Bergman — Nathan Borck/Jac Tracbac — an assumed name after his dead partner at that — stands for the author, and the clown's experiences approximate his own. The novel provided the author with a forum for expounding Borck/Tracbac /Bergman's philosophy and views on life. It served him as an outstanding device for further puns of all kinds as he told his audience a few "truths" about themselves as he saw it.

"We live with our memory" and "through our memory" he began his novel, marking it clearly a memoir. Karin Petherick argued Bergman's posturing, his hiding a deep hurt underneath his mask, calling it Bergman's "clown syndrome."[20] Through Tracbac, Bergman declares in his catechism, "We are all clowns. We don our sly masks and pronounce untruths, cherished lies that turn to gold when people discover that they've been had. It gives them a chance to feel good because they've outsmarted the other fellow."[21] A rather sarcastic view on human nature, to be sure, but Hjalmar Bergman never pretended to be a lover of mankind. Still, Tracbac needs to function in this world of clowns. Thus Hjalmar Bergman alias Nathan Borck/Jac Tracbac disguises his misanthropic feelings behind the jovial funnymaker's mask of the clown who finally dares to tell his fellow humans what he thinks of them and their absurd, clownish behavior.

Young Benjamin/Benbé Borck is yet another, younger Bergman/Nathan clone. Benjamin's mother, a straight-laced, stern Pietist, was a younger edition of Grandma. The description of Benjamin/Benbé's family fits their common ancestors. They were born into a family of "strict Pietists, notorious for mauling their fellow humans to shreds with their pike-like jaws."[22] Only Benjamin was luckier and fate dealt much kinder with him than with his uncle. He is no bastard. He inherited no sickly afflictions. He developed no kleptomaniac tendencies and is not prone to repeat the old grandfather's mistakes. Sly, crafty and inventive like his uncle, he has additionally the good fortune to get help from his family. Eventually he lands a suitable, bourgeois job. Instead of teaming up with a lowly gypsy, healthy Benbé has the good sense to marry a healthy, bourgeois Borck girl. He may remain part of the clan and plant healthy offshoots on modern soil. Benjamin/Benbé is the person Hjalmar Bergman/Nathan Borck would have liked to have been — if fate had let him.

In contrast, Nathan needed to fight fate from the very start. His mother's lowly status might not have been too much of a burden if she had played her cards right. After all, Grandma started as a servant in the Borck household. But Grandma was a strong-willed, full-blooded native peasant, shrewd enough to become Mrs. Borck before bearing her children. She managed not only to rule the clan with an iron fist, but also prevented others from pushing her aside. She made the servant girl leave the household before giving birth to the child "conceived in sin." Even though Grandma eventually took Nathan in and supervised his upbringing, it was in the strictest Pietist tradition. He could never shake the stigma of his "sinful" birth. Her strong-willed upbringing bred terror in him which marked him for life. This relationship is later repeated in the novel between Lillemor and Sanna.

Nathan inherited nothing of Grandma's strength. Marked a bastard and a disgrace, he grew up sickly, extremely fearful, physically and emotionally weak. A true neurotic, he resembled his epileptic grandfather Borck. His grandmother's stern, autocratic upbringing upset him. He became a kleptomaniac and brought disgrace on the family. They tried to hush up his theft of trinkets from the neighbor, jeweler Gavenstein. But after helping himself to Grandma's hidden cash he found it wiser to disappear from the scene.

Years later Nathan turns up in the United States. With a new identity in a new land, Nathan/Tracbac has become a famous entertainer, a clown with considerable wealth. But emotionally he cannot not cut himself loose from his bourgeois upbringing. The various prejudices instilled in him as a child linger. To make things worse, he hates the land, the people, their banality, their business practices. Though it made him famous and rich, he loathes his profession. In his family's tradition, he considers himself just one of those questionable clowns in the hands of a scheming, money-obsessed syndicate. He may not realize that he leads a masked existence. But his frequent escapes to his secret rooms stuffed with Swedish furniture brought over from Sanna after Grandma's death indicate a need to search for his identity. His childhood desk and Grandma's mementos function as substitutes for a lost childhood dream that never materialized.

Twice he tried to return into the fold of his family. Twice he failed.

His first visit after a thirteen-year absence turned into a fiasco because Grandma could not forgive him. He blamed Grandma's senility for the failure. What he did not know was that she had been willing to forgive her grandson had he returned as the Prodigal Son — hungry, poverty-stricken, remorseful — needing her. Instead, he arrived wealthy, in furs and with gadgets his Swedish family had never seen. Being a clown made the situation worse. A common jester was hardly a person to do the Borck clan proud, in spite of wealth and fame. In true Bergmanian sarcasm, the juvenile delinquent secretly bought back Grandma's lost (squandered) family estate.

After Grandma's death he tried a second time. Was it an attempt to "come home" through his relative? Or was it an innate urge to self-destruct that made him seduce his married cousin this time around? Either way, adultery was hardly the Borck way of atoning for previous sins and certainly no road to return into the Pietist Borckian fold. For years afterward he cherished the impossible dream of happy, star-crossed love. In the end he must face the truth that Lillemor was every bit as hard and unforgiving as his grandmother. He remains no more than "a boil on my body, loathsome, disgusting, a dirt, a stain on my honor, an eternal punishment."[23] Learning that the daughter born of this union inherited his flaws adds to his anguish.[24] Sanna Sanna turns out to be physically and emotionally as deficient as her biological father. Like her father, she lacks self-confidence. Like him, she repeatedly falls in love with the wrong person. Like him, she remains alone, prone to general ridicule. At the same time, she symbolizes the truth. Through her, the clown learns some important, never openly acknowledged "truths" about himself and his life.

Nathan's inability to love is his most striking problem. It permeates all his relationships. He has kept Siv and then Benbé at an emotionally cool, weary distance and one wonders about his professed love to Lillemor. It seems almost as if he had wanted this relationship to his married cousin on the other side of the Atlantic because, bound to someone else, she never presented any threat to his insularity.

It is interesting to trace Nathan/Tracbac's reaction to his own child. He initiates Sanna's coming to the United States with a convoluted, outright underhanded scheme, expecting her presence to alleviate his loneliness. After anxiously looking forward to having her with him, the relationship turns sour as soon as he gets his wish when she arrives. The clown cannot love his child, although she makes every effort to please him. He is aloof. Taking care of her becomes a chore, living with her a nightmare. It was all a mistake. He remains the unhappy loner he has always been.

Sven Delblanc observed that throughout his life Hjalmar Bergman remained "the well-bred youngster" and his "tremendous freedom from prejudice exists only in the symbolic home of his prose."[25] Bergman lived in his own world of pretense. Likewise, the clown's essential problem is that he remains a Borck — a bourgeois moralist at heart, emotionally handicapped. He can neither forgive others, nor accept himself. After Grandma, Lillemor best expresses the clan's viewpoint. A clown is no real man.[26] Bergman/Tracbac is the object of his own contemptuous ridicule.

By marrying Siv, the Gypsy, the clown further compounded his emotional/social predicament. Beautiful, talented, Siv remains the half-breed Gypsy nonetheless. Throughout the story Bergman/Nathan/Tracbac never fails to emphasize her lowly origin, even to her face. He does not love her. To have children with her is out of the question. He may need her company, yet he prefers divorce. Accepting her overriding love to him, he wants her to return whenever it suits him. It is all a matter of his convenience.

No longer married, he callously sends her off a second time when he is too embarrassed to explain their cohabitation to his daughter. He readily admits, "We Borcks are really pretty bourgeois, old-fashioned, . . . outright bigoted."[27] Did Bergman hate women? The novel abounds with hateful, sarcastic remarks, especially against older women.

Like the author, the clown may think that he stands outside the Borck bigotry. But his actions belie this assertion. A true Borck at heart, he not only despises his need for Siv, but even more his association with her. Considering that he regards his profession socially degrading and himself a mere "whoopee artist,"[28] teaming up with a gypsy compounds the clown's problem and having to accept the gypsy as partner in the end is true Bergmanian irony. There is no escape from the need to hide behind the mask. He has no choice but to accept his existence as a two-faced horror to himself in his hated, adopted land — "in his modern, artificial labyrinth" of a house, "a prison for him and other Swedes, . . . where the clown runs around like a frightened and gaudily rigged-out rat."[29]

The clown's relationship to his former neighbor, now secretary, Swedish-born Abel Rush, alias Gavenstein, the son of the jeweler he once robbed, is as ambiguous as his bond with Siv. Supposedly Bergman modeled the young Jew after his good friend, brother-in-law and publisher Tor Bonnier. The secretary is extremely capable, efficient, honest, and utterly devoted. He is one of the few people who understands his employer's emotional needs. Yet, Bergman never fails to refer to Abel Rush as "the clown's Jew" or "the Jew." His bride is likewise stereotyped as "the Jewgirl."

These epithets in the novel parallel Bergman's decision to name his play about the Jewish Mengs *Patrasket* (The Rabble). Defending the title before the Jewish Academic Club in Stockholm on October 29, 1928, Bergman declared that "he wanted to show the truly human character of a different race," and that the servant girl in the play used the term in a good-natured way. And while the play portrays some human characteristics of the Meng family, as Jews they are rather cliché and one may question the author's attempt to write a play of a people he admitted to knowing only from outside.[30] Whether good-natured or not, the servant girl's talk seems a strange reason to use the derogatory term as a title for his play. Putting the title between citation marks in no way takes the sting out of it and Bergman knew that.[31] Additionally, in the novel Longfellow's long diatribe against the Jews seems totally uncalled-for in the context and is unnecessary to the plot.[32]

Bergman's description of the black man Longfellow and his family belongs in the same category. Terms like *svartingar* and references to their curly hair, their low status, their strange habits, their unrefined behavior and cheap taste abound in the story.

With regard to Longfellow, during his short stay in the United States Bergman may have seen blacks as mainly a servant class. Consequently, he described the Longfellow family from his superficial European vantage point of the 1920s with all his preconceived notions. On the other hand, the question remains why the clown's secretary in the United States had to be a Jew in the first place and why this fact needed to be emphasized time and again.

Erik Hjalmar Linder explained Bergman's opinions as "a sort of naive and somewhat innocent small-town anti-Semitism in Sweden."[33] His novels and plays were directed at a local audience where his attitudes and beliefs were nothing out of the ordinary. As mentioned, Bergman may not even have been aware of his prejudices when describing the socially mixed society the clown encountered in the New World. The clown's assurance to Siv that he is not intolerant can be seen as an honest self-deceit, applying not only to the clown, but to his creator-author as well.

Today, more than sixty years later, these epithets and opinions sound dated and quite objectionable. Society has greatly changed since the time Bergman wrote his novel and we may look at them with a great deal of hindsight. It is to the credit of our multinational and multiracial societies that prejudices in general and Bergman's biases in particular can be openly discussed in an honest effort to improve relationships between all human races and traditions.

Bergman's opinions belong to his time, his upbringing, his social environment. They in no way detract from the greatness of this novel. On the contrary, Bergman's incisive, probing search for the truth and presenting it as he saw it adds yet another dimension to his characters. Underneath the mask of the funny, foreign, solitary clown hides an unhappy, wounded man. Hurt, he paid back in kind.

Bergman provided a "happy tail" to his story, American-style. In a self-effacing gesture the clown intends to cope with his fate "because he is a clown." He will wear his mask. Siv accepts with a kiss. But Bergman could not refrain from letting the narrator intrude into this idyll. The scene is like "a well-made movie." Yet another stab at common Hollywood practice along with the picture of the tragic clown forced to live in a strange, hostile world and smile at it.

The ending is an escapist's pipe dream. The superficial entertainment world calls for happy endings. But the reader is left to wonder about the psychological make-up of an author who felt compelled to lash out at himself and the world around him.

Bergman's honesty about his own life as told in the Jac Tracbac story is amazing. Elaborating on the growing friction between the author and Stina, their estrangement and their frequent separations, Erik Hjalmar Linder saw a great similarity between Siv and Stina.[34] In an additional analogy, the clown's adulterous affair with Lillemor and her destructive remarks about him strongly remind of Bergman's relationship to Werner Fütterer and the many nightly casual encounters with "sweet little boys"[35] where Lillemor and Stina become another parallel. Lillemor's caustic, unforgiving letter to the clown and his suicidal reaction resemble Bergman's love-hate to his wife, described in a letter to Tor Bonnier who had been married to Stina's sister Greta. They divorced in 1927. Turning to his companion in suffering, Bergman complained about "the terrible Lindberg girls." Stina had just left him after a heated exchange of words, "unnecessary accusations because I know my shortcomings well enough without having them pointed out to me over and over again."[36] Given this equation of Lillemor and Stina, Lillemor's letter in the novel comes through as a not so veiled come-back at his wife for causing him such anguish for his "unforgivable sin."

The novel's "happy tail" was the mask Bergman/Tracbac needed to cope with his unnerving reality. Inwardly he had been slaughtered long before and he had died on a meat hook. He was Jac Tracbac, "born human — he lived a clown — he sold his heart — he died poor . . . a *fatalité du coeur*."[37] His heart, indeed. He knew that what he had done was unpardonable. "The man dies, his deed lives on," he wrote. There was no return home. If he had to wear a mask, the clown hated wearing it and he broke under its weight long before his physical demise. He was a clown with a broken back, as Longfellow explains. "The sudden reversal of action in the Tracbac comedy makes it similar to the Classical tragedy."[38] A modern Oedipus, Tracbac/Bergman was human, flawed. He had hurt and ruined those closest to him and in the end himself. Brought up in a Lutheran milieu, Bergman harked back to the Bible in the story. Tracbac carried the Cain's mark on his forehead. Though unintentionally, he had destroyed others. He deserved to die.

Johannes Edfelt pointed to Hjalmar Bergman's lifelong preoccupation with death.[39] The theme runs through Bergman's adult work, but is especially prominent in the clown's tale. Tracbac was obsessed with the thought of death even before he read Lillemor's letter. After getting her message he turned suicidal. Bergman's message here leads to the conclusion that, subconsciously at least, he wanted to die.

As early as 1922 Bergman developed the theory that no one dies unless he is ready to die, claiming that illness and even accidents come only to those who want to die.[40] Hjalmar Bergman himself explained what he meant in his short story "Ergo sum": the little man can defy death because he was dead already.

Clownen Jac is the horrifying tale of a deeply unhappy human being. It describes Nathan Borck alias Jac Tracbac, the man torn between his two souls, the man full of masked bigotry and self-hate in a hopeless search for love and acceptance. Donning his mask, he gives up struggling for sense in a senseless world. Through the clown, Bergman lashed out at the world and everyone in it, including himself. Most of all himself.

Hjalmar Bergman stands as the great teller of truth in the literature of the twentieth century. *Jac the Clown* invites us to reexamine what humankind is all about.[41]

Notes

[1] Marianne Tivenius, "Av oäkta börd — ett tema med variationer," *Hjalmar Bergman Samfundets Årsbok* 1976, 62.

[2] Sverker R. Ek, "Hjalmar Bergman och Frederick Böök," *BLM* XXIII, 1964, 272.

[3] Letter in Bonniers Archives.

[4] Erik Hjalmar Linder, *Se fantasten: Hjalmar Bergmans liv och diktning från Eros' begravning till Clownen Jac,* Stockholm: Bonniers, 1983, 294–5.

[5] Linder, Se fantasten, 294pp, 334.

[6] Ek, 273.

[7] Ek, 278.

[8] Ibid., 294.

[9] Gunnar Qvarnström, "Clownen Jac's krleksbekymmer," *Hjalmar Bergman Samfundets Årsbok* 1976, 93.

[10] See Hanna Kalter Weiss, *Archetypal Images in Surrealist Prose: A Study in Modern Fiction*. (New York and London: 1988) for a discussion of surrealist prose.

[11] Per Lindberg, "Bakom masker" (Stockholm: 1949), pp 125–152. (Reprint of "Clowen Jac," BLM, 1946, 24–26).

[12] Hans Levander, *Hjalmar Bergman* (Stockholm, 1957), 95.

[13] Linder, *Se fantasten*, 291.

[14] Levander, 95.

[15] Erik Hjalmar Linder, *Hjalmar Bergman*, tr. Catherine Djurklou (Boston: 1975), 143–9.

[16] Ek, 272–280.

[17] Bonniers Archives, #000419 [Sept. 1926?].

[18] Per Lindberg, *Bakom masker* (Stockholm: 1949); Linder, *Se fantasten*, 295.

[19] Bonniers Archives. [Some letters are numbered, others are not.]

[20] Karin Petherick, "The Farewell of a Secular Mystic," *Scandinavica* 31, 1(May 1992):73–82.

[21] *Clownen Jac*, 260.

[22] *Clownen Jac*, 13.

[23] *Clownen Jac*, 223.

[24] Gunnar Qvarnström talks about an "inheritance motif" in Bergman's work. I Lejonets Tecken: En Studie I Hjalmar Bergmans Symbolkonst, Lund:1959,16.

[25] Sven Delblanc, "Clownen i labyrinten: Kring några motiv i Bergmans prosa 1924–1930," *Årsbok 1975, Hjalmar Bergman Samfundet*, Stockholm, 1975, 9–30.

[26] *Clownen Jac*, 197.

[27] *Clownen Jac*, 243.

[28] Ibid.

[29] Delblanc, 23.

[30] Myryam Ehrenpreis, "Hjalmar Bergmans judiska komedy," *Judisk tidskrift*, 1928, 241–242; Olga Raphael-Linden, "Före 'Patrasket,'" *Judisk Krönika*, 2(1933), 1:12–13; Erwin Leiser, "Judiska motiv hos Hjalmar Bergman," *Judisk tidskrift*, 1945, 183–188; Linder, *Se fantasten*, 248–260. See also Erik Hjalmar Linder, "Hjalmar Bergman och judarna," *Hjalmar Bergman Samfundets Årsbok*, 1984, 92–121.

[31] Bergman mentions the "Jewish sensitivity" and his need to defend the play in a letter to Tor Bonnier shortly before his talk in 1928.

[32] *Clownen Jac*, 77.

[33] Linder, "Hjalmar Bergman och judarna," 104.

[34] Linder, *Se fantasten*, 72, 157–173.

[35] Linder, *Se fantasten*, 72, 157–173.

[36] Letter to Tor Bonnier, August 1928. Bonniers Archives.

[37] *Clownen Jac,* 118–119.

[38] *Clownen Jac,* 141.

[39] Johannes Edfelt, "Hjalmar Bergmans dialog med döden," *Kring Hjalmar Bergman,* Sverker R. Ek, ed. (Stockholm:1965).

[40] Ibid., 224.

[41] Quotes and page numbers are from *Clownen Jac* with introduction by Uno Florén, Höganäs: Bokförlaget Bra Böcker, 1982.

1: The Dear Relatives And What They Knew About The Clown

MEMORY, OUR MEMORY is a remarkable commodity. Capricious, unreliable, facetious, wily, often painfully inadequate, it is yet a comforting and indispensable asset. We live through memory and in memory. We rate it highly — and rightly so. Our daily servant, it is our master. Let it fail and random chance will take its place, leaving us at the mercy of impulsive, on the spur of the moment reactions. Well, occasionally that too may work.

Young Benjamin Borck came from solid, old bourgeois stock. His family and friends called him Ben or Benbé. His father, a merchant, had died young and left his wife and son in rather poor circumstances. His widow was a Längsäll, of the Norrland Längsälls with the big, poutish lips — notoriously strict, straight-laced Pietists. The standing joke among the neighbors was that the Borcks with their poutish faces always looked as if chewing on sweets. But the Längsälls used their wide, strong, pike-like jaws to maul fellow humans to shreds whenever they saw a chance to do so.

Steeped in this tradition, the widow Borck, neé Längsäll, was a strict mother. Raising her son meant nipping all signs of pride and wantonness in the bud.

Benbé's talents were less clear-cut. He was twenty years old when his mother died. By then he was a Ph.D. candidate. He had also been to a business school, convinced that his talents lay in that field. Extremely imaginative, he loved to tinker with new plans and projects. Though usually well designed and functional, they were highly irrelevant to modern needs.

After the burial of his mother he decided to go to the United States. Problem was that he had no money. He consulted his list of close friends and relatives and decided to visit his mother's brother to remedy his predicament. He informed his Uncle Längsäll of Sanna that he wished to emigrate and say farewell to his dear family before leaving. His uncle's response was friendly enough. He was welcome to visit Sanna, provided he would refrain from a. turning his girls' heads and b. trying to borrow money. Benbé went, hoping to accomplish both.

Mrs. Längsäll, Benbé's aunt, was a Borck too, but she came from a different branch of the family. Her father had once owned Sanna. Like Benbé — he had been full of new project ideas. But his were of a more technical nature than those of his younger relative. A few of the old man's ingenious, highly impractical waterworks were still gracing the banks of the

1

Sanna rapids where, useless and unused, they were rusting in silence. This Sanna-Borck had eventually been forced to sell his beautiful farm and his son-in-law Längsäll had bought it a few years later. But unlike his father-in-law, Längsäll was not interested in any project other than keeping a tight fist around his money pouch. Slowly and efficiently he kept on filling it.

Benbé's cousin Sanna was born on the estate and named after it. A shy, unpredictable, high-strung and easily frightened girl, she stood waiting for him at the station. People considered her rather "strange" and teasers called her Sanna-Sanna. Benbé greeted her courteously and planted a cousin's kiss on her cheek,

Hello, little Sanna-Sanna, are you glad to see me?

Sure. And I hope never having to see you again in this life, the girl told him sullenly.

Well, there's supposed to be a better life after this. You're good at keeping your true feelings under wraps, Benbé answered politely and patted her lightly on the cheek. That's when he got his first ear box for the season.

The farmhouse was a rather small, green building surrounded by maple trees. Red fall leaves covered its broken, black double roof and climbing grapevines its sides. The good aunt stood at the top of the cracked, worn stone steps, her genial Borckian smile welcoming him. Sanna's older sister Caroline stood next to her, gentle and kissable. From inside the entrance hall came Father Längsäll's impatient mutter,

Get the boy inside and kiss him while we're having our coffee. I'm hungry. I want to eat.

The crucial moment came half an hour later. They had finished their soup — the ladies one plate each, Benbé two and father Längsäll his customary three. His huge paws, freckled and red-haired down to the knuckles, rested on the table. His large, muscular body rose and fell in rhythm with his sighs of relish. Their owner kept staring profoundly into his empty dish as if meditating on the possibility of a fourth helping. Suddenly he said,

Cackle on, you chickens. Just keep on cackling. A young cock has come to the estate. And, as usual, only you, Sanna, seem upset. Has his cock-a-doodle-doo offended you already? Take it easy, my girl, he's on his way to the States. It's a smart move. Shows that you're cut of the right stuff, young fellow. Why waste your youth and ambition in this bum country? I say, Go ahead, Benjamin, and Godspeed.

Another burp of delight after the warm soup followed. Längsäll bent his plump fingers and explained with the mien of the know-it-all,

Apropos emigration — I divide boys into four categories: First, ambitious boys without money; they shouldn't go because it's a waste of ambition. Second, boys with money, but lacking ambition; they shouldn't go either because that's a waste of money. Third, boys with both ambition and

2

money — they ought to go if that's what they want because no one forces them to leave this shabby land. And finally, my friendly advice to those who lack both gold and competence is that they ought to leave. Because, you see, they can't. So, my little Benjamin, go through with your plans. Just don't think that I'm going to pay for your ticket. And now that we've discussed the subject, let's have our roast.

Afraid to upset the giant, the ladies dared not disrupt his far-flung diatribe against poor Benbé. Längsäll proceeded carefully to clean his plate. That done, he wiped the gravy from his bushy red whiskers, leaned heavily back into his chair and pronounced,

Come to think of it! Once you're there, you may even say hello to that famous clown relative of yours. What's his name now, as clown . . . ?

Full of lively indignation both girls spoke up,

His name is Jac Tracbac! Really, Dad, not to remember that! Jac Tracbac! How uneducated you are!

Come to think of it, yes, of course, that's right. His name shows up here and there in newspapers and movie ads. But I'm not interested in clowns and tawdry entertainment. Can't say feeling flattered being related to the fellow.

You aren't! Sanna cut in superciliously. Really. That's from the Borck side and not the Längsälls. Besides, Mom is hardly related to him either because he is from the other branch.

That's what you say, my little impertinence! father Längsäll shot back, visibly annoyed. But let me tell you, I know him personally. I've even had dinner with him. Lord knows, we might have become drinking brothers at that. So there you're completely wrong, my young lady.

Caroline interceded,

Hearing that tremble in your voice, dear Dad, you must still be pretty proud of being related to that cheap entertainer person. By the way, you aren't alone in knowing him. Mom met Jac too.

Längsäll gave a deep, comical sigh,

Benjamin! Never depend on women! Especially regarding their memory, be it time, space or event. I've fully explained that my dear wife could never have met that famous clown when he visited Wadköping two years before Grandma Borck died — because we lived in Johannisberg at the time.

I know that! Sanna snorted angrily. But Mommy met him the very year Grandma Borck died, not two years before her death. And you were in London at the time, Daddy, so you can't know much about that.

Your Mom just dreamed that up, her father explained with authority. She herself admitted that much.

Her memory thus questioned, the beleaguered mother finally spoke up,

Now, you've said enough, all of you.

With a smile she turned to Benbé,

3

Benjamin, you must think we've nothing better to do here but to discuss our famous relative. That's hardly the case. Actually, we rarely talk about him. I once mentioned that I met him, but your uncle said that I imagine it all from hearing his vivid description of his own meeting Jac. That may well be so and he might be right. Of course, the girls' interest in movie stars is only natural, but that our serious Squire Längsäll . . .

Well, that serious Squire Längsäll wants his coffee and his smoke, the master of the house declared.

The family left the dinner table and moved to the living room, its pompous, heavy, overblown furnishings a fitting frame for the fall colors in backyard and park visible through the window. After the coffee the women left to go about their tasks, leaving the two men to themselves. Squire Längsäll gulped his coffee with the same gusto as he had eaten before. With a grunt he resumed his conversation,

Well, the reason for my interest in that famous clown rests on my better knowledge of the past. Now that the girls are gone, let me elaborate a little . . . I'm sure you've heard of Grandma Borck, your father's aunt? Well, no one can deny that she was a rather remarkable woman. The daughter of a small tenant farmer, she first was the maid and then became the wife of one of the wealthiest and respected burghers around. She managed not only to be a powerful force in the clan, but to maintain it with the tenacity of a genuine Swedish peasant girl, so to speak. Then her oldest son Gabriel Borck got a might too close to one of the servant girls and the upshot of that encounter was none less than our famous Jac Tracbac — called Jonathan after his grandfather for the first twenty-five or thirty years of his life. Conscientious young fellow that he was, Gabriel actually wanted to marry the girl. But his grandmother nixed that. One servant marriage in the family was enough, she said, meaning herself. Yeah, she was that kind of woman. She sent the girl off into the countryside and Gabriel to Switzerland on the pretext that he had tuberculosis. Strange, to see that excuse really coming true. Gabriel died in Davos a year or so later — Have another cup.

Anyway, the death of her son must have weighed heavily on grandmother's conscience. She took the little guy into her house and it wasn't long before he became grandmother's favorite, her pet. It's known to happen to grandmothers. She must've spoiled him no end. Then again, he might have been born with this disorderly disposition. If you ask me, I think it's a Borckian family trait. Take our own little Sanna . . . she's a lot of trouble, capricious, whimsical, even quite nasty at times. Other times she's so naively good its worrisome. But, we aren't talking about her, are we?

Well, the boy grew up a real devil, as we say here. That's because Grandma had a tough time disciplining him. He frightened so easily. She needed only to raise her hand in earnest and he'd have hysterical or epileptic

4

fits — just like his grandfather, the chairman of the Chamber of Commerce. Playing his dirty trick on the goldsmith next door didn't improve things either. The goldsmith shop was next door to the Borckian estate. So one night our good fellow squeezed through a crack to the other side. He had quite a few trinkets in his pockets when he eeled out again. The only consolation about the sad affair was his unbelievable naiveté. What d'you think he did with the loot? Gave it away the next morning, tie pins to his male classmates, rings and such to girlfriends. Sure was easy to find the thief, mind you. Why had he done it? He explained — wanted to treat his friends. They were always so nice to him —

What a lofty, decent reason to steal, Benbé interrupted with a grin. But father Längsäll remained serious and continued with a sigh,

No, it's pretty bad. Their goodness makes some people irresponsible, so to speak. Yes, the same with little Sanna. God forbid, she's never given away things that belong to others. No, just her own. Imagine Mama seeing our old servants, or the farmhands' wives wearing the old family heirlooms she'd passed on to Sanna. No, it's not funny. She's too generous with her presents. The servants don't appreciate it. They are nice to her face, but laugh and snicker behind her back.

Anyway, as I said, we're not talking about her. Goldsmith Gavenstein reported the break-in to the police. — But he was a decent little fellow, that Jew. It would've been terribly embarrassing if he had not denied later there ever was a burglary. I got the story from him. The Borcks never mentioned the affair, which is logical. The poor boy — I think he's off his rocker, if you ask me — well, to top it off, a few days later he disappeared and a substantial sum of money from Grandma's desk with him. I don't know how he made it to the States. He wrote a few times to some relatives and it was clear that he was having a rough time. They sent him some money, but after a while they stopped hearing from him.

Needless to say, the whole affair was hard on Grandma. She was never the same afterward, if you ask me — though others considered her sane and lucid. She never mentioned Nathan, and as far as I know he never wrote to her. Not until some twelve, thirteen years later did he contact some relatives about possibly visiting Grandma. Well, the Borcks weren't exactly thrilled about the bum visiting here. They had conveniently put him out of their mind and now resented having him on their neck again. Anyway, upset or not, they had no choice but to tell Grandma the prodigal son had returned.

What happened? Benbé wondered excitedly. Was Grandma angry? Happy? Upset?

Upset, of course, though she didn't show it much. Buzzing about like a busy bee, she informed everybody that finally she was going to tell that boy a thing or two. It was necessary to have some clothes and some money ready

5

for him. She would see to it that he ate properly, and got something worthwhile to do, and so on. In short, the old lady really saw him returning in rags, starving — the prodigal son, you know. I'm convinced the rest of the relatives thought along the same lines, although their picture of the prodigal son was less biblically simple than Grandma's. Well, what do you know! On the appointed day His Lordship arrived — but not in rags. No sir. Wrapped in furs, he brought various other amenities the good old Wadköping citizens had never even seen. The fact that Grandma's finances were in a shambles and that she had been forced to sell her beloved estate did nothing to improve the situation. Well, it turned out that a certain Mr. Gavenstein bought it. And who was behind the deal if not our prodigal son who invited Grandma to take up residence in her old home again? Imagine the reversal of roles in the old drama!

Of course, it would seem a stroke of luck that the prodigal son had returned so posh. But you may forgive that old lady for not getting the drift. The good gentleman had been a pilfering juvenile when he left, if you please. Now, how had he come up in the world? A clown, mind you. The old lady had seen clowns before in seedy circuses, perhaps had even fed some wandering jesters in her fine kitchen. But to make a fortune as a clown? Nonsense! That didn't fit into her scheme of things. She refused to understand.

How was that, uncle?

I like to think that she was getting senile. To be precise you'd have to say that she refused to get the facts straight. The rest may slowly disintegrate in the great confusion. The good lady had always been too inflexible — and finally she failed to understand anything. That was her punishment. The same goes for the boy. She upset the whole clan by showing her wealthy, fine grandson the door, literally. There was no visit with dear Grandma. Jonathan Borck, alias Jac Tracbac, visited on Sanna for a short while as guest of your father's cousin. That's when I met him. He was a nice fellow, not special in any way, somewhat shy and quiet, but his unfortunate experience with his adored grandmother could have caused that. Then he went back to his country to reap further laurels and riches. Two years later he returned — shortly after Grandma's death. I never met him then because I was in London on a business trip. Womenfolk just have no brains and get times and places all mixed up.

Well, that's the way things are, father Längsäll concluded his tale. Just in case you happen to meet this famous clown in the States you tell him hello from cousin Längsäll. Though I'm sure he's forgotten me and my name a long time ago.

Look, Uncle, Benbé said, I don't think that I'm going to see this gentleman, because poor relatives are never really welcome —

One never knows, Längsäll countered, I think that this fellow is basically goodhearted and family-oriented. Besides, I don't mean that you shall ask him for money. No, damn it! But he could possibly get you a decent job, through friends perhaps — as sign carrier, if nothing else, ha ha ha —

I don't mind, even sign carrier, Benbé conceded. But you forget that there won't be a trip because a certain Squire Längsäll refused to lend me the money to go.

The large, ungainly, red-haired master heaved himself out of his rocker and paced the floor for a while, now and then cautiously touching his nose. Finally he snuffled,

That's true. I'm not going to lend a red cent to an old emigrant. It's against my principles. But I just happened to look at the inventory of your mother's estate. I'm her administrator — and I found that I sold certain shares at rather unprofitable prices —

May I ask which shares? Benbé interrupted quietly. Mom didn't have that many shares.

That's none of your business, Längsäll shot back, frowning. I made a mistake. And it's my fault that the estate, that is you, came short about three thousand crowns. I'm going to reimburse that sum.

Stupid administrators are kinder than I thought, Benbé said softly. Längsäll said,

Keep quiet when I'm talking, my boy. Actually, without the women it's lonesome here, so let's do something about it . . .

Planting himself in the dusky room, his feet wide apart, he stuck two fingers in his wide mouth and produced a piercing whistle.

What a considerate way of calling the ladies, Benbé remarked.

Well, it doesn't hurt them. Those who have their mind intact must do the whistling, squire Längsäll muttered, adding shrewdly, Let's see who of the young ladies is most anxious to meet cousin Ben.

They waited a few moments, Benbé with a certain suspense. Otherwise a rather flighty fellow, ever since dinner he was vacillating between the two sisters. But neither one answered the call. Only their mother appeared in the door like a beautiful, mild summer evening.

How far have the gentlemen come, if I may ask? she wondered.

Up to and including the shares, squire Längsäll muttered. His wife smiled reassuringly and said,

Well, then I came at the right moment. Turning to the young man, she continued, Benjamin, we checked your wardrobe. The girls cleaned the worst spots and mended the torn pockets. It's all in good shape now.

My dearest aunt, those spots — they were mere accidents for which I'm not to blame. And the holes in my pockets — they're my ingenious saving accounts. Something like the old-fashioned stocking. I fill my pockets with

7

banknotes, gold and silver when times permit. A good part automatically drops through the holes. Then, whenever I need it, I merely rip the pockets open and help myself to the nice sum I find in the coat lining. Its called 'stabilizing the money market'. As far as I'm concerned, all the world's banks may stand on their heads for B.B.P.L.M. — Ben Borck's Pocket Lining Method, the young man declared with an air of dignity.

Master Längsäll burst forth,

He must emigrate! Patriotism requires to get rid of this youngster. All right, Sweden's greatest crayfishing expert is going fishing now. Whoever wants to learn the craft may come along.

Tugging at the young man's arm, the great crayfisherman's wife whispered,

Wait a minute, Ben. Here, take this and keep it safe. But not in your coat lining.

Ben blushed when he took the little red purse, decorated with a gold imprint of Stockholm's coat of arms. It contained a letter of credit for three thousand crowns in his name.

It's not necessary to thank him. We've already discussed it. But take good care of the money, my boy. I assure you, three thousand crowns are nothing to sneeze at in this household. If you're ever able to repay it, by all means do. If you can't — well, know that we'll forget it, Mrs. Längsäll told him.

Grateful, but too stunned to talk, Benbé bent down to kiss the little woman's ear — the way he used to kiss his mother. She nodded and smiled, but her gaze went far out into the glowing sunset in the park. A certain awkward anxiety seemed to envelop her and she swayed faintly as she crossed her arms. Eventually she said,

Well, what I wanted to say — ah, yes, I remember now. That about meeting our relative Jonathan Borck — I think it's a stupid idea. We really know nothing about him, so you can imagine how much he knows about us. No, don't even consider it. Your uncle is going to give you a letter of recommendation to some business friends in New York and Chicago. Let's hope they help you if you need it.

She fell silent. Benbé had a feeling that she was by no means at peace. And indeed, her eyes wide open toward the rose-colored evening sky, she continued

Should you by any remote chance happen to meet him anyway — well, yes — in that case you may remind him of us — I mean of your uncle — that he and his family — well, that we all are doing very well here — about Sanna —

No, she continued out of breath, I'm going to see about your clothes. You go ahead with your uncle and cousins. He simply loves to pass on his considerable knowledge on fishing. He's taught the girls ever since they were able to walk. I'm sure he'll appreciate a new apprentice.

They both laughed and then Benbé ran out, just in time to grab hold of his two cousins. So they wandered in the dusk down to the reeds which stood straight, still and black against the oil-like shimmering water. They chatted carelessly and left serious matters untouched. Benbé could not make up his mind which one of the girls he wanted to marry. He felt drawn to Sanna, but that ear box made him consider the gentler Caroline. Sanna helped in this decision process by saying,

Oh, dear Caroline, can't I have Ben in peace for a little while, please? —

Oh, by all means, poor Caroline said. Disengaging herself, she ran off to join her father, whose large, dark bulk was moving back and forth among the reeds.

Sanna pressed herself lovingly against her cousin, arousing in Benbé the notion that she definitely ought to be his choice, especially when she whispered in his ear,

Dear Ben, I'd like to give you something.

She pulled a small package out of her pocket and pushed it into his, instructing him,

Don't open it until you get to the United States.

I can't promise you that, because it's totally against my habit not to open packages, Benbé told her.

Then we'll have to shake hands that you won't, the girl said gravely.

They shook hands to seal the deal. His uncle's warning about Sanna's strange generosity flashed through his mind. Ogling her suspiciously, he said,

Listen, little Sanna-Sanna — this isn't anything you've swiped from your mother, is it? —

The girl's large, light blue eyes, like shimmering red-flaming opals, stared at him. Then Benbé got his second slap . . . and ten times harder than his first slap that morning.

Funny, I had a feeling that something like this would happen, he muttered. It took no time for him to transfer his devotion to Caroline.

Father Längsäll stood among the reeds, his substantial catch laid out in a neat row next to him. With a happy sigh he blew up his huge chest and stared at his newest apprentice,

Benjamin, my vast experience permits me to give you a few pointers in the art. My twenty rules sum it up. It may be hard, but above all, you must keep absolutely QUIET. Even the slightest noise will ruin your luck.

His mighty bass rumbled over the sleepy waters and his fists pounded in rhythm. Whether no life was left in the reeds, or all creatures suddenly turned shy, or whether they escaped to other waters was difficult to say . . . But what good is people's wisdom if they don't act on it?

9

2: Benbé In The Gutters Of Paradise

BENBÉ CAME TO the United States and landed in the gutter, literally. Not immediately, of course. As long as his soul's beloved — the little billfold with the letter of credit — had not abandoned him, things went swimmingly. He liked New York for a month, but found no job. He disliked Chicago for another month, still without a job. In beautiful San Francisco he began to get nervous. Still, a job proved impossible to find.

It was certainly not for any lack of merits. He was a Ph.D. candidate who had also graduated from an institute of technology, had attended a business school, a massage institute and a fine arts school. His credentials would not have hurt his job search — if he had kept silent about them. But he was proud of his background and rattled off the entire list every time he applied for a mere office job. The personnel officers found it too much, or not applicable to what they had in mind. They would thank him for applying and give him the brush-off. Benbé considered them idiots and would leave, none the wiser. It was only logical that the ensuing interviews produced the same result.

He left Frisco and went to Los Angeles — the city of horrors where his luck finally ran out. Like a card player throwing his last trump, he threw his letter of credit through the teller's window at the Citizen's Bank

A hundred dollars, please, he demanded.

The fat man with the hornrimmed glasses sitting behind the bars kept on chewing his gum while leisurely scrutinizing the letter. Then Benbé did something he had never done before. He carefully computed the various withdrawals. With a husky chuckle from his gold-speckled mouth, the teller said leisurely,

Young man, take my advice and turn yourself in for attempted fraud before I do. Assures you milder punishment. Your credit is up.

This was how Benbé landed in the gutter. For the moment he still had a roof over his head which he had rented first thing on his arrival in the coastal township north of Los Angeles. His rent paid one month in advance, he was not homeless . . . yet. His landlady was a stately, beautiful, red-haired divorcee from Canada. Far from denying him his rights, the woman seemed anxious to add her heart into the bargain. But the memory of his Längsäll cousins bothered him. Benbé had no desire to start an affair with a beautiful woman he actually liked extremely well. He was simply too poor to afford

10

her. Trying to escape her charms he took to walking the streets. That's how he wound up in the gutter.

His life was not too bad. The scenery was beautiful. The street whose gutter he occupied looked like a palm grove. Behind it were a row of homes moored in asphalt like a Noah's Ark. The palm fronds were teaming with shimmering, colorful birds. Colibris were flapping around gorgeous flowers as if suspended in midair. The roller-skating and scooting children in the neighborhood reminded him of earthbound angels. And he liked waving at the many honorable patriarchs driving by with their golf clubs. Occasionally some of them even stopped for a chat about the grand weather in this Californian paradise. They invited him to join them. Benbé agreed wholeheartedly with them about the great weather. California was a paradise. He considered it a great honor to sit in its gutter. That pleased the gentlemen and they rode on. Then there were charming young girls in bathing suits that drove past. Benbé waved again and the girls stopped to invite him for a swim at the beach. He would have loved to accept, but here his courage failed him.

Seeing him daily on the same spot, the girls began wondering about him. Before long they stopped to chat. They inquired whether his religious beliefs bade him sit here every day. He told them he was a follower of Taoism, an ancient Chinese religion, which among other things taught the seven hundred and seventy-seven ways of arousing curiosity in girls. He firmly believed in its sublime doctrine of suffering young men, who, like him, hurt for seven days. They received their just reward on the eighth day — a visit by seven gorgeous, well-dressed and well-mannered beauties. The girls cheered,

See, ancient Chinese wisdom is as valid today as before.

They brought all kinds of goodies from their cars — fruit, candies, cigarettes, even drugs. They passed around mixed drinks in silver pitchers.

The girls liked the name Benbé. But they preferred to call him Funnybunny. Their own names were more flowery. To Benbé the girls all looked alike with their heavy make-up. He had a hard time to keep their names straight. To distinguish between them he found it simpler to call them after the cars they drove — Miss Nash, Miss Ford, Miss Cadillac, Miss Packard, etc.

More cars stopped. The mothers and grandmothers, even scantier dressed than their daughters, soon joined the group. They fell in love with the true, ancient Chinese maxim and gossiped as if they had never heard of a generation gap.

In paradise the concept of time is vague. Women in paradise are angels and timelessly beautiful. Only the foolish, insensitive newcomer Benbé became concerned that the worthy matrons might catch cold. He borrowed his Canadian landlady's shawls, robes, even furs so the dear old ladies could wrap

11

their aging limbs. He had never expected many thanks for his innocent troubles — and he certainly didn't get any. Besides, he waited in vain for useful mature wisdom from them. Trying to keep up, the ladies prattled as much nonsense as the younger set — if not more.

The Canadian landlady watched these paradisaical gutter parties with great unease. She had second thoughts about her roomer and warned him,

Benbé, the police is keeping an eye on you. Luckily these ladies are members of the local women's club. You'd be in deep trouble if the policeman weren't afraid of them. What kind of behavior is that anyway — to sit out there, waiting for girls? —

Solemn and dignified, Benbé corrected her,

My dear lady, I'm not waiting for these girls. In fact, their ice cream sodas give me heartburn. I sit here to atone for my sins. I'm waiting for Jac Tracbac.

Oh, indeed! the landlady said scornfully. Why not wait for President Coolidge, or Thomas Edison, or good old John D. Rockefeller —

These gentlemen would be very welcome, but I'm not related to them, Benbé countered.

Pulling her pin from her shawl, the landlady picked her beautiful white teeth with it and mused for a while. She said,

Is it really the Jac Tracbac you're waiting for?

Some of my family members think he's a nut. But that doesn't faze me. I owe my father's cousin the courtesy. I'd be heartbroken if he ever walked past my door . . . , Benbé answered.

She sat down beside him and argued,

Tracbac lives in Beverly Hills. You ought to visit him there — instead of waiting for him out here —

I did, Benbé said gloomily. That's to say — I never got past the black fellow in the gatekeeper's cottage.

Oh, for crying out loud — he didn't let you in, is that it? the landlady sneered.

No, he kicked me out, Benbé admitted, blushing. The guy is bigger than I. When I told him he's a scoundrel he let me know that Tracbac had more relatives than hair on his head — to the tune of about ten thousand former school buddies between the ages of twenty-five and seventy, he thought. Well, you know what he meant —

Oh, now I remember, the landlady smiled, suddenly full of compassion. That must've been the day when you fell off the streetcar, or so you said.

Right, Benbé muttered. I lied. Sorry.

You don't have to be bashful with me, the landlady encouraged him, patting him under his chin. Don't be bashful. I graduated from a girls' school.

12

I sent this famous clown a letter with greetings from our mutual relatives and friends. But my father's cousin cared not to answer. What do you make of that? Benbé said.

Oh, you little greenhorn, the landlady answered, pity in her voice. Don't you know that his secretary checks his mail? With instructions to keep moochers away.

Benbé's dark tan deepened a few shades as he muttered,

How d'you know? I mean that I was begging?

The landlady shrugged her shoulders and closed her eyes. A roguish smile lit Benbé's face,

You'll never guess what I did — Want to know?

Tell me! Tell me! she urged, her eyes full on him. Remember that I'm a girls' school graduate — you can confide in me —

All right, Benbé said. Hear my tricks and lies. Listen and learn. There was this article in the newspaper about my relative's hobby. Apes. He keeps them all over his place. Well, not that I can afford an ape, but I bought a monkey travel cage with a window in the best pet store in town, pasted the store's business cards all over the cage and took it to Beverly Hills. There I waved a dollar bill under a boy's nose and asked him to find me a big, beautiful cat —

He returned soon enough, mind you, with a large, savage tomcat. We had a hard time and got all scratched up getting him into that cage. Then I told the fellow to get Tracbac's black guard good and curious . . .

What a tale! the landlady snickered.

Well, it wasn't a bad idea, Benbé admitted timidly. Imagine that fellow taking off with the raging cat. Sure was a sight to behold.

Your boss ordered an ape from our store, he told the guard. For immediate delivery.

You should've seen the black fellow getting clawed sticking his face down the cage opening . . .

That's a cat! he screamed.

I had prepared the little fellow beforehand. So he answered,

Be careful with this new cat-ape from Orangutania. He tends to scratch a bit. So have fun, you two — Mr. Tracbac wants you to keep the cat amused. Imagine that black fellow really sticking his finger down the box and letting the cat bite him —

I praised him for a job well done, Benbé assured her. I knew the black fellow would want to please his boss and take care of that cat. I had hoped . . . hoped . . . hoped that . . . Benbé grew silent. The landlady shook him impatiently,

You idiot! What did you hope to accomplish? Do you really think for a minute Tracbac comes here just because you played that trick on his guard?

Benbé whispered,

13

See that man just turning the corner of Washington Avenue? That's him.

It was noontime, lunch hour. The street lay deserted. The palm-lined sidewalks were shady and cool, but the wide center was baking blindingly white in the hot noonday sun. Only the two sitting on the sidewalk saw the lonely wanderer approaching. Breathless with excitement, the landlady stammered,

Tracbac? How — how do you know?

I've a gut feeling it's him, Benbé said quietly.

The man came closer. For Benbé it was at too slow a pace. His landlady called it crawling in the extreme.

I've seen a few pictures of him in our family album back home, Benbé whispered. I don't remember them. But my guts tells me —

I only know him from movies and magazines. I would think it's hard to recognize him without his make-up. He looks so common, so without distinction, the landlady whispered.

Well, what of it? Benbé whispered with growing excitement. Why should he look special? See, it's his job to be original, out of the ordinary. Now he comes without his professional paraphernalia. No car, no golf clubs, no chewing gum. He must have walked all the way from Beverly Hills, or taken the streetcar to Ocean Park. How stupid of me to imagine him pushing a wheel-barrow or riding on a motor scooter. So silly. From where he sits, it must be much more original not to be average. But, he's my father's cousin. My gut feeling tells me —

His excitement was infectious. The landlady stared ahead, frowning between heavy eyebrows. Benbé put his head between his knees and whispered,

Dear landlady, mind your manners. Stop staring at him. And remember, he'll have to talk to us first. We won't utter a word unless he does.

They waited impatiently, he his head between his knees, she frowning so as not to seem bad-mannered. But when the slow wanderer finally reached their spot he walked on behind them without stopping. Benbé became angry. Convinced that this man was the clown, he got up, stretched to his full height and called in Swedish,

My dear friend! My father's cousin! What's the rush?

The stranger turned abruptly and stared at the young man with his large, very light-blue eyes that glittered like opals in the half-shade. He seemed annoyed and muttered something in English. The landlady hid her face behind her hands. Benbé raised his cap with a respectful smile and said in English,

I'm terribly sorry for my mistake. You look so very much like my relative. The heat must have touched my brain. Please, forgive me.

Of course, of course, the stranger said and disappeared quicker than he had come.

14

Benbé was crestfallen, angry at his erratic gut feeling. It was all right to err on rational deduction. But a gut feeling must work out. The landlady was upset. She considered Benbé an idiot, yet didn't want him to be because she liked him too much. Like unselfish women everywhere, she excused her own mistakes rather than those of her friends. Therefore she said harshly,

Benbé, you and your idiotic gut feelings. Can't you use what little brain our Lord gave you? Whatever made you think Tracbac would want to see you just because you sent him a cat?

I didn't send just the cat. I stuck a letter to Jac in its collar. And I included a package, Benbé explained.

So what! You've written him before without getting an answer, the landlady said.

That's true, Benbé conceded, smiling roguishly. I've done that. But I never mailed it with a wild cat. A cat functioning as mailman draws attention, you see, and everything in this world needs an advertising gimmick. Then there was that package . . .

What was in it? the landlady pursued. Not that I'm the least bit interested in your idiotic schemes, but you ought to come clean to ease your conscience.

Benbé sighed and mumbled,

A ring . . .

A ring? the landlady repeated. Her curiosity was aroused. An expensive ring?

Benbé hesitated. It took a while before he answered, rather meekly,

It cost me a great deal of anguish, if you want to know.

Oh, for crying out loud! the landlady grinned. Come inside and have lunch. Bacon and eggs, what do you say?

My rent doesn't include meals! Benbé shouted. Trading sweets for bacon and eggs was tempting. But he didn't have a cent and he certainly did not want to take anything for free from a woman he liked too much. Besides, he was afraid of leaving his spot. Tracbac might still show up — in spite of it all.

The landlady went inside, slamming the doors so hard the building's paper thin walls buckled under the impact. That's the way houses in paradise were built. Benjamin Borck resumed his position of hugging his knees. His stomach was growling in tandem with the mouthwatering sizzle that wafted from his landlady's kitchen. She soon reappeared on her front steps, wagging her skirt alluringly and humming softly,

Bacon and eggs, bacon and eggs — if you please!

Tempting and persistent, tempting and persistent — if you please, Benbé shouted back without raising his head.

She pondered for a while. Then she said,

How about roast beef with cucumber and lettuce. Is that better?

15

Brazen and conceited red-haired dame! Is that better? he called sullenly.

The landlady disappeared with a slam that straightened the walls in a hurry.

The cars returned and with them candies, girls, mothers and grandmothers. When they saw his sad face their sympathy increased and their candy rations with it. Benbé gnashed his teeth. These women made him feel uncomfortable, a discomfort resembling fear. He knocked over his cocktail and huddled against a palm tree. Its lower frond stubs cut into his back and he felt as if strapped to a torture pole he had once seen on a visit to an old Indian reservation long ago. The noble Indians of his childhood had been courageous and cruel. These ladies were noble and cruel too. The more he frowned, the happier were the girls. Their beautiful eyes radiated an ominous vivacity.

For goodness sakes, will you ninnies please leave me alone! Benbé shouted. But they refused to listen. Miss Cadillac, the most stunning of them all, threw herself into his arms. The others encircled him in a gradually tightening eclipse, their smiles a blend of cannibalism and motherly affection. Funnybunny was their pet, their darling. He could feel their stares, undressing him, then dressing him up again, occasionally chastising him the way little girls chastise their dolls. What good-for-nothing bum was he anyway? Didn't he feel honored and grateful that a bunch of beautiful girls patronized him? Many learned scholars, famous artists, brilliant actors would envy him, possibly want to share this — dubious — honor . . .

Fed up with their game, he thought how strange he would look getting angry over the attention seven gorgeous girls paid him. He needed a scapegoat. His victim appeared soon enough — the slow-moving stranger on his return to Washington Avenue. Benbé appreciated his foresight of having moved the scene of action to the opposite side of the street. Pulling beautiful Miss Cadillac close, he kissed her and whispered something into her ear. Surprise in her face, she murmured,

Do you know what Funnybunny says? The man over there is Jac Tracbac.

Full of cunning, Benbé added,

What a pity that we have no camera. Lost opportunity to get a snapshot with him.

His remark challenged one of humanity's basic instincts — the big game hunt our modern culture helped so greatly improve. Smelling big game within shooting range aroused the ladies' unbridled desire. Within seconds they were back in their cars to get their Kodaks ready to shoot. Benbé drew a sigh of relief. Suddenly a policeman approached him,

I'm not surprised to see you tired, young man. I need to talk to your landlady because I don't approve of what's going on in my street. Only, it's unpleasant to talk with her — she has a violent temper.

Very violent, Benbé agreed, all sympathy.

The policeman straightened his body and flexed his honest muscles. Thus fortified, he stalked into Mrs. Canadian's house, careful to spit his chewing gum out on his way there . . .

At that point the cars came racing back. Benbé cringed and hid his face behind his hands. Miss Ford ground to a stop and called,

Funnybunny, you're a phony. That was a decent fellow and not even close to an artist. Here's his card. Throwing the card at him, she amplified her assault with an assortment of oranges, grapes, chocolates and whatever else was near at hand.

Supporting the bombardment, the other young ladies started a war-cry and drove their cars in circles around the young man. Half a pineapple smashed against his skull. The gooey liquid dripped down his face. Eventually the wild horde left, leaving the spattered, dirty Benbé sitting in the gutter among heaps of crushed fruit and sweets.

He looked ridiculous. The policeman trailing her, the landlady came out and looked him over, frowning. She was glad that not she but other women were the cause of his disgrace. She turned to the policeman,

I'm awfully sorry for screaming at you, sir. I can see now — you were right. This fellow is a bum.

I'm glad you finally see it my way, the policeman answered, relieved. This sidewalk occupant is not fit to live in the United States. He ought to return to his own country.

Are you going to pay for the trip, Noah? Benbé challenged him and held his hand out like a beggar.

The scene turned unpleasant. A few people were gathering around the three, among them the slow stranger. Reflecting on what he had just heard, the policeman smiled and said,

So you don't have any money?

Isn't it obvious? Benbé snapped back.

Well, that makes my case, Noah declared with obvious relief. If you're too poor, you'll be deported.

The curiosity seekers around them heard that the fellow in question was a pauper. Shaking their heads, they walked off in disgust. The simple truth was that it was against the laws of the United States to be poor. Nobody must be poor. At last only the policeman, the landlady and the stranger remained with Benbé.

Softhearted, the landlady tried to make her protégé apologize. In vain. Finally she turned angrily to the policeman, declaring firmly,

17

I don't want a scene in front of my house. Please leave at once!

Mumbling, the policeman tried to keep a professional aura about him,

I'll leave. But this young man will have to go with me. He's under arrest.

At this point the stranger intervened. Compassionate, he offered to put up bail.

And who are you? the policeman interrogated sternly. May I see your identification?

The stranger rummaged through his pockets, but was unable to find what he was looking for. Distressed, he blushed and mumbled at long last,

I had the card just a while ago.

Benbé came suddenly alive. Fumbling frantically through his goodies, he unearthed the card. The policeman read it, loud and curt,

Mr. Jonathan Borck, Beverly Hills. That you?

The stranger nodded. Benbé pulled out his pocket mirror, trying to clean his smudgy face. All of a sudden the policeman straightened up. His muscles bundling under his khaki uniform, he formally saluted the stranger and said,

I'm very happy to meet you, Sir. May I keep this card as a souvenir, please? Politely waving good-bye to the landlady, he took off with a pirouette-like trot and disappeared without taking further notice of the arrested Benjamin Borck.

Borck? the landlady gasped. You mean you are related to this boy?

Without looking up from the mirror, Benbé said,

Whether we're related? Can't you see that I look like a clown? This gentleman is my father's cousin, the famous Jac Tracbac.

3: The Scheme With The Cat, The Ring And The Clown

I CAUGHT HIM, Benbé thought. My scheme paid off. Now I better play it smart and take advantage of the situation. I ought to flatter him, soft-soap him with courtesy to reach my goal. Speak up! Don't be afraid, Benbé! You're a natural cheat and rogue . . . . Out loud he said,

Why don't you come in, Mr. Tracbac. Make yourself at home. I consider your presence here a great honor, I assure you. Whether you believe me or not.

Ingratiatingly, but decisively taking his uncle's right arm, he led him into his room.

Sit down in this nice rocker, he said, coaxing his guest down.

The famous artist looked somewhat puzzled. Gazing back and forth between door and window, he gave the impression of someone caught in a net. Benbé patted his shoulder soothingly,

You're with a friend and kinsman, he said, mindful that the nerves of famous artists merit special consideration. Nothing unpleasant will happen to you here.

I'm not too sure, Tracbac mumbled. Or I would've come earlier. You were waiting for me, I assume?

Benbé admitted truthfully,

I've been dying to meet you. I feel that you'll become an important factor in my life. A boy in my predicament needs to find an anchor wherever he can. Your permission to call you uncle, or cousin, or just simply by your first name would make me proud.

Disgusted with himself for uttering such blarney, he added quickly,

Actually I don't care. Did you like my present? How's our cat doing?

Thus far not much, Tracbac answered good-naturedly. But it's an unusually beautiful cat, I understand . . . the kind of cat I would have liked to get . . .

Benbé was angry. Of course, the clown never wanted a cat. Mailing the animal was meant to startle him, make him chuckle . . . It wasn't necessary that he should beat his drums . . . or grovel! For crying out loud — a clown should understand a joke. Who else if not he?

Benbé threw him a packet of cigarettes. But then he remembered that he ought to flatter the man and hurried to provide fire. Inexperienced in the art, he sided up to the clown and bowed,

19

Just think, having the honor to light Jac Tracbac's cigarette. I'm sure many good people envy me. Yes, sir, this is a strange land. People are interested in ludicrous matters. At home you're awfully popular. The newspapers are full of articles about you. A first-rate Nobel prize winner doesn't get a fraction of the attention. You'll agree that it's completely out of whack. People admire you into the skies and then some. There's no one as hilarious as Jac Tracbac.

Hilarious, the clown repeated, nodding with delight. Yes, I remember as a child using that word about stupid or ridiculous persons. Smiling, he repeated the word several times, Hilarious . . . hilarious . . . hilarious.

And just today I have to be in a foul mood, Benbé thought. I grovel, but my groveling is uneven. My behavior is even less endearing. I must keep in mind to get straight to the heart of the matter . . . and be shrewd about it. He said,

Well, let's talk about our dear family. I assume there's a lot you want to know . . . ?

Nothing, the clown said laconically.

Nothing? Benbé repeated, coughing up smoke as if someone had hit him in the stomach. No . . . oh . . . oh . . . thing? Do you mean nothing at all?

Correct. I couldn't care less about the family, the clown assured him.

That's all I needed to hear, Benbé called out, naively forgetting his tact. What am I then doing here? All I've ever heard at home was, There he is in far-away America, remembering us, but too embarrassed to write because of that incident. Well, you know what I'm referring to . . .

Really, out here we need other things to consider, Tracbac said almost apologetically. One forgets what brought us here.

Of course, Benbé agreed, shaking his head in disapproval. He had very strong moral convictions. A boy who filched and ran away ought to send home penitent, sad letters occasionally. Sullenly he declared,

You've been staring at my beloved, jovial Borck face for the last half hour or so without taking your eyes off. You must be wallowing in old memories. So much for that . . .

The clown cast an evaluating glance at Benbé, closed his quiet, tired eyes and shook his head. Benbé continued,

Your head-shake and your dignified behavior throws me totally off. That's what I get for trying to butter you up and for my brilliant cat idea.

Did you come here to meet me? the clown asked, a certain interest manifest in his voice. Benbé waved deprecatingly with his hand,

Oh no, not at all! Don't get conceited! To tell you the truth, I'd almost forgotten about you. But in Frisco I had a revelation — call it superstition or whatever. In a bank. When I discovered that my letter of credit had run out.

And that led your thoughts my way? How odd to call it superstition —

No, not really! Benbé assured him eagerly. Something made me think of Grandmother. I saw her walking on clouds, and you, Nathan Borck, the old lady's little pet, were hanging from her apron strings.

Oh, is that so? the clown mumbled, nodding.

Benbé continued, sarcastically,

Or, do you want to say that you forgot Grandma too? If that is so, I've really come to a crazy person. I could've saved myself stealing cats and doing other clever tricks . . .

Tracbac closed his eyes again and continued rocking in his chair. It was the first time that Benbé saw his famous relative smile — a smile accomplished with pouting lips that gradually pulled outward into a narrow line. My goodness, if this isn't an honest to goodness, patented clown's grin, Benbé thought.

Forgotten? Grandma? How absurd. How can I ever forget her. She scared the daylights out of me. I was afraid of her.

Afraid! Benbé shouted. You make me laugh! You want to tell me that you were afraid of the old lady? Listen, I don't buy that. Your memory is rotting. All Borcks know how crazy you were about her. You loved her.

That's true, Tracbac agreed. I liked her. But the one doesn't preclude the other. Without Grandma's powerful protection my life would have been much harder. She took me under her wings. But she inspired fear at the same time. Goodness, that woman knew how to put the jitters into my bones . . .

Benbé perceived an unpleasant mixture of fear and pleasure in the clown's tone of voice.

You seemed to have liked it. Your face beams with delight just remembering it, Benbé muttered.

Tracbac frowned. His answer was dry and gruff.

It's not unusual for children to form a strong bond with the strict parent or grandparent. Leniency is soon forgotten. That's my experience.

Here I am, exchanging banalities instead of begging outright, Benbé thought. One ought to learn begging in school. Sooner or later a person is bound to practice the art, in some way. Knowing Latin is nothing compared to knowing how to beg. Out loud he said,

I have a question. Perhaps you can tell me what is more difficult — to sponge from a rich relative who doesn't want to admit that he's taken for a sucker, or to be that relative who's conscious of the poverty-stricken moocher, who's on to your predicament and who's out to make you that sucker. Surely you haven't forgotten the cat and the facts that led to it, have you?

How true, indeed, Tracbac mumbled with alacrity. He dug deep into his wide pockets and pulled out a small box and a letter.

Here's the beggar's letter, Benbé remarked with an air of satisfaction. You probably wonder what the cat meant? I sent it to arouse your curiosity. If I had had the money I'd have sent an elephant. To drum up interest is most important.

Right, the clown mumbled. When I was your age — perhaps even slightly younger — I was a drummer. I stood by the tent entrance, drumming. I've learned to handle the instrument . . .

Anyway, he continued gravely, returning to this letter. It's not really begging. You're sending me Grandma's ring — or to be more precise, a ring with Grandma's hair. You'd like to give it to me as a present. However, you need to sell it . . . for financial reasons.

For crying out loud, why else would I be doing this? Benbé screamed angrily. Hasn't it sunk in yet that I'm sharking on family love?

You especially mention the ring's low commercial value . . . , Tracbac continued, disregarding the interruption.

I would say it's about eight dollars and fifty cents, the seller announced hesitantly.

Right now its commercial value is not the issue. As far as I'm concerned, this is a pure business deal . . .

If you want my opinion, this whole deal stinks. You seem to think that you frightened me when you said that you didn't care about our relatives. What do you expect? Need knows no laws, his young relative answered quietly.

Tracbac rose, eyeing his relative through halfway closed eyelids. He continued fiddling nervously with the letter and the box — as if assessing their value with his fingertips.

I take it then that all this is a mere joke you wanted to play on me. Not a very good joke, I dare say. Still . . . it's better that way . . . , he said.

Better this way? Better for you perhaps. I can't afford to contrive these practical jokes for nothing, Benbé repeated gruffly. He wished fervently for his landlady to show up with her ice water. In a hurry, too, if she wanted to catch a glimpse of our famous Tracbac, he thought.

The clown walked toward the door. But there he turned, irresolute and strangely agitated. He began to scamper back and forth in the room in that typically stumbling, frightened, rat-like, hilarious manner for which he was famous. His voice was subdued when he said,

Benjamin Borck, that's enough. A letter or messenger would easily have taken care of the ring business. But I got a strange idea to send you on an important mission. Of course . . . there's still the ring. Now I've second thoughts about that too. After all, you're not my son. I'm not responsible for your conduct.

He meditated for a while, fingering the box. Then he asked,

22

Benjamin, did you ever meet Grandma?

Benbé shook his head. The old lady had died one year before he was born. To him she was a mere household word in the family, important now because the runaway Jac Tracbac liked her. Staring at the floor, the clown continued,

Under the circumstances the ring can't be of great value to you. I have a collection of family mementos at home and I'd like to add this because it would fit nicely in with the rest. In short, I want to buy the ring.

Benbé, the hardened opportunist, took an audible breather through his tightly closed nostrils. It sounded almost like a sob and was probably meant to be, though his eyes remained decently dry. He was a very young man raised by a strict, well-meaning mother and verbs such as beg, bluff, cheat had never been part of his vocabulary. With a certain throatiness he declared,

Listen, Mr. Tracbac, if you're not completely densed up you ought to understand that I sent you ring, cat and the entire caboodle because I wanted a personal response. I wanted to talk to you.

So far the clown had quietly swallowed Benbé's rudeness. But once provoked, his anger was sudden and lightning-swift,

Talk, nothing but talk! I've listened to your bull, boy! And what did I get to hear? Nothing but rubbish and insolence! For a moment he was silent, then continued, far gentler now,

I'm going to buy the ring. It's just that I find it awkward to mix money and emotional matters. I see that you have no close emotional ties to Grandma. So there remains only the problem of setting the price. Have you an idea?

His gall at the boiling point, Benbé was ready to shoot off his big mouth again. It was hard to suffer humiliation for which he could blame only himself. Immature, he thought of acting bold and cocky, even cynical, important, to assert his masculinity. Stroking his beard, the symbol of his masculinity, he played the speculative salesman with great cunning,

Let me see . . . it's not easy to set the price . . . you are so right . . . to evaluate something like this . . . Grandma's hair . . . dear old Grandmother . . . is a hundred thousand too much?

Benbé's strange behavior convinced Tracbac that the young man was trying to pull his leg, which was hard to explain. He had wanted his relative to help him and had met him halfway. Now that he had succeeded he was torn between his need for help and old ingrained biases and scruples against accepting help. In fact, he was doing his best to ruin his chances. This dilemma is less a sign of the past than of modern time where the gospel of modern heroes teaches to outsmart fellow humans, especially in financial matters. These glorified roll models of contemporary youth may be legally correct, but they ignore morals and ethic values in their dealings. Benbé's desires were at odds with his old-fashioned, strict Längsäll upbringing.

Carrying her tray with ice cubes and cocktails, the Canadian landlady arrived just in time to ease the tension Benbé's rude behavior had caused in the room. The paper-thin walls had allowed her to overhear the two argue heatedly. But, not understanding a word of their language presented the temperamental, highly imaginative woman with a certain dilemma. She believed strongly in certain obligations. Whenever "her boy" sounded rude to the famous clown she lifted two fingers as if to threaten him. Whenever Tracbac seemed arrogant, nasty and impudent she pressed her fists so hard into her sides that her blood shot up into her cheeks. Finally she became too aggravated to remain passive. She took her tray and resolutely walked into the room of her boarder.

She gave the clown a polite welcoming nod and asked him to forgive her for leaving him alone with this boorish boy. That done, she turned quietly to the agitated youngster. She stuck two fingers inside his collar to check his temperature to make sure that he was physically all right. Then she assured the great Tracbac that this was the greatest and most interesting day in her entire life. Imagine, one of the most famous men in the United States visiting in her house. She told him,

You're awfully funny, Jac Tracbac — every time I see one of your movies I'm sick laughing for the next two days. Well, funny you may be, but life is more than a bunch of jokes and clowning. So shame on you, Jac Tracbac. Even a jester has human and Christian responsibilities. What kind of relative are you? This poor boy is about bankrupt and too proud to eat my good food because he can't pay! Mark my words, if he goes to the dogs, I've seen the last of your movies. And let me tell you . . .

See here, the rescue squad in action, Benbé interrupted quietly. Politely, but decisively, he offered the lady his arm. With a quick smile she told the clown,

Don't forget that this is the proudest day in my life, Mr. Tracbac.

Her gold-fluffed head gracefully bent, she followed her knight back to the kitchen. Their ensuing conversation was unimportant. But when Benbé hastened back to his room he found that Tracbac had quietly taken this chance to leave. Benbé felt relieved at first, but he soon began to worry. All his craft had been in vain. The famous, hard-caught relative had slipped through his fingers. I'm not good at being smart, he thought. I may be an unscrupulous joker, but when things come down to the nitty-gritty I lose my guts — I get angry and that spells the end of the deal. A good cheat has no business getting angry.

He emptied his glass of ice water and contemplated. Then he downed his cocktail and contemplated some more. Absentmindedly he fingered a piece of paper that was left on the tray which, as it turned out, was a check for $8,508.50.

Benbé understood well that this large sum was meant to absolve Tracbac of any responsibility toward his needy relative. But this merely stimulated the youth to greater efforts in his con game. His early moral education had taught him not to cheat or steal. Even if it meant dying of hunger would he consider accepting the money. Then again, since the first commandment in this modern catechism of opportunism taught him Don't miss your chance, it forbade him just as strictly to let this chance slip through his fingers. Benbé grinned at the valuable check in his hand,

What a clown! A real joker. I told him the ring was worth eight fifty.

Propelled by a sudden urge to ease his heart, he went to the kitchen and showed the check,

Mrs. Canadian, I sold that ring I told you about. He paid the tidy sum of $8,508 for it.

She took the piece of paper. Rather unseemly, but fully in line with her current frame of mind, she took the fork and scratched her head. Reading the sum over and over again, she shrieked,

Can you imagine! Some ring! Why did I never get to see it?

Because I sent it to Tracbac right after buying it in a Los Angeles junk shop. For eight fifty. Talk about a deal!

He hurried outside and ran up and down the tangle of palm-lined recti- linear asphalt streets, his hands deep in the pockets of the same suit he had worn on his visit in Sanna. Suddenly his left hand happened to slide through the ripped pocket lining and his thoughts shifted away from the clown. He held the small package wrapped in white paper which his cousin Sanna- Sanna had given him on the sly and which he had promised not to open be- fore coming to the United States. With an absent-minded smile he tore away the bright red string the girl had tied around the box addressed to him. Ex- pecting some kind of love token and wondering what it would be, he un- wrapped the outer layer. He found a second wrap underneath, this one addressed to Jonathan Borck.

Benbé understood that the package was not for little Ben and smiled. It was for Big Nathan. He turned it over. On its backside was another note,

"To be sent to him after my death."

What a little neurotic, he mused. Then it hit him — like a flash of revela- tion — the handwriting on the outer wrapper was not the same as the writ- ing on the inside cover . . .

4: The Negro Longfellow Lectures On
Modern Psychology

BENB GREETED TRACBAC'S gate-bouncer loftily, careful to hide his intimi-
dation,

Well, here we meet again. I was looking forward to seeing you.

The Negro produced a patronizing grin,

Please come in, Mr. Borck. No fresh rolls today — forgot to bake them,
Sir. You sure got me into trouble. A lot more than you're worth —

It's reassuring to hear you say that, Benbé countered. I hope your boss
gave you a good piece of his mind —

My boss? the Black closed his eyes and shook his head. Not at all, Sir!
Mr. Tracbac never scolds. If something needs to be said, he tells his secretary
in Los Angeles. As soon as he gets the message this Yahoo shows up in a
hurry. The fellow's not bigger than a common flea, but he sure knows to
bite. Worse than a bedbug.

The Negro opened the gate,

Please, sit down on that bench in the shade there. You look hot. You'll
need a rest before we start.

Wiping the perspiration off his face, Benbé sat down. The black man sat
down beside him, puffing on his fat, dark cigar with great relish.

I have no idea whether you'll be here often from now on, or never again,
Sir. How could I know? Anyway, it won't hurt to tell you a thing or two
about my dead father. A remarkable man — a teacher in Florida — knew
more poetry by heart than anyone I know. Good poetry, mind you, no
spirituals or pop. Mother used to say that he lived and died for poetry. I
never really understood what she meant, the black man declared.

I wouldn't know either, Benbé told him. But we're not discussing your
father, are we? We're talking about your boss.

I'm telling you about my father, the Negro interrupted. He sure was a
very generous man, especially to his children, all eleven of them. No prefer-
ences, you know. Treated us all alike. Generous to a fault in naming us. Gave
us the very best names he could think of. Names ennoble, Sir. And they're
inexpensive too. Christened me Edgar Allan Fennimore Longfellow Harriet
Bret Hart Whitman Irving. All winners, you know. Leaves me plenty to pick
from, Mr. Borck. My brothers had to make do with Homer, Dante and
other such common names. I like all my names, except Harriet. Sure, the

woman was pious and good like me, but there the similarities end. In general, I'm known as Longfellow. And rightly so.

Without doubt, Benbé agreed. But we're still talking about your boss.

Were we? Indeed. Longfellow said. Well, that's not surprising. After all, we're on his grounds. That's his house there behind the palm trees — a Mexican-style ranch house with fifty-eight rooms and nine courtyards. Well, perhaps one hundred and fifty-eight. If you're curious about details ask the reporters. They keep track of such stuff. I bet you anything you'll get lost in that building, more than you ever did in your whole life —

Okay! Let's try, Benbé said, rising quickly. But the black man was quicker. Grabbing Benbé by the seat of his pants, he pulled him back down— a move so sudden and hard Benbé's neck nearly crashed against the wall.

Take it easy, the black man told him. The secretary ordered me to entertain you best I can during the time you care to stay. I think I do, don't you agree, Mr. Borck? Let me know when you get tired of me. The grounds are large enough and there's plenty to admire to keep you entertained for a day or two. See these Japanese. The best gardeners in California. They take care of Tracbac's botanical gardens. He spent over a quarter of a million to design them, mind you.

Is he that interested in plants? Benbé inquired.

What do I know? Longfellow said. If you're not interested in plants, there's more. This path on the right leads to an artificial creek that feeds an artificial stream full of trout. Along its banks stand several unused water mills and -wheels. The most ingenious, ineffective contraptions that cost more than a quarter of a million just to install . . .

I'm not at all surprised, Benbé remarked, remembering his father's cousin on Sannafors who went broke tinkering with all sorts of strange constructs. Not at all. Mechanical genius runs in our family.

I'm not so sure whether genius is the right term. But mechanical sure is, Longfellow said, coughing on his puffs. If that's not your cup of tea, take the path to the left. Walk about ten minutes and you'll see ape city — a big pit with all sorts of monkeys in the trees. They're without leaves because these rascals chewed the foliage off a long time ago. Some of their cages look like Christian dwellings, others like pagan huts, and some like incubators. They're for the chimpanzees, gorillas and such — the best apes.

He's crazy about apes, Benbé interrupted. I read that in the newspapers.

What do I know? Longfellow said. Crazy or not, he's afraid of them, that's for sure. He doesn't get near these beasts without his guards. And whenever he dares getting near them, the apes growl and snarl. Just like humans. I suspect the guards put them up to it. They never growl at me. At any rate, you should see my boss then — ducking backward into a corner, crouching down, growling and snarling just like these apes. If they weren't animals and he a Christian, one might think they're siblings or halfway related in some way. I'm telling you, Sir, no other human on this planet can do these apelike tricks as well as my boss. Really, he outperforms these apes. And he earns millions doing that —

How utterly strange, Benbé mumbled.

Strange or not, who's to say? Longfellow said. I'm instructed to keep you entertained as long as you want. I can tell you stories I wouldn't repeat to just any junk collector or oil king. I'll even stick to the truth —

Oh, promise not to try too hard, I beg you, Benbé said politely.

I assure you that I'll keep my personal opinions out of the picture, the black man grinned. I'll fill you in on how these three global marvels — the botanical gardens, the mechanized waterfalls and the ape compound — came here. They cost millions, but my boss doesn't care too much about that. Might give you some insights into human nature, Mr. Borck, in case you're interested —

Longfellow lighted his second giant cigar before he continued,

When I came here just about ten years ago there was nothing here except the villa, a barn and a garage, the gym hall, the tennis courts and the pool. Some trees here and there, but nothing out of the ordinary. In his sort of uncultured, amoral way Mr. Tracbac seemed satisfied with life here. People in his category rarely know what they want out of life. They create syndicates and hire directors and secretaries and such to disentangle their wants and needs. Otherwise they'd never know they have any.

See, a lot of people from all over the States come to shake Jac Tracbac's hand, snap pictures, etc. Nothing wrong with that if you're strong enough to take it. But my boss isn't, and his art even less. So, I'm here to get rid of riffraff and violent, shady characters quickly — you found that out already. But, Sir, some don't belong in that category. My methods are sometimes too simple, outright unpopular, see. That creates problems. Before long people found this place sorely lacking in civil behavior, organization, culture, morals, etc.

I couldn't care less about those highfalutin things, but that about morals really got to me. Morals is a tricky issue, Sir. A person without morals is a danger to himself. If he has them, he's dangerous to others. That's where our problem got started. Unless his secretary had checked them inside and out and found them worthy of shaking hands with our great Jac Tracbac, people weren't allowed to enter the grounds. And how many were there who could? Not more than ten percent, I'd say. Those who got a complimentary free kick in the pants became vocal. And soon reporters got into the act. The papers devoted almost as much space on that subject as on presidential issues, kidnapings and famous murders . . .

28

Why can't Jac Tracbac open his gates for decent fellow citizens? What's he trying to hide in his secretive villa? Orgies? If so, what kind? Mr. Borck, they imagined all kinds of carousals — liquor, sex, other stuff — whatever kind a dirty mind can think of.

People are stupid, Longfellow continued calmly. Certainly are. Only exceptions are you and me and our dear relatives. Once I saw a movie about the lives of famous circus artists — how they live, work, love. Supposedly real life pictures, Sir. What did they show? Unbelievably heroic performances at night. Lewdness and disorder the rest of the day — the real fire and brimstone stuff preachers love to condemn.

D'you really think a circus artist or famous sport hero can live like a pig? D'you really think guys and dames can properly swing on the trapeze, or handle a gun, or kick a ball when they're stoned? You don't and neither do I. We know better. Perhaps a king, or a president might possibly get away with it. Not that I'm saying that it happens — not at all. I can't remember, Sir, ever having shaken hands with a drunken king. All I'm saying is that it's possible that a king drinks gallons of whisky without disrupting his country because he has a prime minister to take care of his affairs. But a tightrope dancer — no siree, Sir, nobody else's legs, body, or brains can do his work! That's impossible. He must guard his body like a miser his dollar, or a holy man his soul because that's all he has.

Well, that's our educated argument, Mr. Borck. But we're dealing with fatheads, see. Getting back to Jac Tracbac — once these rumors got started the papers began asking questions. Why is he so secretive? Why does he throw people out? His place must be full of floozies and other trash. Others knew of stealing innocent children on travels around the world. Or that he would if only he weren't spending his days drunk in bed.

You see, Mr. Borck, such rumors threatened not only our daily lives. Our Tracbac stocks took a terrible dive on the stock market. (See, we aren't just simple private persons, but a corporation listed on Wall Street. We have our bullish ups and bearish downs.) I'll tell you, Sir, our secretary deserves a lot of credit, poor fellow, considering where he's spending his summer vacation. His name is Abel Rush, though I prefer to call him Cain — my sneaky way of pegging him — though, truth to say, he's a better judge of human character than the two of us put together. He had the bright idea to keep Jac Tracbac's private life out of the public eye because there's nothing to see. It would hurt him professionally. Of course, you can't separate the clown completely from the people. That's why I'm here — to keep people from seeing what we don't want them to see. We show them the essential Jac Tracbac — his soul and his morals.

The eight largest rooms in his home are chock-full of old paintings, marble guys and wooden guys, stuff made of iron, books and other such junk from a grand past that's dead, so to speak. He hired an art professor from Boston to organize the stuff and lecture the crowds coming through. This professor declared our collection the most accomplished in the States, next to that of Mogens J. Piergans — not just old trash, but first class stuff, properly worm-eaten, moldy and warped, all in line with the latest research.

But, Mr. Borck, the whole idea was stupid, Longfellow continued, lighting his third cigar. Cain emphasized art, but he ignored moral standards. It wasn't long before honorable Mormon preachers sounded off against ancient depravity and temptations of the flesh. Puritanical prohibitionists preached against showing pictures of carousing Dutch peasants playing drunken jokes on each other, convinced that seeing such wickedness would lead to imitation. Background and example determine people's characters they said. Believe me, enough people listened.

Well, once these wise men started, the whole world chimed in. But all this fuss sideswiped Tracbac because he never looked at newspapers or came near the gate. His secretary got the blame and the board threatened to kick him out. Of course, our Cain wasn't born yesterday, Sir. He wanted a round million from the board. That's when our botanical gardens, the artificial waterfalls and the ape compound came in.

I can't see what they're for, Benbé said, nonplussed.

Longfellow smiled triumphantly,

For sure. You're not supposed to, Mr. Borck. They would lose their intended effect if these idiots understood what gardens, apes and waterfalls are for. But as a guide of these hordes traipsing through here I can see the Cainite ideas work. Listen! When my little lambs have seen the gardens and all the great and small things and have finished their admiring Ah!'s and Oh!'s there's always some good-looking, romantic female among them that comes forward — may even climb on a stone if there's a big one nearby — and declare,

To grow flowers is to worship our creator.

Or she might say,

Planting herbs is the noble man's poetry.

Or something like that. I don't need to tell you that Jac Tracbac gets all the credit, though he never even sets foot in these gardens. Yeah, famous persons reap all the merits — it's like that here. I imagine in other countries too. There may be a hundred, or even a thousand talented Japanese working on his plants — people will still think he digs the dirt, plants the bulbs, waters and nurses them along. So, you see, this is the way our smart Cain wants us to look — God's helpers in Nature and poets in the Gardens of Paradise. That's the impression people get.

What about the ape compound? Where does that fit in? Benbé wondered.

Same thing, on a more solid moral level, Longfellow said. When the whole caboodle — men, women, oldies, children — are done unmercifully teasing the apes and they have laughed their fill, some tenderhearted woman will declare that loving animals is the trademark of civilization. Meaning that our boss is highly civilized —

Do they get paid for that?

Who? The women? Oh, no, no. A fellow might do this for money. But not a woman. She acts on some inner inspiration. And then she can't shut up, even if she wants to. Then come the waterfalls — they strike my lambs with awe. Serene and hushed, people try to figure the underlying reason for this collection of contraptions. I explain that my boss reassembled them after drawings he brought home from the old country. When they see no practical reason for the falls, some old general will tip his hat and declare: Edison. One word. No more.

Oh, well, Longfellow continued, lighting his fourth cigar. After the artificial waterfalls there's no danger taking the caravan to the art collection. Sort of heightens the all-over effect, like putting the dot over the i, as it were. One thing I have to remember above all — never show the art first. People look at the artist with a lot of suspicion. The same applies to the art lover, unless he plays the solid citizen. But things are improving. Some experts see our exhibit on a par with the Mogens J. Piergans collection.

Really! Benbé burst out, impressed.

Oh, yes! Indeed! Longfellow said, closing his eyes in inordinate pride. The crux of the matter is that the man himself is less important than what surrounds him. A person with a weak spot in his past can make up for it with his surrounding. It makes people wonder about him, especially if he's a big cheese. A noble environment ennobles the owner. Untold examples in the history of the world show that. Take Napoleon who dubbed counts, dukes and even kings at will. He and his relatives became high society.

Benbé got down to business trying to win his guardian over to his own ends,

Now, when can I meet Tracbac? Listen, Longfellow, be reasonable — I simply have to see him in person —

Have to is a most compelling reason, Longfellow agreed. If you have to, you have to, said the thief and grabbed hold of the moon. Mind you, he never went beyond his good intentions. His ladder was too short, see. I think that every human gets his personal ladder cut to size from the start. Some have short, others long ladders. This birth ladder sets the stage for the person's life. The short-laddered people stick to their low rungs and long-laddered persons climb to the stars, so to speak. It may seem unfair, but let me tell you, things even out in the end. Those with small, handy ladders scamper easily through the world. They soon find their target and are happy.

31

It's far more difficult to drag a heavy stellar ladder about. Raising it in its destined place and then anchoring it there is difficult enough, even before climbing its many rungs. When they finally reach the enviable top, they may admire their star-studded reflections in the floodlights. But I think that many top stars have broken their backs getting there. Their ladders wobble underneath them.

The Negro bent suddenly forward and put his hand on Benbé's knee. Glancing furtively right and left, he whispered,

Mister Borck, your worthy relative, my boss, is one of these star-sitters with a broken back. No one knows it, and no one must ever know. But I have eyes. I can see —

Snuffling the way troubled people often do, Benbé stroked the tip of his nose with his forefinger — an ugly habit, a sort of rudimentary clearing of the brain. With stolid determination he pulled out a check and said with a heavy heart,

I shouldn't show you this check because the way I got it was rather embarrassing. I'm doing it now because I must return it to your boss — personally. Really, Longfellow. I'm telling you the truth.

The black man thought for a moment, then he said in a friendly tone,

I understand, young man. You've goofed and now your conscience haunts you. Not that you were dishonest exactly, but you want to come clean. That's honorable. You'll look like a second George Washington in no time at all — a sort of cheaper edition. Let me see what I can do. This thing may take time so you better spend some time with the apes and the waterfalls. It's not a piece of cake to straighten a fake. Walk this way Sir — Mr. Borck — take the falls first, They're worthwhile. Look at them —

Benbé got up and trudged rather reluctantly off in the direction shown. He saw Japanese workers in the hills, a flock of children clinging to their sides. A group of black children played between the white jasmine bushes further on. From the steps of her gatekeeper's lodge mylady Longfellow was trying hard to coax her curly-headed offspring home,

Elynor! Sinclair! Carra! O'Neal!

Art lovers, these Longfellows. Surely kept their poetic traditions alive — ingrained, superficial outer trappings for a family unfamiliar with literary pursuits. The black smallfry came running to their bungalow. It was time for lunch.

My business will have to wait until their onion soup is properly digested, Benbé thought. My problems must in no way interfere with his bread. A sound principle.

Rather depressed Benbé ambled toward the mechanical falls. But he was wrong doubting Longfellow's determination. The black man spooned his soup with one hand; with the other he dialed the telephone.

5: King Clown And His Dancer

OPPORTUNITY MAKES THE thief. Or, opportunity knocks but once, or, better yet, grab chance by its tail! The person's character rather than good luck determines a man's fate! That was it. Like many young people, Benjamin Borck liked taking shortcuts. Not because he was lazy. No, it was more a matter of impatience. Unfortunately, waiting was not one of his virtues. In a hurry to get to his famous relative to present his cause, he had devised the scheme with the cat and the ring.

But his easy success turned his head. He had been very rude to his relative when he should have flattered him. He was desperate to straighten things out.

His usual shortcut-method should have led Benbé through the palm-studded property straight to the large, black entrance door of the somber, flesh-colored, rather bulky residence of the clown. But experience had taught young Benbé the strangely reversed logic that the shortest distance between two points is often a crooked line, the curvier the better. Thus he strolled up Jasmine Path at the safe distance of about two hundred meter from the villa.

The decision greatly improved Benbé's disposition. He merrily juggled his buckled hat. The small creek below the falls with its lively sprattling fishes was really super. He inspected the strange mechanics of the waterfalls from up close and admired their ingenuity. Giddy like a boy playing hooky, he yelped,

Oh, Sanna, Sanna!

Here stood the exact replicas of the crazy contraptions at Sanna. Even experts considered them products of genius.

A man dressed in plain work clothes came briskly walking down the banks of the falls toward Benbé, wiping his mouth as if he had just disrupted his lunch. The revolver on his belt suggested one of the supervisors. Benbé expected another interrogation. Much to his surprise, the man offered to run the machines, smiling his typical, friendly American smile.

They're amazing, Mr. Borck, he told him.

Benbé was surprised to hear the man addressing him by his name. Had the black gatekeeper alerted everyone on the estate? Could his luck have taken a sudden turn for the better? He thought to detect a certain deference in their behavior toward him. Or was behind all this merely an order to keep him under supervision? The supervisor disappeared in one of the man-made dripstone caves and after a few minutes the entire assortment of machines clunked into action. Benbé was impressed. The invention was ingenious. Back at pristine Sanna these contraptions had looked like the expensive tinkertoys of a grown-up child. In their new location they performed a valuable service — bluffing a curious, powerful public into thinking that this strange Jac Tracbac tinkered with a legitimate, worthwhile hobby.

Trained and knowledgeable, the supervisor explained the mechanics of the machines while Benbé pondered his upcoming meeting with Tracbac. He would readily admit to having lied about the ring. But he would emphasize that he was not an ordinary crook. No, necessity had driven him to cheat. There was a fine line, a definite distinction between the two kinds of crookedness. Just like the difference between an ordinary and an "extraordinary" clown.

The Negro had left Benbé forty-five minutes earlier. Full of impatience Benbé strode past the falls. The supervisor caught up with him, grabbing his arm with the force of the typical American supervisor. Benbé tried to wrench himself free. What was this fellow up to?

Nothing special, the man answered. We could go to the ape compound and have a good time. There comes my colleague on the other side.

Indeed — the head of the foreman's twin rose over a dense aloe hedge. Benbé cringed. This supervision was getting too much. Stretching to his full length, he spoke up,

What's the matter with you people? Mr. Tracbac is waiting for me.

The twin coming from the ape compound crossed the bridge and the supervisor introduced his protégé — or was it prisoner?

Ah, yes, I know, Supervisor No Two said, smiling just like No One before. I know all about him. Nice weather today, Mr. Borck, isn't it?

The three crossed the bridge. Once on the other side, the aloe hedge concealed them from anyone spying from the main building.

Benbé was right. His friend Jac was indeed anxiously waiting for him. Tracbac had seen Benbé playing with his hat on the jasmine path. Now the clown was pacing nervously back and forth on the terrace surrounding his villa.

One of several doors on the opposite side of the terrace stood open. The terrace itself led to a large backyard with a square pool in its center. Vines climbed over the pool's edges and water splashed softly from its fountain in the center into the waters below. Chinese ducks with shiny, steel-blue bodies and yellow-red heads fluttered about, their hisses frightening the smaller, colorful Japanese sea-ducks. A sack hung over the balustrade, embroidered with the words "The needy beggar thanks God for old bread." It was a keepsake from Sanna, now filled with stale bread to feed the gorgeous waterfowl beggars. A long bamboo stick in his hand, Jac shouted at them, trying to establish fair dealings between Japanese and Chinese,

34

I find your behavior disgusting, my little darlings. Beautiful garments hiding ugly character traits. There are rewards for neighborly sharing.

Tracbac himself wore a rather strange outfit — old-fashioned, starched chokers under a long black coat; a wide, flowery shawl; and tight yellow nankin pants with straps. Across his stomach hung a heavy, golden watch chain. Bundles of charms dangled from its double links. He looked like a well-to-do burgher or the chairman of a Chamber of Commerce from the early nineteenth century.

He put his stick aside and resumed his walk up and down the veranda. His hands were folded under his coat tails whose ends flared out like a rooster tail. Visibly impatient, he mumbled

Well, why isn't he coming? How long am I supposed to wait here? I wonder whether he came only out of curiosity? It's a much stronger drive than honesty. People are curious —

Impulsively he walked toward the open door. Leaning back against the door post and his left arm twisted and slanting backward, he looked strangely crooked. He spread the fingers of his right hand stiffly against his face as if trying to ward off a strike and thumb his nose at the same time. His mouth opened as if in convulsions, like the square orifice of a tragic mask. Except for some slight, hardly discernible twitches in his upper trunk, he remained motionless in this position for four or five minutes. Eventually his impatience got the better of him and he shouted,

Now, isn't this long enough? I'd say it's enough already, don't you agree?

An easel stood on the other side of the open door. In front of it sat a young woman painting the clown the way he had looked in his very first role. Neither his dress nor his behavior was all that strange, considering that the outfit had become the famous trademark of Tracbac the Clown. He hated to stand model, but he had two valid reasons for doing it. Years ago the woman had been his wife. The marriage may have been short-lived, but he still loved her deeply. Her name was Siva Yala, the dancer — offspring of an Irish mother and a gypsy father.

With a diffident air about her as if she were asking for something outrageous or dangerous, she said,

May I ask you to resume that position just once more?

His fingers raised, Tracbac walked over to her, cupped her head between his hands and kissed her eyelashes. Softly blowing through her hair, he said,

My little gypsy, your pitch-black hair and your brown skin may show your lowly origin. But where did you steal these beautiful, amber eyes? I can't help kissing them — irresistible amber orifices full of cigarette smoke — strongly scented and slightly nauseating.

Get back into position, if you don't mind, the girl insisted.

35

Not for a hundred dollars, my little one, not for fifty, not even for twenty-five.

Muttering under his breath, he resumed his pacing across the gallery,

Why doesn't the rascal show up? What'll I do if he doesn't show at all? Send for him? That wasn't in my plans. This is his test. If he doesn't come on his own I can't use him.

On a sudden impulse, Tracbac stuck his head inside the door and declared harshly,

Siv, did I tell you that Abel Rush wants to get me on the road again next month? My last tour was two years ago, he tells me. Well, it's fine with me. But I won't do it unless that certain person comes and not only agrees, but completes what I want him to do to my full satisfaction. No, I definitely won't.

He trudged on, his coattails swinging. Dressed like this, he resembled his grandfather — a small, wiry, nervous man, slightly epileptic. His grandfather had had the same habit of wandering about, coattails flying while contemplating large sums of money and the pros and cons of weighty bank dealings. In comparison, the transaction his grandson had in mind was far more important.

Siv's sigh sounded habitual. As a dancer she had made quite a name for herself by the time she was sixteen years old. She had hoped that marrying Jac Tracbac would ease her way to the pinnacles of stardom. A publicity stunt for her, the marriage for Jac Tracbac was hardly more than a case of innate lethargy. It was during a conference that the dancer's manager had cornered Abel Rush about a marriage between the two. Rush then invited her to one of the famous clown's garden parties at his estate. To the secretary's later query whether he liked Siva, Tracbac's answer was a dispassionate,

Great.

She wants to marry you.

Outstanding, Tracbac said. He loved the contrast of pitch-black hair and amber eyes.

Shall I arrange it then? the secretary inquired.

Fine with me, Tracbac responded.

The two were married. Tracbac liked it. Their subsequent divorce was just as okay with him. Their problem surfaced a few months after the wedding while they were having tea on some hotel veranda in Florida. Pressing her hands to her heart, Siv suddenly fixed her amber eyes on her husband and moaned,

Oh-o-o-ooh —

Startled, the clown vaulted out of his chair, his face contorted in one of those ugly grimaces for which he was famous through movies and circus appearances.

You must forgive me, Siv said, knowing how expensive these grimaces were. Sorry for acting up like that, Jac dear. It suddenly occurred to me that I'm in love.

No harm done, so it's easy to forgive, Tracbac reassured her, easing himself back into his chair. With whom, if I may ask?

You, Mrs. Tracbac answered without a moment's hesitation.

Tracbac stroked his chin, assessing the situation. Trying, as usual, to make light of serious predicaments, he declared with a smile,

Oh, well, we're on our honeymoon, so this may pass. But please, Siv, don't make it a permanent habit. You mustn't. I've been in love once and regret it still. Just take it easy and it'll blow over.

Siv's love did not pass. Her marriage did. That this marriage never advanced her own career deepened her disappointment. Both secretary and manager realized their mistake too late. She was well-known all right. But when Siva Yala the dancer became Mrs. Tracbac, her husband's fame pushed hers aside. Just that.

But fame was no longer the issue. Having children was. Siva wanted them. Tracbac did not, arguing with misguided, dogged bullheadedness that children would interfere with his career. In truth, his hostility ran far deeper. The sickly offspring of a strong-willed grandmother, he was afraid of passing on some inherited infirmities, couching his misgivings carefully with the rationalization,

Siv, you need to consider your career. Or we'll have to get a divorce —

You're a jerk, Siv said and filed for divorce.

Marry someone else and you'll be fine, Tracbac advised her.

But she was spiteful. She remained single and childless just to show the great Tracbac that her willpower was equal to his. Preferring her comfort, she stopped dancing altogether and destroyed her career just to make Jac feel guilty.

She took up painting, a former hobby, which became her second career. Her art showed considerable flair and a certain boldness, but it remained superficial, a handicap she never overcame. In her personal life, she continued to monopolize her former husband. To spite him, she signed her works "divorced wife." He overlooked her shenanigans. Yes, he was easily frightened. But he would never respond to provocation and he was forgiving to a fault. She established several studios, but did most of her work in Tracbac's villa. Friends maintained that she stuck close to him just to keep other women at bay.

37

Repeatedly checking his watch as if it held some urgent message, Tracbac continued pacing the veranda — muttering all the while,

What's the matter? Why doesn't he come? What shall I do?

Now and then he raised his eyebrows, or arched his arms in a wide sweep. He looked like a village shopkeeper praising his wares, or talking politics with friends from behind his counter. Without stopping his pacing, or even looking up, he suddenly burst out,

You want to know of course what all this is about. I want to establish contact with a woman. Now, I hope you're satisfied?

Indeed, Siv answered quietly. Is it something like your last affair?

My last affair? Tracbac repeated, insulted. What do you know about that? When did I ever confide in you? Do you know of any love affairs in my past? Please, don't say such things! My last affair? Sure, a romping delight that was.

Delight. Indeed! Siv said.

It's true, the clown said, rubbing his hands with a satisfied mien. But this is something else. I'm waiting for my relative. He's the only one able to help me — and now he doesn't show. How d'you like that! And I know he's on the grounds. I saw him earlier. Within arm's reach. But he doesn't come to see me. It's really something, don't you think?

Why not send for him, Siv suggested.

Tracbac kicked the floor hard. The splinters of the worthy old planks taken from an old Spanish-Mexican mansion whirled high into the air,

No, no no! He must come here on his own. Here's the case. He's a poor boy, a distant relative. He wrote me a letter, which Rush dutifully confiscated. He tried to visit me, and Longfellow threw him out. After that he sent me a cat, a ring and a letter. That prank finally clicked. Why? Because I can't stand cats wearing collars around their necks. Well, when Longfellow brought me the cat I removed the collar and let the animal run free. But I found a letter inside the collar and in it a locket ring containing a lock of hair from my grandmother. Well, you know about my grandmother.

Sure. You described her. Even had me paint her portrait no less than three times —

From someone who's never even met the old lady the pictures were excellent, Tracbac agreed. Benjamin, my relative, can't have seen her either. It's only natural for the boy to imagine an eighty-year old woman with white hair. The lock in that ring was white. Problem is that grandmother had black hair when she died, see? As black as yours.

A real con-artist, this relative of yours! Siv mocked.

Sure. A real little fraud. But, I did look him up, pretended not to be wise to his sham. I left him a roundly sum for the ring — and disappeared. Look. If that boy is really a low-down, incurable joker, he'll run off with the money. If he's not, he'll show up and say that what he did was a youthful prank to get my attention. Well, he got my attention all right. Now, my argument runs like this: one — he is shrewd; two — he's relatively honest. Add to this that we're related and that he expects me to help him — well, that makes him exactly the person I need —

Need? Siv mocked indignantly, her eyes flashing wild sparks. Need what? That woman you were talking about?

Tracbac shook his head, trying to explain,

You're some woman, indeed, and I wish I could love you. But I can't. I need another woman. Now hear the truth. I can in all honesty say that there is no one and nothing I love, neither woman, dog, cat, horse, ape, nor anything else. I'm burned out. It's all the same to me. I'm asked to perform — and I'm wondering why I should. Do I care about the applause? The whistles? Not in the least. Do I want to heap up money? For whom? The Tracbac syndicate? Or myself? I have no ambitions, no vices, no hobby, no desire to do good or evil. Name one thing that I want or desire?

Sure, the woman answered quickly.

The clown shrugged his shoulders.

No, my doll, you can't. Neither you nor anyone else. Why should I work? Ah, yes, I see that triumphant smile on your face, you little wretch. Why not get married again, Jac Tracbac? I'll bear you twelve healthy kids! That'll give you something to work for, clown! Yes, have them first and reflect later! Twelve little Tracbacs, six males, six females! How utterly ludicrous. No. Bringing children into this world would do my colleagues a lot of harm because I'd create an enormous oversupply of clowns and a colossal slump in earning power on the clown market. Buffoons for sale to the lowest bidder.

He kicked again in Siv's direction and went on,

Well, my little, gold-eyed animal, pray tell what I want and desire! Didn't you say you knew? Let's hear it! What is it I want?

Her heart pounded with fear, but she feigned total disinterest when she quietly answered,

What you want, Jac? You want to perform.

For an instant he stood perfectly still. Then he came wildly alive, grabbed his bamboo stick and hurled it like a spear out into the water. The flustered ducks ran noisily quacking in all directions. As in a frenzy, Tracbac turned around and faced the woman now standing stiffly pressed against the wall. His shoulders moved up, then down again. His arms hung loose and his legs wobbled as if his hip joint were broken. He looked like an ape trying to walk upright. Edging closer to Siv, he grabbed her wrists, brought his face down to hers and said,

Do you know what it costs me to perform? Do you know the price I have to pay? Oh no, you don't! You couldn't possibly know! No one knows, except me! Me! Because I have to pay the price —

He said it calmly, but there was a whiny, rather bitter undertone, just as old businessman Borck must have sounded complaining about hard times in an effort to undercut some frivolous expense. The woman stood still, utterly frightened, the wings of her nose trembling as she caught her breath. His hands drew slowly a caressingly investigative arc over her naked arms all the way up to her shoulders. She tried hard to keep her muscles still and loose. He lifted her hand, but let it drop again. Her arm dangled loosely down her side as if she were a corpse, or asleep. He quieted down.

He began to undress in a hurry. The woman giggled — as much as she dared under the circumstances, then scolded,

Well, aren't you ashamed, Jac? How shocking! Do you want to undress out here, in front of me?

How right you are! So thoughtless of me, the clown roared and limped off. He looked like a boy on his hobby horse, both hands holding on to his pants, one trouser leg dangling on the side as if unhinged. Siv's pealing laugh was audible until he disappeared through the door at the end of the veranda. As soon it fell shut behind him, she stopped as abruptly as the machines of the artificial waterfalls.

Longfellow's black curls appeared at the bottom rim of the staircase, his rolling eyes and fleshy lips framing silent questions while motioning her. Siv nodded and the Negro slunk forward to give her a note.

From Mr. Abel Rush, he whispered.

Surprised and alarmed, Siv read the note. Then she said decisively,

My regards to Mr. Rush. Tell him I absolutely agree.

The Negro nodded, dashing off as quietly as he had come. Siv tore up the note. The pieces were still in her hand when Tracbac returned.

The picture of respectable Wadköping citizen, he was dressed in a floor-length, kaftan-like black silk gown with Chinese embroideries. On his head he wore a Mandarin cap with a blue button on top. His good old golden watch chain was draped across his stomach. Dangling the watch from his hand, he chanted off-key: Ring, thou Corneville's clocks — ring all day long — ring, all thou clocks — ring ding ding dong —

He stopped in front of Siv and declared,

That relative I mentioned has obviously vanished. I saw him play ball with his hat on Jasmine Path over an hour ago. Did I see right? Perhaps it wasn't he at all? What do you think?

How should I know? the woman snapped back.

He sneezed.

Gee, I must've caught a cold. The ducks splashed so hard, I got all wet. Do you know *A Thousand And One Nights*? I mean the tales about Sindbad the Sailor. Well, the gentleman suffered various shipwrecks. But he survived each one and finally managed to wash up on some island. He really survived, poor guy, without any advertising and executive board. So all alone one morning on his island he was planning his next shipwreck when to his dismay he discovered an ugly troll sitting ever so comfortably on his shoulders. His spindly legs were ever so tightly wound around Tracbac's neck. Impossible to dislodge. And he ruled Sindbad from then on. Sindbad had to do whatever this pest told him. Yes, my little girl. Once there was a young man. Jonathan Borck was his name. Me. I'm that Sindbad. I suffered shipwreck and washed up on a beach with an ugly old fellow riding my neck. He's still there. They call him Jac Tracbac.

He caught sight of Siv's balled fist. Catching himself, he pointed at it,

What've you got there?

Without blinking she showed him the paper bits and said,

From Mr. Rush.

Great. Outright fantastic, the clown beamed. Well, well, the lady and the gentleman write notes to each other, he? Haven't I told you to marry this Abel Rush? Saves me from having to put up with you. Take him! He's young, intelligent, good-looking. And in a few years we'll have twelve little Rushes with all the modern improvements. The market can easily absorb them —

He consulted his watch again.

Oh well, he isn't coming, our young man. By the way, Siv, please tell your friend Abel Rush that I do wish to perform — if I'm alive and healthy, that is. But not in three months, as he wants it. No, in three years. Then I'll perform, provided I've been able to take care of the business with that woman I mentioned. My, my, I can just picture your jealousy! Well, my regards to Abel Rush —

You tell him yourself, Siv mumbled sullenly.

Tell him also that I don't want to see his face or hear his endearing voice for the next six months. Don't forget! I'll hermit for a while to do some research. I want to find out how Sindbad finally managed to shake this Jac Tracbac. He's been bothering me long enough.

He checked his watch once more. Then he said,

Oh, well, the fellow won't show.

Whistling the tune from the operetta *Corneville's Clocks,* he walked down the stairs into the garden, leaving Siv to muse,

Rush will have to take care of this. Soon. His women affairs are not my business. Not the least.

She went inside, her hands tightly pressed against her beautiful amber eyes.

6: The Clown's Jew

WHILE TRACBAC WAS anxiously waiting for his young relative, a confused Benbé was trudging about with the two supervisors. Nothing made sense to him. Was he a king on display with two escorts, or a criminal held at the place of crime, two sleuths at his heels?

One of the men tapped Benbé's shoulder,

Well, Sir, we've done our duty to our worthy guest. We may head back to our work in good conscience. Here comes Longfellow, so you won't be lonely.

Longfellow approached, sweating profusely, cap in his hand — not out of respect, but to wipe his forehead. Pompously, Benbé shouted,

This is getting better and better. Longfellow. Friendly nigger return to smoke peace pipe, not false nigger, lowly park attendant.

Mr. Borck, the black man sighed, folding his arms across his chest. I'm doing more than that; I came on my own. Mr. Rush has evaporated. Scrammed, Sir. May I invite you to my house, Mr. Borck? Mrs. Longfellow is expecting us.

Politely opening the door, he let Benbé enter. The hall led into a large room. Its furniture looked cheap and gaudy. A sideboard with shiny brass-work stood along the wall. On a chair next to it sat Longfellow's wife, gorgeously plump and shining like a polished stove top. She exuded an aura of peaceful, sated cannibalism. Her large hands rested quietly and good-naturedly on her apron-covered stomach. Her seven children crowded around her. The oldest was a twelve-year old spitting image of his father. The entire scene was a blueprint of decent family. Mr. Rush stood among them like a sorry photographer who had lost his equipment.

Mr. Rush was a very young man, hardly more than two or three years older than Benjamin Borck. A Jew, he looked more like Happy Arabia than Palestine. In his demeanor he resembled a poet or spiritual leader. He had the reputation of a shrewd businessman. Striding into the room, Longfellow introduced with grand gestures and an angrily rumbling voice,

Mr. Cain Rush!

Abel Rush, the secretary corrected the Negro with a gentle, searching, slightly impatient smile. His gaze glided to the huge black mama and her cute children, then back again to the master of the gatekeeper lodge. With a sudden, growling sigh Longfellow walked up to his wife, shook his fists and thundered,

Mylady, can't you see what's going on, you stupid, simple-minded woman? You're not wanted in your home! We're shown the door, see! You, and I and our poor children. Thrown out! So, get going!

It's beautiful outside, Mr. Rush volunteered good-naturedly. Smiling softly, mylady swept out of the room — a black comet, her magnificent tail of small, black meteorites trailing behind her. But Longfellow grabbed his oldest boy quickly by his shoulders and pushed him back on the chair his mother had just left vacant,

Hiawatha, my son, you stay here. Hiawatha may stay, right, Mr. Rush?

Fine with me, though I don't know why, the secretary said.

If you want to know, Cain, it's because there's a crook, a Jew and a cabinet full of silverware in this room. That's why, Mr. Rush. Hiawatha, keep your eyes peeled!

The formidable gatekeeper stalked out. The door banged shut behind him. The secretary gave a low, easy chuckle.

Oh, well, there we got as much as we can take, he said.

To Benbé's utter surprise, the secretary switched to perfect Swedish for their ensuing discussion, a slight Yankee accent barely audible,

Don't think that our good Longfellow is as angry or as hateful as he sounds. Negroes are good actors. He didn't leave young Hiawatha here to guard any silver spoons, or even to annoy us. He's here to report to his father.

The secretary's allegation proved correct. When the young man found himself unable to understand what was said, he looked for better entertainment. His eyes fastened longingly on a large jar of preserves in the buffet. His eyes pleading discretion, he pulled it out.

Rush remained standing, but offered Benbé a chair.

You see, I am Swedish. I was eight years old when my parents moved here. You may not remember, but we have met before. Our backyard was next to the Borck estate. Once we even got into a fight. My father was jeweler Gavenstein. He changed his name to Rush when we moved here.

That sounds like a car make, Benbé put in.

Perhaps. But Gavenstein sounded like an apple. I used to get into fights for both — Gavenstein in Sweden, Rush here. Well, it doesn't really matter what boys fight over, does it? Prepares them for life.

Speaking softly he turned to the black boy,

Go ahead and eat, Hiawatha! There's a lot more where that came from.

That's right, the boy said, obviously relieved, his red mouth wide open. I'll lock the door to be on the safe side —

You see, Jews are supposed to be vindictive and unforgiving. So I've decided to live up to that reputation and punish Longfellow and his family for insinuating we're two cheap silver thieves. We don't deserve that.

Benbé gave a sigh of relief. He smiled, reassured. The secretary was Gavenstein's son, Grandmother's next-door neighbor. He remembered the short, chubby, jovial jeweler and his occasional bankruptcies. What did the secretary want from him? He decided to treat him like a childhood friend. True to the ritual, he warmly stretched his hand out,

Abel Gavenstein, or Cain Rush, or whatever you're called, how wonderful to meet you again. Let's drop the formalities — it's ridiculous to be formal with a boy I once clobbered.

But Abel Rush countered with a subtle, rather melancholy smile,

Well, Mr. Borck. Those who hold the titles may drop them. But in our case I think it's best to wait. Suppose we regret it later on —

People even barely familiar with Swedish etiquette know that refusing an offer to drop formal address between young men is the ultimate insult. Benbé lost his temper. His face turning crimson he breathed heavily,

As you wish. Damn it, just tell me what you want.

Personally nothing, the secretary answered with composure. I'm just a delegate of the gentlemen who manage Jac Tracbac's professional finances. Your arrival has caused some alarm. As for me, I'll be satisfied with a discussion leading to a mutually satisfactory agreement.

Agreement? Benbé repeated furiously. Mind your words, Abel Gavenstein! Are you insinuating that I'm out to blackmail?

The secretary smiled as if he were addressing a child,

We're not concerned about blackmailers. I felt free to confiscate your first letter . . .

Oh, so you admit that! Benbé screamed, happy to have a reason for his ire. So, you owe up to stealing your boss's letters?

Tracbac knows. Or rather, he ordered me to censure his mail. You want to call it theft — fine. Mr. Tracbac gets a lot of mail from so called relatives. We never answer them. Your case is more complicated. I knew right away that the writer told the truth and I can assure you that you would have been more than welcome next year. But to have you here right now is rather inconvenient. Tracbac agreed to perform in the near future —

I don't want to disrupt your plans, Benbé said loftily. The secretary sighed and closed his eyes like someone trying hard to manage an impossible task.

Mr. Borck, once Tracbac gets hold of you, you won't have any say in the matter because you don't control these decisions. You must remain under our supervision. And, when I say we and our, I mean my bosses, the Tracbac syndicate.

The problem is this, Rush continued, Tracbac finally promised to perform, which really doesn't happen too often. We know that with his acute sense of duty he will do everything in his power to fulfill his obligation and it would bother him a great deal if for some reason he would have to break his promise. We know too that he'll wangle out if he sees a chance to do it without breaking it outright —

In the States you call it good logic, Benbé said. Europeans call it paradoxes —

We call it damn extra trouble, the secretary said with a deep sigh. Well, don't get the impression Mr. Tracbac does it out of spite. No, he's not that way at all. It's simply that every performance drains him emotionally. That's why he hates to perform. He literally shies away from it.

Oh well, Benbé rationalized, he shouldn't have any difficulty to get out from under. He could get a doctor's statement. Whooping cough, for example. That'd do the trick.

The secretary burst out laughing. His black eyes sparkled with boyish delight.

You know, he said, there you hit on the strangest clause in Tracbac's otherwise straightforward contract. He himself insisted on including that: no illness of whatever kind may prevent the undersigned from performing according to contract; neither his death nor interment may be exploited, artistically or commercially, if the syndicate has the slightest reason for suspicion.

I'll be darned, Benbé said.

Actually, the syndicate first refused to include this seemingly cynical and outright brutal proviso, but Tracbac insisted and would not sign the contract without it. So it's in there. Cynical businessmen, my bosses suspect that Tracbac wanted this clause in there as an ultimate weapon he could hold against them if necessary. But I know your relative better — he's more childish than crafty in business matters. He has this innate aversion to perform and I'm convinced that he wanted to eliminate any temptation to find excuses to get out of the contract.

See, my problem is that underneath it all Mr. Tracbac is a moral perfectionist. He'll never agree to manipulations. If he did my job would be much easier. Other top performers do. But he keeps us on constant alert because, on closer inspection, his morals are twisted. He's an old-fashioned, hypocritical Swedish bourgeois and his comic act is strictly family-oriented. Nothing even faintly suggestive of immorality may be included. His pity is boundless. Problem is his unpredictability. He's unbelievably imaginative and could find some reason for doing the impossible. And once he does, it's impossible to talk sense to him. For example, if he for some reason finds it his moral duty to break his contract — he'd tear it up without a moment's hesitation. It's hard to explain, really, Mr. Borck, but he's impossible in this respect, the secretary suddenly burst out, stroking his hair in despair. After awhile, he added reflectively,

That's why we'll have to be on guard about relatives. Luckily, you're the only one on this side of the Atlantic.

Do you think that I . . . ? Benbé screamed in a sudden flush of wounded pride. But he was smart enough to catch himself before blurting out, Do you think that I'm out to get his sympathy? He closed his mouth tightly, lowered his head and muttered instead,

Thanks for the jab, I'm getting the message. You mean that check he gave me . . .

The secretary interrupted him angrily,

Such utter nonsense. That almost slipped my mind. Do you think we're interested in how Mr. Tracbac spends his money? Actually, my bosses would be only too happy to see him squander all his millions — down to the last penny. That would leave him at their mercy. Or so they think. I don't share this view. Poor Tracbac would be as difficult to handle as wealthy Tracbac. No — if he wants to ruin himself he may, for all we care. But we can't permit him to ruin the syndicate. He would by refusing to perform.

You don't make sense, Benbé said. You just told me that he always sticks to his decision once he promises to perform.

Well, it's not I who doesn't make sense, the secretary countered. Sure, Tracbac will perform, but where? when? and how? Oh well, the how we can dismiss because that's his business. We don't have to worry about that and we hardly do. It's the time frame! Arriving five minutes late for rehearsal puts him in a tizzy. But to be five months late for opening night wouldn't bother him the least.

That must be embarrassing for you, I can see that, Mr. Syndicate Secretary, Benbé agreed. Now, what I'd like to know is whether you work for the syndicate or Tracbac? There's a slight difference, you know —

I can't see any. The syndicate can't exist without Jac Tracbac. By the same token, he can't exist without them. We plan the tours and reservations in fifteen or twenty cities two years in advance to beat competing performers. There are risks involved and we're very discreet. Planning ahead takes a lot of effort and money. That's why it's tantamount to disaster should Tracbac suddenly decide to perform six months later after all the contracts have been signed. We would have to pay immense fines without compensation. Add the financial losses, not to mention the embarrassment he's causing us —

Right, Benbé agreed. Generous. I can see the need to revise my provincial notions of syndicates, corporations and such.

It's not generosity at all. That would be unforgivable. No. It's the fact that six months of planning the tour's every detail comes to nothing. Contracts with the various entertainment centers become legally binding three months before the performance. Changes after that are liable to fines. As a rule we set aside half a million in case Tracbac won't be able to keep the dates. But that sum is arbitrary because we have to renew the contract time and again until Tracbac finally declares his readiness.

Now, what would happen if you told him, This is the date for your performance?

The secretary shook sadly his head,

What would happen? The performance would be a catastrophe. Tracbac would oblige and try his best. Dutiful to the hilt. But we'd be done for, so to speak. A fiasco spells the end of Jac Tracbac.

Listen, doesn't he know that? Benbé wondered.

Who knows? I think he still sees himself performing in a portable tent, two spavined horses dragging it from one market place to the next. At heart he knows better, I'd say. He's emotionally extremely acute and a very sensitive performer. We have to advertise in all the dozen or so cities on the very same date we settle the dates of our tour. If we staggered it one place at a time, other places could jump in. Imagine the mess if we'd be forced to change our set route. No. We include all successive performance dates and the localities on the day the tickets go on sale. That way we can figure our earnings by the time we perform. We can deposit the money in the banks without further delay.

On opening night Tracbac always tells me to count the curtain calls. Just for fun I've tried to give him the wrong answer — too many or too few. Exhausted he may be, but he invariably corrects me and, with a laugh, calls me a lying cheat. Mind you, even when there have been close to a hundred curtain calls, he knows the exact number. Also, he never leaves his dressing room — throughout the tour. Eats and sleeps there. I think it's because he hates staying in those circus cars we have at our disposal. After every performance he waits until everyone has left. When the hall is completely empty, he will say, very secretively and somewhat embarrassed,

Gavenstein, how about checking the proceeds? —

Then we sneak through the corridors to the ticket office where a girl, hired for just his performances, pretends to be busily adding receipts. Cordially Tracbac announces,

I'm Jac Tracbac. Would you mind giving me the total?

The woman scribbles the sum on a paper and shows him. Tracbac nods, hesitates momentarily and says,

Not bad. Could have been better. Of course, could've been worse too. We'll have to be satisfied. Come, let's drink to that in my dressing room.

There he uncorks a bottle of champagne and muses,

Really, we earned the right to binge a little.

Then he undresses, empties his glass, pulls the blanket over his face and falls asleep, instantly .

What an act, Benbé snorted.

I prefer to call it a game — or rest, if you want. His memory harks back to his first years with a circus when Jonathan Borck's clowning wasn't the big money maker it now is. Actually, that's all we know about him, which is in fact very little. When I started as his secretary, Chicago was our point of departure for the tour. The schedules were set months ahead of time and nobody even asked where Tracbac wanted opening night, although our contract stipulated his right to make that choice. Actually he doesn't much care where — Australia, Asia, Africa — as long as it's not Europe.

Why not Europe? Benbé wondered.

The secretary shook his head,

It would hurt us because Americans are against it. As long as it's in the States, he's free to choose. The choice in general is between New York, Los Angeles or Chicago. Well — this time, a month or so before the start, he got the crazy idea to open in Topeka, Kansas — a godforsaken hole of no more than forty or fifty thousand. The syndicate is dumbfounded. Why on earth Topeka? they want to know. If he wants certain people to see him perform, it's easier to bring them to Chicago. Tracbac, embarrassed, remains secretive, but stubbornly insists on opening in dear Topeka. No one has a clue. That's what makes him hard to handle. I have a notion that he simply closed his eyes and willy-nilly put his finger on the map. That's how he discovered Topeka.

Confusion among the syndicate. I had to collect my nerve and confront Tracbac who at the time had just moved into his new villa. He was in a genial mood — even joked, calling me "apple Gavenstein" — homonym of Abel Gavenstein — the first and last time I ever heard him crack a joke. Well, I dared to cut through all this geniality and inquire what all this stupid Topeka-business was about. What, a crazy idea? Jac's white face turned copper-red. He was utterly calm and very gentle when he corrected me,

Outrageous? Not at all. It's no more than fair to have my first-nighter there! Why favor the Chicago meat packers! Or the Wall Street jobbers in New York? These big cities have plenty of diversions and sights small places don't have. Topeka, or any other little hole and its people deserve the same chance, right?

It struck me how naive and reasonable your uncle looked when he said that. As well-meaning as the wealthy little girl on Christmas eve when her parents remind her to distribute her gifts for the poor children fairly. I felt like hugging that good little clown, or bowing down reverently. But I was an immature young show-off, ambitious, anxious to get ahead in this world. So, I turned mean and shrewd,

Mr. Tracbac, you sound off about justice and fairness. Do you really believe the good citizens of Topeka hold you in such high esteem? Sure, you're a well-known artist, and your art is original and worth a lot of money — but you must agree that people in Chicago or other metropolitan cities appreciate you far more!

I was never as ashamed as when I said that, either before or since, the secretary continued, blushing all over his tanned, beautiful poet-face. His eyes sparked flames.

I knew how cruel I was when I said it. I have only one excuse — my job was on the line —

I remember it so well, he resumed. We were sitting in a small sparsely furnished room right under the roof among the old furniture he had shipped over from his childhood home — a sofa sleeper, some Windsor chairs, a small bookcase, a pine desk scratched full of initials and old men's faces. Tracbac just sat there, his hands gliding across the scribbles. He reminded me of a blind man trying to read with his fingertips. My heart in my throat, I don't know how long I sat there waiting for his answer. Eventually he said calmly,

You're right, my art is good enough for Chicago hog butchers and their likes. My sort of art must make a lot of money, an awful lot of money, to have any merit.

I slunk out when he said that, feeling like a mouse who is looking for the nearest hole to creep into as quickly as possible. I was certain of two things: my job was more secure, but hardly more pleasant. I had earned the syndicate's goodwill and trust. But Tracbac turned cold, resentful and full of contempt.

Abel Rush looked dejected. A faint smile on his lips, he pondered the pros and cons of what he had done. Full of his precious ego, Benbé appraised his own situation. Why did the secretary wish to meet him in the gatekeeper's lodge? What were his reasons? Rush was seemingly nervous and ill at ease, moving his lips slightly as if having an internal dialogue or reviewing a lesson. Meanwhile, the boy Hiawatha was absorbed in his own sins — using a ladle to transfer pineapple jam from crock to mouth. He looked drowsy and his muffled belching signaled a vast overload on his digestive tract.

Abel Rush spoke up, impatience in his voice,

I'm fed up with the schemes this syndicate secretary is hatching. You must be too! Let me get to the point.

His wrinkled forehead showing his discontent, he continued,

I declined your friendly offer of informality because underneath all this I'm a very sensitive fellow. You realize that, don't you?

Oh, really? Benbé retorted, uncomfortably curious.

— rr-m-m-ph-ph. The young black man in the room ejected a loud, sated belch. His job was complete.

7: The Labyrinth

THE YOUNG JEW pushed his fists deep into his pockets, raised his shoulders as if trying to work up steam, or to convince Benbé that their discussion was extremely important. He said,

Well, Mr. Borck, you want to know what this is about. Simply put, we want you to leave California. Now — preferably this afternoon. Board the first boat in New York bound for Europe. I took the liberty to book passage, first class, on the Gripsholm. She leaves in six days. At the same time I reserved two tickets on the Santa Fé to New York. I'm sure you've nothing against my company to see you off. In a nutshell, that's my message —

A tall order in a few words, Benbé said calmly. How very considerate to suffer that long a trip just to keep me company. Permit me fifteen minutes to think this over.

By all means — take the entire day. You have the right to think all you want. There's plenty of time. The train to make the Gripsholm won't leave before tomorrow evening. You may consider us pretty nasty, my bosses and me. I can't help that. As long as you understand that our decision is final, Mr. Borck.

Controlling his temper, Benbé said calmly,

You never consulted me on this matter!

Actually, Benbé found the proposition quite expedient for several reasons. Having failed in the United States, he could simply go home. Traveling first class like a gentleman was also tempting. Still, it was damned insulting to let some wealthy cads push you off— without even bothering to tell you why. He wanted to get an explanation, if he so had to set fire to the building and search the ruins.

The secretary eased himself comfortably into a huge velvet chair. His very dark blue eyes glittered with impatience like cut, burnished coals. Benbé remembered the Negro's warning: he stings like a bedbug. This fellow spells trouble, Benbé thought, but I'll crush him between my fingertips. Rush cut into his thoughts with a sad, bitter smile,

Your worthy uncle Mr. Tracbac considers himself a slave to the syndicate. Indeed, owning slaves presents special problems and risks. Really, these days it's hard to say who's master and who's slave. It's called democracy.

Benbé cut in acridly,

I don't want to delay my departure unnecessarily. But I ought to know why you prevent me from meeting Mr. Tracbac.

Simply because we don't think very highly of you. You lack principles, the young Jew told him with ruthless honesty.

Lack principles? Where does that fit in here? Benbé stammered.

That's the basic difference between us and Europeans, the European-born American told him. In Europe, as long as you have a certain expertise and some skills, principles and morals don't count for much. Not so here. Europeans are wrong thinking we're a ruthless bunch. Americans value principles above all. True, we might use methods you'd be too cowardly, or too lazy, or even too stupid to apply. But that doesn't mean we're more ruthless than you. Actually, ruthlessness has its pros and cons. We consider it admirable to reject ingrained old prejudices and modern follies. If there's anything new and good about us — and heaven knows there's plenty — then it's our tendency to value highly principled people. In order to borrow money here a person needs a good reputation more than expensive property. People with a debatable background usually have difficulties in getting loans. Our business dealings, really our entire social life, is based on mutual trust. That's what's new here — if there's anything that's new under the sun anyway. Of course, you can say that's a figment of our imagination — childish American conceit. But even if it were, my good Mr. European, it's preferable to your senile, nauseating cynicism.

What do you mean? Me? Cynical? Benbé burst out, sincerely indignant.

The secretary gave a boyish, contemptuous laugh at his heated response,

Perhaps I ought to correct my statement. Childish rather than cynical. My relatives in Sweden informed me of your coming long before you arrived. We've kept an eye on you ever since. You failed in the East. And why did you then come to California? I'll tell you. You had this crazy notion your connection with a celebrity would get you an in with the newspapers. Correct?

What of it? Benbé snapped back. Anything wrong with that? I could write some articles about Tracbac's private life. The syndicate would love the extra publicity. I'm not a bad writer, I have you know —

Oh dear, the secretary sighed. My young fellow, the syndicate wants nothing more than to avoid that kind of publicity. It's bad policy for an artist as famous as Tracbac. They need to wrap him in silence, like a precious insect in cotton, between blows. Of course, you could have written a few articles — under our supervision. But we don't think you're reliable or trustworthy enough. Consider the many reporters who would welcome the chance to discredit success. And you would make that an easy job. Indeed, it's already happened —

What? Benbé screamed. I assure you, I never even saw a journalist.

Well, let's say you got a slight glimpse, the secretary countered, facetiously flipping his eyelids. Good-looking young girls, Mr. Borck. I drove past you a few times and recognized at least two professional reporters among them; the others may have been friends, or quite possibly even free-lancers for the press. They made it look like a joke. Mark that you didn't merit their attention until you had contacted your uncle. You were hardly off the boat when the papers announced that a Tracbac relative, a Mr. Borck, had arrived in New York. You were famous before you ever knew. But not before you came close to your uncle did they notice you.

Now, look here! Benbé called. I must correct you. Those chicks never even believed me when I told them who my uncle was. Didn't even talk to him —

Oh, they didn't believe! Indeed! The secretary smiled. They knew only too well. Long before you did. But they knew better than to ask him for an interview. I caught on some years ago. Since then no one may interview or photograph Tracbac without permission from the syndicate. Sure. That creates other problems — like hiring people to supervise. As I said, he has complete "freedom." Any little reporter may interview him — provided Tracbac agrees. He's so damn meek. Every old or young whippersnapper can talk him into it. Luckily, he doesn't know much about himself, at least nothing a reporter may want to report. Besides, we supply our own information on various matters and take pains to get that printed in a dozen or so papers. This takes the edge off any interviews. Of course, people close to him are always a desirable target. That's why a naive relative like you is dangerous. Flattery could easily pull all sorts of Tracbac news out of you — and ruin us. Just imagine them pumping you for details on Jac Tracbac's next tour. No, a young rogue like you is easy game for a dozen or so good-looking, scheming babes.

Well, that's true, Benbé agreed, docile and humbled. To think that those good-looking dames were nothing but frauds —

With a bitter smile and a businesslike tone the Jew explained,

I've praised us Yankees so far. Now let me add a codicil of truth. We are by no means paragons of innocence. Semi-paragons perhaps — but certainly not more.

This just to make you understand why you have to leave. You can publish all you want about us in Europe. Americans know that nothing written about us in Europe is true. Your publications don't count for much here.

That leaves the question whether you want to travel at our expense, including some additional compensation . . . within reason, of course. Or at federal —

Federal expense? Benbé repeated, wide-eyed.

Rush explained coldly,

It would hardly be difficult to have you deported as an undesirable alien. All we need is a few decent, influential citizens alerting the police about your

52

doings here and you may kiss the good old US of A goodbye. A very unpleasant goodbye, I dare say. All around, it's easier and cheaper through the syndicate. We don't want to be too harsh —

Rush stopped abruptly. Benbé, hurt and humiliated, burst out,

Oh, how magnanimous, your syndicate.

The secretary did not answer. The sound of a galloping horse in the park compelled him to mumble instead,

That's him. I assume he's leaving the grounds.

He was unnerved, his face distorted. In a hurry, he ran to close the window facing the park. Full of revenge, Benbé meditated,

Well, well, Mr. Syndicate Secretary. Now let's see how easy it is to kick me out of this paradise. I just have to open the window and call my father's cousin.

Outside, Tracbac was shouting,

Hello there! Longfellow! Asleep? Come on, open the gate! Can't you see that I want to get out? Open up, you black psalm book.

Longfellow answered leisurely from the steps outside the lodge,

At your service, Sir. I'm always ready to open the gate. This human disgrace, this Rush would kick me out if I didn't.

Is Mr. Rush here? Tracbac seemed surprised.

Inside, Rush stood rigidly pressed against the wall, much to Benbé's delight. Outside, willfully loud, Longfellow continued shouting to his boss,

Use your eyes, Sir. I can't see him if you can't. Why should my eyesight be keener than yours?

Benbé noticed pearls of sweat glisten on Abel Rush's forehead. With an embarrassed smile on his face Rush said,

I am pretty nervous. All I need now is that he sees you. He and the syndicate'll give me the boot, you see —

His fists were fiercely arched down his pockets, hard enough to crack the seams across the narrow shoulders of his jacket. Benbé pulled his right fist out and shook it hard,

Whatever happens, Abel Rush, I'm going to leave tonight. I won't let you lose your job for my sake.

They heard the Negro open the gate and loudly complain about its faulty mechanism. Impatient, Tracbac kept clicking his tongue at the horse, a warm-blooded slender, short black mare. Suddenly he called out,

Hi, Longfellow, what's this? Isn't this Mr. Rush's car?

Abel Rush slumped down with a sigh, mumbling,

Well, that's the end of me. I'm done for —

Outside Longfellow said,

Stay out of my problems. As long as I don't interfere in yours, you mustn't mess with mine, Sir —

Great! the clown screamed, where is he, my dear friend Rush?

Inside, Benbé whispered excitedly, his unrepenting boy's soul aching with enthusiasm for lies and shams,

Now, you go out and face him. I've given you my word that I'm not going to show my face. Tell him any lie you want.

Abel Rush wiped his forehead and stepped quickly up to the prancing mare.

The clown began to shout,

Great! Then, dryly polite, he added,

Are you looking for me, Mr. Rush?

The secretary shook his head and Tracbac rode through the gate, turned in his saddle and said,

As all-knowing as you are, I'm sure you know whether my nephew has been here. He seemed pretty happy when I saw him on Jasmine Way a short while ago, playing with his hat. I wanted him to come in, but he doesn't seem to need me. I let Fate decide. I'm going to his place. Is he at home — fine. If not — just as well. Fate will make the right decision. See you later.

Behind the window, Benbé listened and mumbled,

Goodbye. Goodbye. There's my super chance riding off on a black mare. Farewell.

He gave a heartfelt sigh. Behind him, his red mouth gaping, his eyelids violently fluttering, the young Hiawatha spewed an even deeper belch. Trying to comfort him, Benbé put his hand over the boy's mouth. He had to pull it back quickly. The boy's moaning continued. Slowly a nauseating smell of pineapple, cinnamon and ginger wafted through the room. Mylady Longfellow trundled in, screaming and gesticulating wildly. On the steps outside Longfellow howled in sympathy with his suffering offspring. With all the commotion around him Benbé could not remain in his hiding place. Yes, he had promised not to show his face, but that was before he saw what happens when black children gorge themselves with pineapple preserves.

The clown jumped off his horse, shouting,

What's going on here?

He stalked through the gate and approached the Negro. Carefully closing the door behind him, Benbé stepped out and walked over to Rush without acknowledging Tracbac's presence. Hiawatha's heartrending moans were slowly subsiding. His mother's first worries about her son's emptying the contents of an entire jar of pineapple jam gradually dissolved in morality lectures. However, her concern for her unhappy offspring eliminated any reason for the rest of the world to interfere in the case. Tracbac stood silently at the top of the stairs while Longfellow tried to keep the horse calm after its master's circus plunge.

How long are we going to stand here? Benbé whispered to Abel Rush. The secretary stopped whistling under his breath and whispered,

We'll have to let him talk first. He's furious, judging from the way he's standing there.

About the same age, the two young men instinctively united against Tracbac who was twice their age. The generation gap can never be bridged, in sharp contrast to other differences that people nowadays have learned to resolve.

Tracbac turned toward the young men, his eyes closed and his nose aflutter like that of a dog on the trail. Rush wiped his forehead and murmured under his breath,

I hope nothing serious will come of this. I had no idea he would get this irate —

Without opening his eyes, the clown said,

Strange. People will ask me what I'm thinking, and I can't tell them because in general I don't think. But now that I do, no one cares to know.

Well, Sir, what's on your mind? the Negro asked bitterly. Please, don't look so unhappy. If it's Mr. Rush, well, go ahead. Give him a piece of your mind. Don't be stingy — the guy can take it. He stings like a bedbug himself. He does.

His eyes still closed, Tracbac acknowledged his gatekeeper's advice with a slight nod. Then he cleared his throat and said,

Excellent, Longfellow. Since you can't manage the gate, you'll have to take care of the stables. Take the horse back there and dry her off. And don't you dare to whack Hiawatha. If you do I'll throw you out. The same goes if you're disrespectful to Mr. Rush — and Mr. Borck. If you're rude to me I'll feed you fat lamb steaks, your favorite dish. Should you want to stab yourself, I'll make you stand in the corner. Now off with you, my black rhyme lexicon!

The clown turned to Rush who lowered his head and sighed deeply,

Come to think of my tour. Is this comedy a draft for my new act, I wonder?

What do you mean? Rush burst out in desperation. For goodness sake, don't get these problems mixed up with your tour.

Why not? the clown shot back with a shrug. It's not such a stupid idea. Seventy hungry millionaires — our so called Tracbac Syndicate — holding one man prisoner. Objective? Butcher him for Christmas. Now, a sympathetic friend comes to free the prisoner. Appears a scoundrel employee — that's you Mr. Rush — locks up young friend plus innocent child, stuffs the kid with enough pineapple to make him explode. Only instead of blasting the prisoner off into thin air, the prison walls crack. The two friends reunite. The real stuff comedy is made of — with a happy ending.

Mr. Tracbac, the secretary remarked quietly, you never stage comedies that end completely happy. Seventy voracious millionaires wind up lynching the secretary in disgrace. How about this noble idea for your comedy?

Outstanding. Simply outstanding, the clown agreed and clapped his hands slightly before turning to Benbé,

You're moving in with me. I need a new secretary.

At a loss at first what all this was about, Benbé understood now that he was pegged to replace his new friend Abel Rush. Relieved, the told his relative,

Oh, if that's what you want, I must decline your kind offer. Your secretary may have no say in the matter, but I am the wrong candidate for the job. I've solemnly promised to leave tonight . . . —

He stopped short and bit his lips, realizing that he had said too much.

Who made you give that promise? Tracbac shot back.

Abel Rush intervened,

I, of course. Don't ask useless questions and don't gloat. You feel troubled enough already. As to your promise, Benjamin — I'm not going to hold you to it. Rather, and I'm speaking here for my bosses too, I would like you to accept the job. If you don't, who knows in whose claws he'll wind up. At least you keep a given promise — and that's a great deal already.

Just listen to him! the clown hollered, grinning, waving his hand. Complimenting his successor in the bitter hour of parting! What honorable, well-meaning young Jews!

That said, he stalked through the gate to the secretary's car, opened its door and bowed ceremoniously,

Appreciate your visit, Mr. Rush. I hate taking up more of your valuable time for free. You're most welcome back when we have seven Thursdays per week. Not a day later, Sir.

Shrugging, Rush walked past his new-found friend Benbé, murmuring under his breath,

Do me a favor and stay with him.

Ignoring the bowing clown, Rush settled into his car and turned the ignition. Tracbac waited a few seconds, then raised his hand in a friendly farewell before turning to Benbé. He took his nephew's arm with intimate friendliness, but dropped it immediately when he felt the young man's resistance, turned abruptly and walked toward the villa, saying,

Follow me to the house. We'll have to find you suitable living quarters.

Benbé followed, surprised, uneasy, beset with doubts and a hazy, inexplicable fear for his friend. Nonetheless, he managed to say,

You did act in a huff and now you're sorry, aren't you? I take it that Mr. Rush may keep his job. Am I right?

But the clown answered quietly,

I never regret anything. Regret isn't my line. My strength embodies fear and compassion. Everyone knows that. I'm not very successful at anything else.

The tiny bell on the rafter tinkled when Tracbac turned the huge, church-key-sized key, that stuck in the lock of the dark villa door. He frowned and muttered,

No, I have nothing to regret. But there's a little lady here in love with Abel Rush who'll give me a piece of her mind. She might as well fall in love with you. If you ask me — in love the love object matters little.

The tinkle of the bell stopped abruptly. Pushing Benbé ahead, Tracbac entered the villa, saying,

May God bless your coming in and going out, my boy.

Several lights came on in the windowless room. A number of gaudily painted Mexican hope chests stood along the wall. An old white and two black servants appeared. Tracbac told Benbé,

Have a look around while I look for that lady. Sort of an old habit before I do anything else — she used to be my wife.

Benbé surveyed his new surroundings. An old, feeble servant with shaky hands and knees spoke to him in Swedish,

Welcome, Mr. Borck. My master was expecting you. It'll be up to you not to let him forget you're here. You're absolutely free here and get whatever you want. Eventually he'll neglect you just the same. My name is Axelsson; used to be the Borcks' handyman in Wadköping. When the old lady died I came here with her furniture — the boy's room, the dining room, the living room and the old lady's room. Now no one cares about me or the furniture. He doesn't, so who else should? At home I used to cut the firewood, do the carpentry and care for the gardens. Now I do this.

He held up one of those racy little feather dusters that flirty little females wave about in French farces. The dainty feathers looked outright ludicrous, if not ghastly, in his trembling, parched, rough fingers. The old man bent forward, breathing heavily,

I'm a lush, Sir, that's what I am. Don't tell anyone, Mr. Borck. I dust and booze. Who cares — about me or the furniture? You'd think that he'd appreciate having us here. No, not him, mind you! Dust and booze — that's all I do.

The old man tottered off through one of the countless doors. His curiosity aroused about the place, Benbé walked through another door. Longfellow was correct — it was easy to get lost in the many odd-shaped, sparsely furnished clusters of rooms grouped together like honeycombs in a beehive. Lattice windows filtered out most of the bright sunshine, but the open spaces between the clusters were flooded with its intensity — aviaries with colorful exotic birds and solaria, which Benbé considered unnecessary in this subtropical climate.

A few times Benbé heard Tracbac's voice, calling, Siv, Siv! Once he even caught a glimpse of his relative far down the hall, but he vanished into thin air when Benbé tried to catch up with him. Benbé felt lost in this maze and became afraid that he might miss the exit. How childish, he told himself, quite embarrassed about such fears and trying to calm down. From one of the dark door openings a dark-complexioned, gray-haired gentleman with an impeccably groomed, waxed black mustache emerged. Dressed in riding garb, he was looking for Mr. Tracbac. Benbé told him that he was a stranger looking for the master of the house too. When he wanted to say goodbye and leave, the dark man introduced himself in a formal, friendly manner: Ilois De Grazy, retired major in the Austrian army. He confided in Benbé,

I've lived in this place for six years, but still can't find my way. To think that I was reconnaissance officer in the Götz army in 1916!! Well, perhaps that's why it went the way it did. I negotiate the building by now, but finding its owner is yet another matter. This maze was built for people to get lost. Only he can find his way blindfolded. Good-bye, Sir. Remember me to our host — in case fate leads you to him.

With a meticulous Schönbrunn bow the Austrian disappeared in the opposite direction. Drifting on, Benbé reached a flight of rooms with typically paltry, hideous American furniture. But upstairs he came to a comfortable, wide, English-style bedroom. Exhausted from the day's events, he dropped onto the bed, thinking,

Take a nap. It'll improve your disposition when you wake up, little Benjamin.

He had hardly closed his eyes when the clown returned. With a smile he sat down by his bedside. Benbé wanted to get up, but he pushed him gently back,

Lie down, young man. You need a rest after today's shock. We have a lot to talk about. —

8: A Flawed Heart

TRACBAC GLANCED THROUGH the room, smiled and announced,

Well, my dear nephew, you picked this room — so it's yours. I completely forgot about its existence, but it isn't too bad. I like to let my guests choose by letting them get lost and then plop down wherever they feel comfortable. There isn't much that children or clowns can enjoy — so this is my fun. I firmly believe that fate ought to be left to chance, quite in contrast to rationalists who reason first and then decide. I wonder about their psychological makeup. I consider them crazy, or about to crack. Chance is the great regenerator. Without it we're doomed to wilt like straw.

The clown's smile was soothing, tender, when he continued,

Well, I really should let you sleep now. Only, I don't want you to worry and have nightmares about my firing Abel Rush. I need him much more than he needs me. The rascal may eventually permit me to make amends. It's not my habit to apologize, but I must bear in mind that he's very sensitive. A wise word from your uncle, Benjamin Borck — it doesn't hurt to go against your grain every now and then. Preserves and cake are for the palate, but the stomach needs potatoes and herring too. I know a lot of wise maxims from Axelsson who spouts them whether I want to hear them or not. He's really an excellent, strict taskmaster.

Checking the time on his watch he went on,

All right, by now Rush has had plenty of time to inform the syndicate that I fired him. I may prepare for an unpleasant day. Well, never mind. Can't say that anything else went smoothly lately. Everything exacts a price. Nothing comes free, my boy. Remember. Easy come, easy go — let your wine vat run too thee, get my company for free, said the gout. That's Axelsson again. Quite a character, he. Well, I hear Siv coming up the stairs. Get up, my boy, smooth your clothes, comb your hair and bow politely —

Benbé flew up and tried to smooth his hair. But Siv entered the room before he finished. She had changed her smock. The dark blue silk cape she wore made her look like a blue dove with cream-colored down under its wings. Benbé bowed. When she ignored his presence Benbé ambled toward the door. But her angry look made him stop short. She turned to Tracbac,

You can hardly be surprised that the syndicate is here to discuss Abel's firing. The gentlemen are in the foyer.

For an instant Tracbac blushed to a deep red. Then he turned ashen and bellowed,

59

Just great! Didn't lose much time, did they? Who's here?

Siv named four prominent bankers — the syndicate's chief executives. Frowning, she added hesitantly,

Henny is here too.

The clown jumped up, visibly angry, and screamed,

Ohhhh! Henny-Denny! Henny-Denny! Indeed! Turning to Benbé, he explained,

The famous neurologist. He only turns up for important sessions when the fellows might give me a heart attack. His job is reviving poor Jac with salts or some such stuff. Just great! he gasped.

Are you tired? Siv wondered suddenly, her eyes wide open with fright. The clown gasped again before answering surly,

Jac is not tired, but he might soon be.

Siv frowned pensively, obviously worried. In a decisive, motherly tone she said after a while,

It would be wise to receive them. They seem very anxious. Judging from the way they're dressed — they want to make it seem like a casual drop-in. Some wear coats, some in shirtsleeves. That fraud Denny came in his bathrobe, no less. They want you to understand that all they want is to shake hands with you — slap you on your back —

Her beautiful eyes sparkling, her teeth crunching, Siv looked like a furious, gorgeous animal. The clown cupped her face and gave her an airborne kiss, exclaiming vehemently,

Excellent, just excellent! Some die because they're stupid, others because they're smart. Yet another Axelsson quote. Great! I know what I am going to wear. Siv, go and tell the gentlemen I'll be with them presently. You, Benjamin, stay here until I call for you.

Tracbac tiptoed quickly out of the room. Disregarding Benbé's polite bows, beautiful Siv turned slowly to leave too, but then turned in the door and finally spoke to him, all sarcasm,

So, you are the fellow to succeed Mr. Rush?

Crestfallen, Benbé could only shake his head. Siv drawled on, deadly scorn in her voice,

Well, all I can say is that your job won't be easy. Poor Abel surely deserves his hard-earned rest. And a piece of advice: Never contradict Mr. Tracbac. Should he tell you to throw him out of the window, by all means do. There's no use in trying to contradict.

She came back into the room and sat down on Benbé's bedside.

Suck your thumb, little Benjamin. Very soothing when you're a child, it flashed through his mind.

Meanwhile, the five uninvited guests lounged comfortably in the huge hall. The star-shaped lamps in the ceiling spread a dim light. Vice president and speaker of the Jac Tracbac Syndicate was tall, skinny, slightly stooping Dr. Adams, senator, doctor of jurisprudence and theology, president of the Farmers and Merchants Bank and distinguished elder of a religious organization. The two in shirtsleeves were short, stubby Judah and short, square, broad-shouldered, mean Mr. Cow. Judah had made his fortune in cultured pearls. An extraordinarily gentle man, he represented the syndicate in business dealings with the large movie corporations. Mr. Cow, vice president of a distinguished New York-based corporation of lawyers and honorary president of the National Steeplechase and Hunting Club, managed the syndicate's legal affairs. The red-haired, lanky man in the tropical suit was Mr. Pech. Outside his family people knew nothing about him.

Finally, the young man in the bathrobe was Dr. Denny O'Henny. A neurologist, he specialized in the Tracbac case. The younger brother of an oil magnate and a tenfold millionaire, he was the only person present who had no financial interests in the Tracbac syndicate. Professionally well-known, he charged three dollars for Tracbac's regular bimonthly consultations, money he carelessly squandered on good-looking minor starlets. Because of their involvement in various religious, moral and philanthropic charities, the four older gentlemen felt far superior and they treated him with a patronizing flair. Only an occasional tremble in their voices betrayed a certain unease, much to the amusement of the doctor who couched his contempt for them under layers of exaggerated deference. They, in turn, saw his behavior as medical supervision and a definite threat. Like many of his professional colleagues, the neurologist himself was emotionally rather unstable. He termed Siv's love for the young man "reserved and quite wanton." His character flaw posed a real threat to Abel Rush. One of the Jew's few personal friends, Denny could easily find a thrill in ruining him.

While the Tracbac syndicate thus camped in the dimly lit hall, the grand illumination in and outside the rest of the villa seemed all set up for a grand reception. Dusk was quickly setting and the park lights dazzled all the way from the man-made waterfalls to the gatekeeper's lodge. Longfellow's small, black-skinned masterpieces began dancing under the arched, bluish lights, the recovered Hiawatha leading the line of moving silhouettes. Considering their informal dress and the unconventional nature of their visit, the five gentlemen saw no reason for the festive illumination. They sensed trouble ahead and felt apprehensive. Sitting astride a Mexican chest, Denny O'Henny amused himself with the Inca-spear he had pulled off the wall. His unruly, curly red hair and bare brawny arms made him look more like a Gothic warrior than a docent in neuropathology. The others were lying about on various rugs, skins and pillows in the center of the foyer, trying to give the appearance harmless, American men leisurely spending a pleasant afternoon with a good friend. Nothing special at all.

Siva Yala's appearance disrupted this leisurely atmosphere. The beautiful hostess remained standing in the door and, without officially reprimanding her guests, she frowned and gave them that disapproving stern-mother-stare that ill-mannered intruders messing up her home deserved. Doctor O'Henny cast his spear aside and jumped off his chest. He grabbed her hand as if to kiss it, but changed his mind and placed his lips on an open spot in the girl's sleeve. The other gentlemen came stiffly off their various skins and pillows in a vain effort to emulate the young man's relaxed demeanor. Siv remained rigid, her arms lifted like a model patient demonstrating before a class of students. Laboriously she pulled out a handkerchief, spit on it and rubbed the spot he had kissed. That done, she slowly settled down on a large, square pillow. Despite her slender figure, it went flat down to the floor. She said,

Dare I ask the reason for this unwelcome visit? In case it's Abel Rush's doing, please tell him that he's in for a good licking. My Negro will take care of that. And you, crazy ruffian on the chest, you're supposed to be Jac's medic. You ought to know how upset this friendly visit will make poor Jac?

O'Henny laughed, again straddling the chest. Young Pech poked his head through the hug of an immense, stuffed polar bear and stammered,

Oh, sweet — little — Siv. You don't mean to imply that Jac — our great, kind Jac — could get angry —

The son of a Kansas farmer, Pech was the syndicate's most trusted press agent and a great asset to the group. His unbelievably simpleminded looks, his cockish, outgoing helpfulness, his seeming integrity combined with a well-masked intelligence made him the favorite of the reporters. Especially ambitious, energetic, unsophisticated greenhorns liked the red-haired, grinning, seemingly naive, simpleminded farm boy. Playing the hotly pursued dupe, he would let them pump him for so called revelations which were nothing but fake.

Dr. O'Henny wondered out loud,

Why should Jac get upset? About what? Our innocent visit? As a medic, I should find it most interesting to watch this attack — if it comes. Might be an excellent opportunity to judge his health on an occasion like this. —

You — you — degenerate bum, Siv burst out, you know well that psychologically Jac is a hundred times healthier than you, you gangster. Dagos, miserable half-breeds all of you, the agitated little gypsy sniffed vehemently, scratching the hollow of her knee. Don't you dare to upset Jac —

The young man she alternately called "degenerate rascal" and "charlatan scoundrel" upset her — and with good reason. The general public's inability to control the increasing power of the medical profession was bound to make it easy for degenerate crooks with the necessary financial and intellectual means to infiltrate their ranks. If Siv disliked the syndicate members, she dreaded O'Henny. He posed the greatest danger to her clown — her "favorite baby" as she once tenderly called the man who was over twenty years her senior.

Tracbac took his time. Major DeGrazy entered in full regalia. The fact that he had never before worn his uniform on this side of the Atlantic intimated that he now wore it at the clown's whim. With a mechanical smile on his face, DeGrazy clapped his gloved hands, bent slightly backward and called,

Madame, and you, my American friends! Both Mr. Tracbac and I were expecting you in the hall of mirrors. No one imagined you sprawling all over the vestibule floor in total disregard of the foolish conventions and dictates well-mannered, dull Europeans observe. Mr. Cow, wouldn't you consider this formidable little scene something for the movies: Group of California Gold Diggers Out To Shock Charming Retired European Officer?

From the depths of his soft pillows and without lifting his square head, Mr. Cow intoned in his nasal phonograph voice,

I am sure it is. May I suggest a better title! More like: The Idiot And His Traitors. I sure hope Tracbac gets here soon. —

The Austrian's face turned an even deeper yellow. Bent over Siv's hand to kiss it, he whispered quickly,

Don't worry. I'll be right back. He was in your studio with his nephew. I don't know what they did there.

Siv stared ahead, her large eyes aglitter with apprehension.

The clown finally arrived. By now no one was surprised at his strange outfit — white tie and tails, breeches, silk stockings and jewel-buckled shoes. It might have been a party suit for his socially prominent great-grandfather. He looked like a snob with his extravagant lace cuffs hanging all the way down to his knuckles. In fact, they were nothing but a cover under which to hide his timidity and a nervous habit of raising and shaking his hands when trying to emphasize a point.

All pretense of nonchalance vanished the moment the clown entered the huge hall. Petrified, silent and perspiring heavily on their pillows, the floorbound gentlemen worried about the clown's frame of mind. Tracbac shook cursorily their limp hands without saying a word. Only young Dr. O'Henny found it necessary to leave his chest again to welcome Tracbac with an energetic bow, the way polite European students greet their teachers. Tracbac recognized him with a smile and a slap on his back. The medic was his favorite. Siv dreaded him.

Having welcomed his guests, Tracbac sat down on a pillow next to Siv. He nodded to the men and said,

Welcome, gentlemen. It's nice to see you.

Mr. Adam, the oldest, came slowly upright and said with a friendly grin,

You're all dressed up, Jac. On your way to a party?

As you see, I do have guests, Tracbac answered, bowing politely.

Oh, come on now! Mr. Cow protested, heaving himself laboriously out of his seat. Do you always wear tails when friends drop in?

I dress pretty informally for guests I invite. But I draw the line for uninvited guests. They make me feel formal, he explained. Suddenly frowning and his voice slipping in falsetto, he added,

And if you care to know, I wore this to avoid hearing your jovial blusters, Hello Jac, old fellow! Listen, my friends! I don't mind my gatekeeper's jovial camaraderie and backslaps. Damn it, I am his comrade, certainly as long as he cares to watch my gate. But, my dear CEO's and VIP's and the likes, I resent your taking liberties in my home. And I'll be damned if I take it from operators like you.

He breathed heavily, his head bobbing backward time and again. Siv stroked his forehead and back, gently, like an anxious mother, whispering soothingly,

Baby — my baby — calm down.

All of a sudden her hand stiffened. Terrified, she stared at O'Henny who had pulled a small notepad from his bathrobe and was scribbling hurriedly while observing the clown. Tracbac followed the doctor's doings with a frown, then motioned him to sit on the empty seat beside him. But O'Henny shook his head to the invitation and continued to write. The clown's face turned crimson with fury and he screamed in high falsetto,

Boy!

The young man shrugged and put his notepad away. Then, folding his arms across his chest, he stalked over to Tracbac's side, jumped into the air with an acrobat's agility and landed cross-legged on the indicated pillow. Satisfied with his performance, he said,

At your command, King Clown!

Tracbac instructed fatherly,

Denny-Henny, I command you to behave. My boy, with your shameless wealth you can easily buy all of us. Not our gorgeous hostess, of course — but certainly the rest of this caboodle. That's why I demand special tact and consideration. Understand?

O'Henny bowed silently. Puffing on their cigars, the reclining men understood that their strategy to settle their differences with the clown about tour and movie rights had misfired. Their smoke hung suspended in the dimly lit hall like a giant orb — incense burning in honor of a mighty god — Jac Tracbac. The small man sat hunched forward, one hand tightly against his chin, the other limply hanging down his side, the long lace cuff covering the slender fingers. Next to him sat the girl with the amber eyes, stiff and straight. Opposite sat the young man, looking like a wild ephebus with his curly, parted, gold-red hair. Behind the god stood his temple guard — the uniformed DeGrazy, a defeated warrior, prisoner in the land of King Midas and indifferent to the general agitation surrounding him.

Tracbac began softly,

Well, gentlemen, obviously you and I need to talk. So — what's on your mind?

The worthy Mr. Adams stood up. The others sat up to listen. Mr. Adams began,

There's one grave issue — your ill-timed dismissal of Abel Rush. He and Mr. Cow were in the middle of negotiating with the twenty places on our tour. Also, he and Judah were scheduled to finalize our contract with the movie company. So, it's most untimely to fire him. Of course, we bend to your wishes. Abel Rush has displeased you; Abel Rush may go —

Taking his good time to reflect, Tracbac eventually said quietly and almost humbly,

Abel Rush is not leaving. He may have infuriated me, but that has nothing to do with my decision —

He stopped short, closed his eyes and with a tired, almost despairing gesture he stroked his forehead. Siv resumed her gentle massage of his forehead and back. O'Henny mumbled under his breath,

Your decision, Tracbac? What decision?

Hush, Denny-Henny, Tracbac mumbled. He cleared his throat and declared,

My decision not to perform. My reasons for that go far deeper than my momentary displeasure with Abel Rush.

Hear! Hear! O'Henny murmured. Tracbac and the gentlemen frowned. Mr. Adam said,

Before discussing your decision, may we ask DeGrazy to call Abel Rush?

Tracbac's face lit up. Waving his hands, he burst out,

Well, well! Abel Rush here! Does that mean he's not angry with me? Great! Excellent!

Following the major's call, Abel Rush entered quickly and sat down without greeting the beautiful lady. Dry and businesslike he said,

Before I leave, I consider it my duty to —

Leave! Tracbac bellowed. His large, light blue eyes popped out like the eyes of a provoked bull. Absolutely absurd! Ridiculous!

Monitoring Tracbac's behavior, O'Henny began scribbling in his notebook again. This infuriated the clown who pulled the notebook out of his doctor's hands and threw it on the floor. Then in a forward lunge he struck the face of the young medic.

Thanks a lot, O'Henny mumbled, collected his notebook from the floor and backed, crab-like, into his seat. There was a short pause before Rush continued,

I feel it my duty to inform Tracbac on the economics of his work since I am slightly better informed than he is. He seems to think that his yearly income runs into the hundred thousands —

Tracbac flapped his lacy wings, apparently deeply insulted, and muttered,

Oh, oh, much, much more!

Rush resumed,

However, I feel obliged to report that the mere upkeep of his villa and his servants amounts to three times that much —

Great, just great, Tracbac mumbled, confused.

Of course, that's his personal money and therefore not our concern. So let's discuss the tour which involves twenty major cities in the States. Doctor O'Henny has limited the performances to one hundred. That means some four hundred thousand tickets sold at an average price of twenty dollars a piece — totaling about eight million dollars.

The clown interrupted him, full of despair,

Great. The total expenses are just as high. Sure, I know. Railways, busses, hotels, restaurants, heating, personal expenses. Listen, my boy, my experience tops yours by far, he concluded with an air of importance.

Granted that it does, Abel Rush agreed, biting his lips to prevent an unmanageable sad smile. Indeed, expenses are enormous, so our gross income must match. Negotiations with the movie company are not finalized yet. Mr. Judah and I insist on a guaranteed sum so that the entire tour, including movie rights, will gross us sixteen million, at least.

Nodding solemnly, the clown said,

Huge sums, Abel Rush, very huge indeed —

Rush shrugged his shoulders, crestfallen, and proceeded,

I don't dare suggest that you bother looking at the sums. But you ought to know that a company our size not only concerns you, but many others as well, including thousands economically far less fortunate than you.

The clown's head sank slowly forward. Behind his back, Siv shook her fist to warn Abel Rush. But the secretary forged ahead, his listeners breathlessly waiting — not for what he had to say, but to watch the effect it would have on the clown,

While you are having fun creating all kinds of problems, Sir, these people are anxiously waiting to see whether His Majesty King Clown chooses to provide for their daily bread —

Hogwash, Tracbac mumbled angrily. Idiot — I'm certainly not the only clown in the world. There are oodles of them, oodles —

Yes, there are indeed, Abel Rush agreed. I don't mean to imply that you're the most outstanding clown either, perhaps not even one of the greater among the lot. But I dare say that you are the best paid. You earn far more than the others. Can't you see that this carries certain responsibilities? Especially toward people depending on you for their income? It's disgusting to see how many decent people depend on the whims of an overgrown child. That's my considered opinion, Sir.

Overgrown child, Tracbac repeated, glowering furiously at Siv. Do you hear that? Your beloved Abel accusing me of behaving like an overgrown child!

I heard, Siv answered quietly. Abel Rush got up and left as quickly as he had come without saying goodbye. Once outside he stopped and listened. Abel Rush had attacked the clown on his two most vulnerable points — his compassion for others and his bourgeois honor to meet commitments. In silent deference to Abel Rush, the syndicate gentlemen waited for the clown's response. But Tracbac remained lost in thought, shaking his head sententiously now and then. Then he turned and whispered to DeGrazy who stood behind him,

My friend, report to Mr. Borck and Longfellow.

Tracbac waited until the major had left, sighed and said,

Well, gentlemen, the fellow reported huge earnings. And he gave me a good piece of his mind too —

All dignity, Mr. Adam interrupted him,

You realize of course that the young man was fired. His anger preceded this outrageous personal attack —

No, I don't believe that at all, the clown countered quietly. Abel Rush has too much business sense to rant. But there's something he does not know, which I tell you now. He is absolutely right about my responsibilities. To quote Axelsson, there's nothing dumber than acting dumb. As a youngster I was greedy about ten dollar bills — now it's thousands. Why am I greedy? I have obligations, to be sure. But there's also something else beyond my powers, a sort of force majeure, a certain emptiness, an inner void, a barrenness — .

His voice became sentimental, lachrymose. Siv stroked his cheek and he leaned his head momentarily against her shoulder. Deeply touched, the gentlemen bowed their heads as if in church. Only Denny O'Henny pulled a face full of visible disgust. Actually he was rather fond of the clown, in contrast to the other men present. Imitating Tracbac's tearful tone, he hummed: The Clown's *force majeure — fatalité du coeur —*

Tracbac chuckled and repeated,

Fatalité du coeur! Well, your words, Henny-Denny. *Fatalité du coeur!* He chuckled again. Grabbing Siv's arm, he tried to get up, groaning, staggering, his chuckle gradually turning into a scream that rent the air like a knife — a lightning shriek, a howling flash echoing through the dimly lit room. Siv jumped up to steady him, both hands under his arms. Momentarily silent, the clown spread his arms, his palms outward as if praying to some almighty force. Presently his scream broke through again, more piercing than before. Raising his eyebrows, O'Henny bounced up and stared at the clown. The others turned away from the scene or closed their eyes, their shielding hands over their ears. In an effort to help, the freckled Pech brought a glass of water. To prevent total disaster O'Henny slapped Pech's face, toppling him along with his potentially dangerous water. Then the doctor began to massage Tracbac's throat muscles. The screams gradually subsided. The clown looked like a rabies patient with his gnashing teeth. Suddenly he gave a deep sigh, put his arms around O'Henny's neck and for an instant hung on the young man like a deadweight.

DeGrazy returned through the opposite door. Benbé, Longfellow and Axelsson followed him. Between them Longfellow and Axelsson carried a cloth-covered painting, one meter high and two meters wide. DeGrazy stopped short when he saw the group gathered in the center of the hall. But he was his old lively, smiling self again when Tracbac waved him closer with his lace-covered wrists, calling,

Gentlemen, I want to show you a sentimental, macabre view of my profession as seen by our famous artist Siva Yala. She painted this picture as a personal gift. It reveals a side of me which I'm unable to put into words — this — *force majeure* — emptiness — void — *fatalité du coeur* as this rascal called it — well, then — let's step back, you get a better view from a distance — don't get angry — just try to understand — Siv, you too, don't be angry — oh, you are — listen to me — oh, you're furious! (He wet his fingertips, pointed at her and hissed. It sounded like a droplet of water on a hot plate.) A flawed character, Siv — help your neighbor, help yourself. Axelsson, drop the cloth!

Axelsson's trembling woodcutter's hands pulled the cover. Longfellow's dark face, eyes closed, his red mouth grinning, appeared above the frame.

It was a charcoal drawing of a modern meat market, its marble walls, marble counters and marble floor covered with sawdust. Five salespersons in white aprons and caps stood behind the counter, three of them distinguishable replicas of Adam, Cow and Judah. The fifth, doctor O'Henny, was busily sawing deep into a heart with a modern meat cutter, under the watchful eyes of the salespersons. To judge from the sad faces, the heart was the last sales item in the store: Judah was shrugging his shoulders, his palms outward turned, much like the real Judah sitting in the hall; the original Mr. Adams and his replica were raising their eyes skyward; Mr. Cow was balling a fist.

Only O'Henny, unperturbed in his investigation, kept cutting deeper into the heart — a bright red blotch in the chiaroscuro of its surrounding.

A skeleton hung from one of the meat hooks, the tip of the hook sticking out through its neck. Two ribbons came snorkeling out of its grinning mouth, the kind that usually display the family's coat of arms. The inscription on one ribbon read,

I was Jac Tracbac.

On the other,

I was born human — I lived a clown — I sold my heart — I died poor —

Aghast, the group, stared in utter silence.

Tracbac whispered,

Do you get the meaning? No, you don't? Then look at this —

He signaled Benbé who stood waiting behind him. Reluctantly the young man walked over and pasted a hastily prepared sign across the butcher showcase in the picture,

Sold Out — Business Closed. Jac Tracbac Syndicate, Ltd.

The gentlemen were upset. Outside, though he had never seen the drawing, Abel Rush could hear himself scream. He lay supine in one of the smaller rooms, crying, his body shaking in convulsions all at the same time. Nothing bad against him. Not just great clowns, but anyone can have a nervous breakdown. And crying is free of charge.

9: Hobby and Glove

B ENBÉ MOVED INTO Tracbac's villa. It took him a full week before he settled in enough to think of writing to his friends in Sanna. So far, he had
eaten, slept, walked through the neighborhood, watched the apes, contemplated the botanical gardens and shot the breeze with Longfellow, DeGrazy,
Axelsson. Writing gave him a sense of finally doing something worthwhile.
Tracbac was nowhere to be seen.

But writing a letter to the Längsälls proved more difficult than expected.
He had to confess to failing finding a job all the way from New York to San
Francisco. Mooching on his wealthy uncle and living in his house complicated the matter. Of course, his stay was only temporary. He hesitated momentarily, then informed the family Längsäll that his uncle Tracbac wanted
to return their greetings. This was an outright lie. But it could hardly hurt
mentioning that he had relayed their regards. Thus he wrote:

Our mutual friend and relative is happy to hear that you remembered
him and sends his regards.

Imagine Jac Tracbac remembering them! He hardly remembered the
relative living in his house! One day Benbé happened to pass by Axelsson
with his featherduster. The old fellow stopped, grinned his toothless smile
and surmised,

Well, well, young master, I see you've been put on ice. Nothing to do —
just collect room and board. Pocket money too — all you need do is ask the
secretary and you get all you want. Just don't imagine you're important in
the scheme of things. Not a bit. He doesn't value anybody. Has no heart,
that kid. Never had, not even as a boy. I've seen him grow up, so I should
know. Sure, he can be kind, mind you. Generous as hell. But heart? — Not
on your life. No one ever means anything to him. Dust and booze, dust and
booze. That's all there is.

Weaving his featherduster airily, the old buffer shuffled off, a dimwitted
shadow drifting through the dimness around.

Benbé felt sorely abandoned. His meals were served in a little hall adjoining his bedroom. Once DeGrazy sent him an elegant note asking for the
honor to share his supper. Mindful of the Austrian's crazy formality, Benbé
dressed up in his tuxedo to welcome his guest. But DeGrazy arrived drowsy
and unshaved, still in his robe. He seemed to have slept through the day.
Only after a cocktail or two and a noisy yawn behind his hand did he finally
wake up. His eyes wide open and grave, he stared at Benbé,

You know, Mr. Borck, you really ought to leave this place; the sooner the better. This environment is not good for a young man like you. My case is different. I am close to sixty. And I am an *uomo finito,* finished, a man without expectations. So here I am, a sort of major-domo, master steward for special occasions. The work is not demanding. Besides, Tracbac likes me because I'm an old soldier who's inhaled a lot more than just gunpowder smoke. His greatest worry is a malicious individual some day stabbing him in the back. That's why he likes having a dependable old soldier like me around. For me it's a convenient retreat. But, young man, it's no place for you, believe me. Try to leave, soon.

Easier said than done, Benbé mused. He sighed, knowing that all penniless persons shared his kind of predicament. Poverty was like anemia, sapping all energy out of its victims. Confused their morals and minds. Take his case. When Longfellow returned the ominous check, he tore it up in a fit of virtuous pride and gave the pieces to Rush. That made it impossible to ask the secretary for money now. Sullenly he said,

Before I got stuck in this maze the relationship seemed easy enough, especially when Tracbac came to see me. Now that we live under the same roof he's become invisible.

Well, the Austrian countered, right now it's difficult to meet him. I am not privy to the problem, but I know there's a lot of animosity between him and the syndicate. They gave him an ultimatum. Later doctor O'Henny blocked further negotiations. And the doctor is all-powerful — no one dares to contradict him. Except Jac, of course. He does exactly what he wants — and nothing else. Trouble is — he likes doing nothing.

Benbé wanted to leave at all cost and he decided to act. Knowing that Jac stood model for Siv every morning, he stationed himself under the palm trees by the duck pond and waited for him. The rash, unsophisticated young man wanted to avoid meeting Siva Yala. Her cool, proud amber eyes irritated him. He had not expected Siv to notice him and was surprised to see her suddenly bent over the veranda railing, calling,

Listen here, Mr. Borck. Standing there, you look like a cat lurking for a bird. If you want to see Jac, I'll send him to you.

Send him to me, Benbé imitated her, offended for his famous relative. Sounds as if I must humbly beg for an audience.

Nonsense! Siv snorted, pulling a face. Our unassuming Jac finds your excessive fawning and groveling so revolting that it might land him in an insane asylum. What time suits you?

Five o'clock, Benbé answered on the spur of the moment.

The woman mused a moment. Then she said,

All right. He'll see you at five. Have the decency to be there. He mustn't wait.

71

Siv returned to her studio.

Benbé checked his watch. Barely three o'clock. Still, he went straight to his room, humming,

It's best to listen to the skirt! She's right. The simpler the better. Groveling is for jerks. Decent people deserve decent strategies. Basta.

He settled down comfortably in his room for a patient wait, even refrained from lighting one of his beloved cigarettes, knowing how much Tracbac hated smoke. But he was wrong expecting the clown to arrive on time and slip into the room without further ceremonies. At four thirty one of the black servants finally came and opened the window to rid the room of all remaining dust. No one considered Benbé or his discomfort. Then Denny O'Henny arrived, sat down, nodded at Benbé and lit a long cigar. The Negro stared at him, horrorstricken. Benbé protested. The young doctor laughed,

Ash, don't give me bull! Siv and DeGrazy compete in spoiling him. They treat him like a baby! Utter nonsense. The aroma of an extra strong Havana will perk him up. I'll let him remain in here for thirty to forty-five minutes. If he stays longer, I'll come and get him. I'm all in favor of this visit. He's to sign the final contract at six and is usually very nervous and contrary before he does. Amuse him. Small talk. Keep him preoccupied and he'll sign without giving it another thought when Rush comes with the contract. Well, now, don't think that we're putting you up to mischief. Goodness no! Rush and I have checked and rechecked this contract for a whole month now. There's nothing in it that can hurt him and his health, I can assure you.

The physician left the room, leaving wads of his thick smoke hanging in the air. They upset DeGrazy when he entered shortly thereafter. Throwing his head backward and his hands up, he shouted,

Calamity John, what have you done! Can't you feed your foul habits elsewhere and leave the air in here fit for breathing when Tracbac comes?!

Benbé screamed back,

The doctor did that. I didn't take a single puff.

The major managed a resigned shrug and dropped the subject, but darted to the window and opened it quickly. Then he checked his watch and announced,

Tracbac should be here in about ten minutes. I just met him by the duck pond. His mood swings may seem precarious, but his calling me Beelzebub's general tells me that it's upbeat for now. Today is a critical day. He's pretty nervous underneath all this joking. The contract — I guess you know. We're keeping the lines of communication open and will spread the news throughout the States about an hour after he signs it. This visit is a gift from heaven. He'll sign without giving it a second thought —

The major's gush ebbed away. He tiptoed out of the room in a cloud of secrecy. Again Benbé waited, still unclear about the roll he was supposed to play in the unfolding drama. The thought of being no more than a passive, ignorant tool in the hands of the players depressed him.

The blue-gray wads hung still thick in the room when the clown appeared in the dark door opening. Dressed in some kind of homespun, he blended into the grayness surrounding him. He stopped abruptly and puckered his nose when he noticed the smoke. Eventually he said cheerfully,

Here I am, but where are you? said the hawk and devoured the cuckoo . . . the gun piff-puffed and shot the hawk . . . This time I'm not quoting Axelsson, but my wet nurse, God bless her soul. She's been dead for forty years. Yes, people move on, but their words live on. How are you, my boy? I haven't seen you in a while. Are you bored? I am. Very much. I'm loafing. No job. Disgusting. People who don't work have no right to eat. I have a mind to follow that maxim to the letter.

He went to the open window and flapped his arms in an effort to ease the smoke out. Snorting and sneezing, he said,

I've met many people out of work, artists and others. It's hopeless. Plain hopeless. They're worse off than galley slaves. I'm out of work too — oh well — perhaps it's not the same. I have still my generous income — and more. At any rate. It's hopeless. People tell me it's my own fault, but the gentlemen are wrong. But you wouldn't understand, as smart as you are in other respects.

He straddled a chair and eased himself down, smiling sententiously and good-naturedly like a humble puck.

Siv sent me here. Is there something you want? Or is this just a simple, informal social call? Let's hear it.

Benbé sighed, awkward, confused. With an all-knowing face the clown tried to encourage him,

Just shoot. Don't be bashful.

It took Benbé a moment to relent,

Well, my case is like yours. No job. I have room and board, but no work. It frazzles my spirits. I'm getting edgy.

Yes, that's it, the clown mumbled. Frazzles one's spirits. Is that a standard expression, or did you coin it? It frazzles your spirits —

The clown mused quietly as if trying to give his thoughts a new direction. Suddenly he perked up,

You know, a man faces two major choices in his life — either he gets himself a toy, a hobby, or he lacks one. I could never find a hobby, though I've tried countless times. Once I even thought I found one. Take the many antiques here, Mexican furniture, religious and domestic articles, and such. They were bought without my knowledge. It struck me later how much all

73

this Mexican junk resembled the rural Dalarna paintings, the old chests and the furniture I remembered from home. I made it a first-rate hobby — even gave it a scientific base. Yes indeed. Formulated a new theory: in the eyes of Our Lord we're all alike. Mexican art derives from the Spanish, the Spanish from Western Gothic, just like the Sicilian from Norman, and both from South Scandinavian tribes. I was immensely proud of my equality theory. If I had handled it more carefully, it would have become a lifelong hobby, you see; something to sew on at night and a decent cloak for daytime wear. You see, clowns don't wear decent clothing. They hate themselves — a person needs to don civil trappings occasionally, to speak professional lingo.

With a cunning grin, the clown continued,

Well, you think that people ridiculed my nonsense. They didn't. I was Jac the Clown, you see, and when a joker is serious for a change — well, then it's to be taken damn seriously. I have it in black and white. A doctorate from two universities, mind you, just for collecting these chests. I hired a scientific old woman with experience in university exhibits and supplied six scientific boys and as many girls, all first-rate. She exchanged the girls for as many boys, and surely put something in between, arguing that males are more creative than females because the male soul is less domesticated and hence more original. I sent them to buy twice as much scientific furniture in addition to what I had already donated to the universities. That would've made a fantastic hobby — if it hadn't suddenly struck me how totally irrelevant it really is whether Mexican culture is rooted in Småland or in some other culture in this wide world. It's this indifference, that's my basic problem. Indifference — my character flaw that keeps me from ever pursuing a decent hobby.

To succeed I would have to overcome such feelings, he went on, gravely shaking his head. Sooner or later one ought to become a child again. Not many people have the strength to keep their maturity on the same level throughout life. Our Austrian, you know, gets up in the middle of the night and pads to a room where he keeps his library. I envied him because I thought he had a secret hobby. So, one night I sneaked behind him and spied through the keyhole. I couldn't see, but I heard him in some kind of ecstasy counting down vast sums — two hundred, six hundred, one thousand, ten thousand, and on and on. Hearing him made me think that the poor fellow, an important commanding officer who lead many bloody offensives during the war and had a lot of his men die on him, now sits, counting, whether he should have adopted a different strategy. A tragic fate, wouldn't you agree? Poor, poor fellow, I thought. Well, I later heard that these nocturnal strolls were to his stamp collection. Not much of a collection, either. He can't afford expensive stamps, so he buys ordinary stamps in bulk. Now, when he feels edgy and down at night, he gets up and counts his thousands, drills them by happily adding new acquisitions to his troops. Poor fellow? Sure. His war experiences were tragic, but he has reached the point where tragedy no longer feels tragic — the terrible edge where pain has lost its sting. That's the time when a person needs stamps or other junk to stuff his mind. Like a wastebasket.

Without losing his serious demeanor he coughed up two or three laughs. He called,

No, let's discuss other matters, dear Benjamin. I feel so happy tonight. It's good to have someone to confide in and talk profound topics in simple terms.

Amiably, he quickly corrected himself before he continued,

Oh! Look who's coming? If it isn't our mutual friend Abel Rush —

Tracbac rose as the secretary entered. Knowing the purpose of the visit, Benbé watched with childish curiosity. The secretary seemed equally tense; his Adam's apple danced up and down in a nervous attempt to swallow his uneasiness along with his saliva. The secretary's career hinged on what would happen during the next few minutes.

Excuse me for intruding, but I would like to have your signature. Our partners are waiting.

Tracbac bowed and answered without blinking,

I'm sorry, Abel, but I'm not going to sign this agreement. I've spent these past days gauging my guts as carefully as my forebears inventoried their warehouses. Empty, my dear Abel. I've nothing to sell.

The secretary sucked his cheeks into hollows. Serenely, politely and businesslike, he countered,

Does that mean you want the tour delayed, or do you want to cancel it?

Bowing again, the clown answered,

The latter, Abel.

For a while the secretary stood silent. Then, timid as if embarrassed about repeating himself, he said,

I take it that you considered all the suffering and disappointment your decision will cause other people?

With an undertone of rage Tracbac informed him,

I did indeed, Mr. Rush, much more than you think. Kindly do not accuse me of being inconsiderate, Mr. Rush, because I am not. I assure you. Take that down in writing.

Rush's face turned pale green. Completely calm, he said,

All right, that wraps up my assignment.

Nodding at Benbé, he left. Tracbac sank back into his chair, breathing heavily. He slapped his face as if to drive off an impudent fly, muttering sullenly,

I'm awfully sorry for the boy. But it's not my fault if he gets into trouble. They want to pressure me — telling me that I cause all the mess and confusion. As if I didn't know! Oh yes, gentlemen, I know from experience. I've had a lot of experience. For many years I ran my own business. Not as big as this, mind you, but not so small either. We had twenty-four men, including the grooms. Pretty good-sized, I would say, he repeated with pride. Including all the troubles that went with it, the responsibilities and cares for details, great and small. I had a little ballerina — gosh was she ever cute. I used to tease Siv with her. A little bitch, that one, when she had a mind to. I've never seen anyone as talented in straining tendons, twisting joints and stretching muscles. Her toes and fingers could turn in all directions. Lord knows! She was our star attraction and I had to cancel time and again, return the money and other such stuff. I used to perspire at night. My sheets were wet like a baby's. And now they're telling me that I don't know what I'm doing when I cancel a tour. I would go through with it even if seven deadly sicknesses struck me — but I can't go empty — that's something I can't do. And here they go, bloated with self-righteousness, against me, an old, experienced circus horse. Shame on those apes. Lice, really. But I say bah . . . !

Angry, he stuck out his tongue at Benbé as if he were one of the apes or lice. Benbé kept his lips tightly pressed to keep from smiling. The clown looked too comical, the way he sat there, rocking back and forth in his chair, not unlike an unruly ape himself. There was something touching in his childish, sulking lament. Tracbac tried another slap at the pesky fly that kept buzzing about his face. It took a while before he resumed his conversation,

Well, ideally, people who've stopped feeling alive should find a hobby. But I find it impossible. I've even tried to get interested in a "sentimental" hobby, so to speak. I had Grandma's furniture sent here, including old Axelsson, one of her live fixtures. What are they to me now? Tell me! People your age treasure things. Love and interest for mementos are intact. Well, my dear friend, they diminish with time. Feeling yourself sliding into that murky area of becoming a relic yourself makes it worse. Any veneration stops. Occasionally a young man shows respect for his elders. But old men never respect one another. Never! Only the future counts — even if you're on your deathbed. Not the present! No, it is dead. Your childhood is forgotten and youth and adulthood follow suit. If they were unhappy years you ought to forget them; if happy, forget them ten times over. To live on memory alone is like living among corpses. Why embalm our dear ones, sit with them, light electric sparks in their eyes, put phonographs into their chests? Of course you don't! Yesterday should be forgotten by today.

Congenially and matter-of-factly he interrupted himself,

Oh well, Benjamin, actually we were discussing you. What made you come here? What are your plans? You've given me to understand you have no money. Do you owe someone something back home? Who paid your trip here?

Benbé's face lit up. Here was finally his chance to relay the greetings, which he considered meaningless. He said,

I got the ticket from a decent relative, uncle Längsäll of Sanna. You seem to have met. Do you remember him?

Tracbac stiffened and stared into the air as if trying to recapture a long dead memory. Benbé scanned his face carefully to detect a glimmer of recollection, but there was not the slightest hint. For a while the clown remained silent. Then he nodded and said,

Längsäll. On Sanna. Oh yes, I sure remember him. I do indeed.

Benbé appreciated the answer, though he could not explain why. He remembered Sanna Sanna's present to the famous uncle and her wish to send her a signed picture and a note from the great Jac Tracbac himself. With his typical, boyish excitement he called,

Wait a minute, Tracbac! O Boy! I have a present for you! A present from a cute girl. You don't get that every day! Just a minute, wait just a minute —

Frantic, he searched the room, rummaged through all his drawers. Eventually, he stopped, dismayed, straightened up and pulled his hair. Suddenly his face lit up. With cocksure certainty he exclaimed,

Sure, as usual. Ben Borck's safety deposit box. The world's best. The present must be in the lining.

Having regained his air of dignity he walked to the closet, dug in his torn pocket and pulled out his little package. He held it out to Tracbac, who sat still staring into empty space, his face more bloodless and ashen than before.

Benbé hesitated. The clown suddenly looked like his picture — a dead skull, artificial lights illuminating his eye cavities. The clown before him gave a jerk, smiled faintly and took the package. Slowly peeling the wrapping, in a low voice he deciphered his own name on it. Benbé bent forward, far more curious than the addressee himself.

The package contained a small lady's glove of brown suède. The clown stared at the strange gift, turned it in his hands, held it up to his cheek as if wanting to detect some hidden secrets. Benbé joked,

What's that? The girl seems to throw you the glove. What a dame — ! Honestly!

The clown's protruding, bulging, light blue, slightly opalescent eyes scrutinized Benbé. Tracbac queried,

Who? Who's sent me this glove?

Oh, one of the Sanna girls, Benbé said.

The clown put his hand over his eyes and slowly shook his head, wondering softly,

Tell me, Benjamin — it says here, "To be delivered after my death." Has Mrs. Längsäll of Sanna died?

Oh no, not at all, Benbé protested animatedly. I told you, it was the girl's idea. Well, of course you don't know her. She's full of crazy ideas, I tell you —

The clown meditated a few minutes. Then he got up and left the room, saying,

Wait a second, Benjamin, stay here. I've something to show you.

The clown to show him? Benbé wondered what on earth that would be. One thing was clear, though. He had not forgotten the good Längsälls at all.

Tracbac returned and put another glove next to the glove on the table. They made a perfect pair. Stroking both with his fingertips, he said quietly,

I don't know what to make of it. I do need an explanation. It's important. Remember O'Henny's quote the other day: The clown's force *majeure — fatalité du coeur.*

Staring wide-eyed at the two gloves, Benbé cried out,

But Jac — that's the mate! They belong together!

Yes. Right. They belong together.

10: The Art Of Selling Emotions

THE SYNDICATE WAS in a bind.

After the clown's refusal to perform, Abel Rush recommended that the board stop to negotiate. Further negotiations would only cause further delay,

But if we leave Jac alone, it's possible that he'll soon regret what he did. Then he'll nicely come to us instead.

His round, tanned, mild face smiling as usual, Mr. Judah wondered anxiously,

Come to us, Abel? He may just as easily approach others, dear Abel.

Gruffly Rush set him straight,

Mr. Judah, you've never understood that Jac is an honest man. If he changes his mind, he'll turn to us. That's just the point. He'll come to us. Not we to him — if we so have to wait ten years, or dissolve the syndicate.

Kind Mr. Adam rubbed his hands and said gently,

Abel Rush is right, as always. Jac himself must resume the negotiations. That'll give us certain advantages —

But Rush interrupted him caustically,

I must warn you. I'll do all I can to prevent you from gaining any leverage over Jac.

The four gentlemen: Adam, Cow, Judah and Pech clicked their tongues the way owls snap their beaks. The fifth, O'Henny, sat by the window, playing with a baby rattle as if the discussion did not concern him. As was their custom, they used the room with the barbaric furniture where Hiawatha's pineapple bomb had exploded not too long ago.

Smiling nervously, Mr. Judah said softly,

Dear Abel, you ought to remember that Jac's willful behavior causes us heavy losses. That includes you.

Rush said,

For one, I don't call it willful when a person suffers a burn-out. It can happen to anyone, including your humble secretary. Secondly, we always provide for unforeseen disruptions in our calculations. I feel sorry if the gentlemen speculated on the pre-sale of our tickets and now face heavy losses. Though I must add that my compassion is rather limited.

Rush had touched on an especially sensitive issue. The gentlemen turned quickly to the other topic of the day. Should they notify the mass media about Jac Tracbac's canceled tour? Ill-tempered as usual, Mr. Cow bellowed like a wounded bull: the press release should inform the media that Jac

Tracbac has turned his back on circus and movies for good. This would set an excellent stage for a "great comeback" after a few years. Red-haired Pech, the syndicate's press manager, pointed out that "comebacks" are problematic. They are risky and often become financial disasters. The general public might find a too hasty "comeback" ludicrous. Interest for an artist tends to fade quickly once he retires. Others take their place. Abel Rush supported his viewpoint. He suggested to keep the whole thing silent — the news about the tour had not been official anyway. Mr. Adam shook his curly white hair, declaring with his fatherly smile,

Gentlemen, don't underestimate the news media. They're not easily fooled. I'm convinced some ambitious reporters already know more about the thing than we do. Besides, they already have the details about our negotiations in the twenty cities. We have no other choice but to report him sick.

I won't accept any doctor's report, the secretary interrupted him.

Mr. Adam said,

He doesn't need to know about it. O'Henny writes a communiqué that the planned tour had to be delayed because of Tracbac's health.

Mr. Cow bellowed angrily,

Write that he's crazy! Short and simple. Crazy! —

Red-haired Pech, his voice flipping in highest falsetto, screeched,

Gentlemen! Gentlemen! I must emphasize that nothing could be more dangerous. People lose interest. Insanity turns them off. He's another leper if he's gone off the deep end. People take pity, but stay away.

His head thrown backward and his face ashen, Abel Rush listened silently, swallowing time and again in an effort to control his nausea. His eyes locked into O'Henny's. The physician raised his eyebrows ever so slightly and the secretary acknowledged it with an imperceptible nod. O'Henny started furiously banging his rattle as if he were the presiding officer. He stood up in the ensuing silence and said with his customary reverence toward the board members,

Gentlemen. As Jac Tracbac's official personal physician I, Denny O'Henny, M.D., regretfully submit my refusal to write any sickness reports. Of course, I can't prevent you from bribing a dozen of my worthy colleagues.

Mildly reproachful, Mr. Adam interrupted him,

Denny! It's nasty to slander your colleagues.

I do no such thing, O'Henny said. But my worthy colleagues may need some extra income. I don't. That's the difference between us.

Conciliatory, Mr. Adam continued,

Oh well, calling it mental illness is absurd, of course. Nervous breakdown, depression, or something like that would be more appropriate. Don't you agree, Denny?

The young physician answered politely,

At your service, Adam. I promise a full and conscientious report on Jac Tracbac's mental health. But not before I've watched him for three years or so in my private clinic.

O'Henny sat down. Mr. Cow flew up, still raging,

There we go! One of your damn underhanded tricks again. Now you want to lock Tracbac up in your private clinic. Boy, I'll see to it that you won't succeed! You're not the only reputable physician in the States! There are plenty others! We'll appoint an entire commission to hound you, if necessary! Mark that!

O'Henny kept his cool and smiled,

Sure. I know you can. If not I would've added dear Jac to my waxworks collection a long time ago.

Abel Rush rose quickly and said,

Well, gentlemen, we've settled two things. One — we won't negotiate with Jac Tracbac unless he contacts us. Two — we won't give the news media anything more than the vague explanation I suggested. And that only when asked. Pech can handle that. If we all agree, we need no longer keep Mylady Longfellow out of her living quarters.

Trying to overlook the jocular reference to Mylady's living room, the good gentlemen managed a golden smile. Lighting their cigars or unwrapping chewing gum, they rose to leave. They found Longfellow outside, dutifully guarding his gate and politely and jovially gabbing with seven good-looking beauties who stood beyond the fence. At the sight of the secretary, the girls locked arms like ballet dancers and shouted in unison,

We want Benbé! Our Funnybunny! We want Benbé —

Miss Cadillac, Miss Nash and other car makes!

The grapevine had been busy with all sorts of rumors about the clown and the value of their doll, their Funnybunny, had increased considerably during the last forty-eight hours. His nephew was worth his weight in gold by now. The gentlemen of the syndicate recoiled, ready to return to their shelter inside the gatekeeper's lodge. But the Negro grinned and cackled encouragingly,

Now, don't be bashful, gentlemen. If the girls get too pushy I'll call mylady with her broom. There isn't much that bites on these chicks, but an older woman with broom should do the trick.

He opened the gate slightly and the board members left single file, fighting their way through the screaming throng in order to reach their cars and leave. Only poor Pech had the misfortune to trip over his running board which made him a prisoner to cruel miss Cadillac and consorts. Longfellow heard the victim complain,

Let me go, girls, let me go. No, there's nothing I can tell you. Oy, oy, oy, don't pinch me, you fashion plates — no, not a single word out of me — not one syllable — will you kindly get out of my — aaauuuww — don't tickle me! — aaaauuuuuwww —

Locking the gate, Longfellow ruminated,

My lady, it'll be interesting to see what tomorrow's paper will have to say.

One of the morning papers announced in bold print,

Jac Tracbac to Europe? The famous clown may have to delay his long-expected tour. His grandmother, on a visit in spa Aix-les-Bains, has suddenly taken ill. Her dutiful grandchild, our dear Jac, rushes to her bedside. The length of the delay will depend on the venerable old lady's condition.

The afternoon editions published a different version,

This morning some enterprising colleagues printed certain news on Jac Tracbac. We know from a reliable source that Jac Tracbac has no travel plans for Europe. His grandmother died some thirty years ago and cannot be ill in spa Aix-les-Bains. He has no plans for a tour at the present time.

Longfellow commented,

Pech is and remains Pech. Those who don't know Pech, just don't know him. If that isn't the truth on the fellow.

The simple truth was that Tracbac felt fine. Exceedingly so. True, he was nervous and roamed through his maze the first few days after breaking with the syndicate. Given his resolute opposition, this reaction was to be expected. But he surprised Siv when he settled into an aura of subdued cheerfulness after only three days. He tried hard to hide his clapping hands like a child when no one seemed around. Or he took some boyish leaps before seriously strutting about the rooms again. O'Henny too noticed this secretive happiness. He considered it an insult to his professional reputation, declaring angrily,

Haven't we become a cheery chap! That's contrary to prognosis. What's happened? Got an inheritance? I'd like to recommend decent behavior as long as you're my patient.

The clown pulled his earlobe, then countered with a condescending smile,

Ah, Sir, you expected a case of melancholy between the sheets, didn't you? Well, consider yourself fooled. Physician proposes, God disposes, see. Don't get stuck up, little Henny-Denny.

It was possible that dressing out as Frederick the Great of Prussia could have tainted his clown's soul. His wearing the costume was Siv's decision. She wanted to enrich the gallery with some more of the clown's portraits in successful roles. One of his most famous was his role as Frederick the Great in nineteen-sixteen. The basic skit was unbelievably silly and rather crude and

82

without the war propaganda against Germany at the time it would never have made headlines. The plot was simple. King Frederick, "the great Prussian," liked to bully his personal guards, a regiment of tall men. The clown, like a cruel, mad ape, pushes and beats them to exhaustion. But the obtuse, docile giants willingly suffer his abuse. Enter Madame la France, neat and pert of course, carrying a small basket. The "Prussian" gives her the same cruel treatment. Surprised, Madame la France drops her basket. Out jumps a small, slender man who starts barking like a furious dog and attacking the king. Panic-stricken, the king tries to escape by climbing up and down these giants like a jungle ape, the dog-man close at his heels.

Using Frederick the Great as a Prussian symbol may seem odd. But the clown with his large, bulging blue eyes, small face and slender body was an ideal specimen for the type. Add to this the utter helplessness of these giant guards against one small man's cruelty was the ideal material for a good farce. Did King Frederick like or dislike dogs? Neither the author, nor the runaway schoolboy Jonathan Borck, nor the audience knew. Tracbac knew no more about the World War than a dumb, deaf and blind man about volcanic eruptions, except that both were earthshaking events. Tracbac was just as ignorant of the fact that the syndicate had used him to promote the war effort. He even asked Rush what it meant when the audience shouted "Boche!" The secretary explained that *boche* was a French term for poor wretch hounded by a pack of ferocious hounds. The poor little devil playing the pack assured the farce-effect of the skit. Satisfied, the clown said sententiously,

Ah, yes, I finally get it. I must say, the farce fits my character to a tee.

He meant his artistic qualities. But the vulgar skit fit the mass psychosis of the time. The plot itself contained all the basic ingredients of the typical Tracbac comedy — danger, cruelty, cowardice, fear. Fear and droll wit create a particular energy, whether in circus, theater, movies, the political arena or daily life. Like tragedy, the Tracbac comedy involved a so-called irony of situation, a sudden, unexpected reversal of the situation at the end. Essentially, irony of situation is tragic, even when it involves comedy.

Tracbac's skits differed from the stereotypical acts of other clowns and comedians. He insisted on a written, well-planned denouement that slowly turns to improvisation, a sudden shift from the comical to a tightening, heartfelt terror, like a hobgoblin's sudden jump out of his box, disintegrating into nothing like an exploding soap bubble. Tracbac's overpowering artistic strength lay just in staging this sudden turn from written manuscript to a sudden unexpected climax on his own spur of the moment. The effect of this terror is extremely comical and much more poignant than one that is carefully planned. That's why he found this paltry skit "a good description of my character traits."

83

His great ability to act out this momentary terror came from the clown's own past. Handyman Axelsson, now spooking through the clown's Californian villa with feather duster in his wrinkled fist, had owned a vicious dog back home. The animal once attacked the five- or six year old Jonathan when he was playing in the yard. No physical harm done. But his helplessness to defend himself against the roaring animal left severe emotional scars. Even now, forty years later, a barking little lapdog could strike the clown with terror. The skit *The Prussian and Madame's Lapdog* built on this very panic reaction.

It was strange to watch the clown recapture this moment of terror in the plots he played. It looked anything but improvised. Rather the opposite. He was like a trapeze artist getting ready for his salto mortale, his master jump — his muscles tight, controlled, gauging the limits of his physical strength, mobility, propulsion. So Jac Tracbac garnered his inner resources in the momentary lull before the storm of terror, heartache and cerebral fire broke loose. Not just the careful, analytical observer, but the entire mindless audience could feel this tension when breathlessly waiting for the artist's death jump. Seeing the tormented little man, hearing his sudden terror-stricken screams had a calculated comical effect. The audience shrieked and howled and thus the terror dissolved in a sigh of relief. O'Henny likened this fascinating play on public sentiment to a lynching where people, especially women, show emotional approval in similar fashion.

Tracbac routinely finished his skits with this comic twist. The mishandled clown either won over his enemies or ended droopy-eared with a funny little revenge in his back pocket. He called it "the happy tail" and didn't think much of it. But critics recognized the artistry involved and it became the focal point of his performance. Once Siv asked him how he managed the effortless, quick change from utter terror to roguish mirth. He simply shrugged it off, almost sullenly,

Oh, silly, I never worry about the happy tail. I'm born a buffoon and have a natural flair for comedy. Later events merely added a knack for tragedy.

He disliked discussing his performances. Found it embarrassing. In contrast, he was very proud of his character portrayals. He would browse through his professional picture albums with a look of naive satisfaction and say,

Well, that sure was a funny character — I wonder whether people understood how good he was? —

He showed his pride in these character sketches by patiently "sit" for Siv. He advised her constantly and quarreled furiously and pedantically whenever he thought she had misconstrued one of them.

Meanwhile Benbé was anxiously waiting for these Frederick the Great-sittings to end. Tracbac told him to be patient,

Don't run around like a sourpuss. I need to talk to you before I can release you from this jail. Just give me time. A free and uncoerced lark can sing its fate in major key. That's not Axelsson, but Aunt Amelia who ran a child-care center in Wadköping. Poor old lady one day fell on thin ice and drowned. Good Lord, Benjamin, your coming here opened a Pandora's box of memories — it's high time for me to kick you out. Let's go upstairs to my place and talk. Right now.

Ignoring Siv's indignant protests, Frederick the Great ran up to his attic, pulling Benbé along,

Calling this my place is hardly correct. I don't get here more than once or twice a year, if that often. But that's perhaps all a person manages in his lifetime — "to enter his own room." Come in.

They walked through the so-called "Borck rooms." Benbé had never seen this furniture. It had been shipped off before he ever set foot on the Borck estate and it held no special interest for him. They came to a smaller room containing the plain furniture of a student — a pinewood table and a rib-backed settee. The clown pointed to some words cut shakily into the desk top with a bowie knife,

GRANDMA ISS THE WORLTD'S CUTESST WIDOW.

Tracbac gave a shrewd chuckle,

I carved that once upon a time to patch things up when the old lady was angry with me. I didn't notice my terrible spelling before I got her into my room — two *s*'s in "is" and "cutest" and a *t* in "world" — I expected another earboxing where I had hoped for a cookie. But I did get the cookies anyway. Guess why?

Grandma was touched, Benbé suggested.

The hell she was. Well, that too and that made for the cookies. As for the earboxing — she was no better speller than I. I tell you — I love poor spellers. They don't waste their brains on nonsense —

He threw himself headlong on the settee. His hat and wig fell off.

All right, here we are in the temple of memory. As a rule I dislike to think back. But there are exceptions. For example when memories are linked up with the future. I feel empty and miserable these days and want to turn my past to some good. At least, I think I can. You may not understand all this. You're too young. Why don't you say anything?

Because you talk nonstop, Benbé told him gravely. I can't get a word in edgewise.

The clown laughed,

Yes. That's a valid enough reason. Well, I'll shut up and be as mum as a wall. Tell me. How was Sanna? Is Längsäll doing all right? He must be a great guy? Yes, he must be. I met him just once. He was a fellow who — well, how can I say that — yes, commanded respect? No, that's not the right word. How can I respect a person I've seen but once? Let me see — I felt — well, I know exactly how I felt. I was ashamed, pure and simple. He was so much better than I was. Far superior. Yes, I do remember. But why in God's name aren't you saying anything?

I must repeat what I said before, Benbé said. I can't speak when you do.

Tracbac frowned and said heatedly,

So give me some time, young fellow. Why come to a decision right away? Yes, I see a chance to be happy — sure, big word, isn't it? — Happy? Let's say glad, satisfied, hopeful or some such thing. It's just a chance, a chance in a thousand. So, let me thumb my lottery ticket for a while before I look at the prize list. Now I'll shut up about that. Absolutely mum. So, you were visiting Sanna. And your aunt Mrs. Längsäll gave you a package for me. The little glove —

Feeling that his words carried some weight, Benbé interrupted emphatically,

Jonathan Borck, you want me to tell you all the trivial details about Sanna. But I must ask you to keep track of what say. And I told you that the youngest daughter Sanna, usually called Sanna-Sanna, stuffed that package in my pocket —

Tracbac closed his eyes, lost in thought. After a long silence he declared with a voice totally lacking its recent forced happiness,

No, Benjamin, that's impossible. You must be confusing what happened here. What you say presupposes that the mother gave the glove to the girl and asked her to give it to you. But that doesn't make sense. Why should she — if she really had wanted to — why shouldn't she have given you the package in person?

Benbé was silent, recalling his suspicions regarding Sanna. Finally he said,

I really don't know. The girl could have filched the package from her mother. She's a strange girl. I remember suspecting something of the kind and told her so. She slapped my face for saying that — .

Again Tracbac closed his eyes, leaving Benbé free to observe him. His face muscles agitated heavily up and down his narrow cheeks, even around his mouth. The excitement eventually subsided, leaving his face smooth, somewhat limp. He did not open his eyes and looked weary when he said,

Ooh — so she is strange — the girl —

Awkward, not knowing what to say, Benbé mumbled,

Oh yes, that's for sure —

Tracbac cut him off, heatedly, as if he had come to a decision,

All right already. Good. Enough talk about her. Now, tell me about her mother. Who advised you to look me up — did she?

Benbé smiled lively,

To the contrary. You got it all wrong. Uncle Längsäll thought it a good idea for me to visit our famous relative. Aunt was decidedly against it. She thought it unlikely that you care about them —

Benbé stopped short, frightened, surprised at seeing the clown suddenly jump off his sofa. He looked furious. His eyes glittered as he shook his finger under his nephew's nose, roaring,

See here — you're lying — you're lying — how could she have given you the glove if she told you not to visit here? You must admit how unlikely that sounds — you're lying like all the others — people spout lies — not just in this damned country — lies — lies — lies — liars all —

The clown stood still, both arms stretched akimbo, his index finger pointing at the young man. Benbé was frightened, less for himself than for Tracbac. He waited a while before quietly answering the clown's charges,

Dear uncle, I can only repeat what I told you before. I never said that she sent you the glove. You said it. What makes you think she did? Why do you keep on insisting? I don't understand.

Tracbac struck back, quick, gruff,

Your tale makes no sense. That's why! It would mean that her mother told her something —

He stopped himself short and sat down again. Subdued, he said,

So, she thought I had forgotten them. Oh well, it's really not surprising that she does. It happened so long ago and we never corresponded. Besides, I've been through so much since and have seen even more. All right, what else can you tell me about Sanna —

Oh, I really don't know whether there's more to tell, Benbé said hesitantly. I stayed just one day. We tried to catch lobsters, talked about my trip, about you —

Benbé hesitated, grinning mischievously at the memory,

Ah yes, something strange did occur in connection with you. Really strange —

Caught by Benbé's excitement, Tracbac grinned roguishly,

Tell me! Come on! Tell!

Benbé continued animatedly,

Well, the good Längsälls got into an odd argument. Aunt Längsäll and the girls were sure that she met you at a certain time. But Papa Längsäll contradicted in no uncertain terms. Called it rubbish, insinuated her memory was flawed —

Tracbac interrupted him abruptly,

How can he say that? He was in London at the time.

Without knowing why, Benbé perceived these violently hurled words like a slap in his face. He leaned his head backward and stared at the wallpaper's frieze, groups of indistinguishable young wrestlers in bold colors.

But the clown saw nothing extraordinary in his involuntary outburst. He got up and walked back and forth in silence. Eventually he planted himself in front of Benbé and said slowly,

You say — well, what you're saying — that she admitted — ?

Admitted? Benbé repeated vaguely.

I mean — well, what I mean — that she confessed? — Tracbac stammered.

Confessed? Benbé repeated, nonplussed. Confessed?

Don't label words! the clown bawled, suddenly in blood-red anger stamping his foot. He sat down at the desk and held his head between his hands. There was a long silence. Finally he declared,

Benjamin, I'm going to send you home on an errand. I hinted at it before, but I needed to think this through. It's perhaps too hasty still. Well, it's extremely difficult. To entrust you, a mere boy, with the task might make me look rather unscrupulous. But I can't help it — I have no other choice — I feel that —

The narrow face shrank deeper into the hands that held it.

I am — I am so — so very, so utterly helpless —

11: Groom and Bride Went to Town to Shovel Snow
Groom and Bride Walk to Town to Unearth Truth

THE CLOWN'S HIGH-spirited activities the following morning were outright alarming. He got up around five A.M., took a swim in the pool, went horseback riding, still half-naked, in the park, then breakfasted solo and finally got dressed in his Frederick the Great outfit. He didn't limit this flurry of activities to himself, but got everyone else around involved. By seven o'clock he decided to get the estate on its feet. To accomplish this he ordered a drowsy DeGrazy to blow reveille. Thus crudely aroused, the victims saw no reason not to vent their true feelings. The ceremony was unheard of. It was awful, despite its simplicity. The bugle was a memento DeGrazy had received long ago from Emperor Franz Joseph for leading his hunting expeditions. More proud than qualified for the task, the major blew at the top of his lungs. It might have done for the Austrian Alps, but the sound split walls and eardrums alike in the limited confines of the Mexican-style gardens.

Servants and guests came scuttling to the duck pond like ants out of their hills, barely awake, smiling or angry about the noisy disruption. Frederick the Great grinned complacently, sauntering back and forth, his three-cornered hat cocked over one ear and his gold-buttoned stick in one hand. Axelsson came, clutching his late wife's monstrously enlarged photography tightly between his fingers. Benbé emerged, still in his pajamas but wide awake. Beautiful Siv arrived, wrapped in her amber-colored footlong dressing gown, flustered at having to maneuver the unwieldy garment like an acrobat. Fingers crooked, eyes flashing, the crowd hurled insults at Frederick the Great who needed all his strength to withstand the attacks. Outwardly he kept calm and told Siv,

Get to your studio, Gypsy, and start working. I want your painting finished by tonight. I'm getting tired of wearing this outfit.

The gypsy responded in kind,

Listen here, my witless comedian. Wearing it has given you a swelled head. It's high time that I speak up. I need at least four more days. Who do you think you are anyway, telling me to work before breakfast and bath?

You get yourself there on the double if you ever want to finish it, the clown ordered sternly. Just listen to her. Needs bath and breakfast! These painterdames! When was it you did not wear worn slippers, dirty nightgown and filthy smock, a cheese crust hanging in one side of your mouth, a cigarette dangling from the other? Suddenly she wants breakfast and bath! My dear Madam, you lack talent. Get thee going! You'll get a cup of coffee, bread and butter and sausage.

Condescending, gross and rude, Tracbac continued his abuse. His harsh words prevented his angry partner from launching a counterattack.

Suit yourself, lady. I just want to emphasize that this is my last free day before preparing for my tour. It's scheduled to start in a few months. My last free day for a year or so.

The clown lifted his hat ceremoniously and bowed to all those gathered around, the ducks in the pond included. The news left everybody stunned and silent. Only Axelsson shuffled off, grumbling, through one of the dark alleys, the picture of his beloved wife still in his hand. Benbé edged over to Siv in secret unrequited adoration, mumbling under his breath,

It's a pleasure dealing with Tracbac. He sticks to his decisions. Whatever he wants today, he's sure to want tomorrow.

What business is that of yours? the gypsy snorted.

Tracbac shook his fist at them, warning,

Be nice to Benjamin, Siv. He's leaving tomorrow.

Benbé crossed his arms across his chest, bowed deeply and said,

In that case I'll better use my remaining time to pack and say goodbye.

Blushing to a deep crimson, Tracbac waved his hands energetically,

No, no, for goodness sake! Someone else can take care of your packing. I want company to prevent this little artist from tormenting me all day. I have a lot to talk to you about before you leave, mind you. Now get dressed, have your breakfast and meet me at Siv's. I'll be there.

I assume that Mr. Rush needs to be informed about the change in schedule? DeGrazy wondered, standing at attention. Tracbac said,

Ask Abel Rush to come here at six this afternoon. But do me a favor and muzzle him. He won't need to strain his voice. I only want him to listen.

The clown threw his tricornered hat playfully into the air, caught it on the tip of his stick and, twirling it above his head, he forged up the staircase into the studio. Siv followed, glumly loyal.

Properly dressed and fed, Benbé arrived in the studio an hour later. The couple's roles were reversed now. Siv was busily at work on the portrait, her beautiful amber eyes glittering with life. Tracbac, on the other hand, was beginning to get tired of sitting model and pulled ugly faces. But his good humor returned as soon Benbé appeared. For the second time that morning the clown's pale face blushed in a rare, deep crimson.

Siv, he said, I don't want to disrupt your valuable efforts so I'll speak Swedish with Benjamin. I hope you don't mind?

Talk whatever gibberish you want, the beautiful lady told him. With a sudden frown she added sullenly,

Actually, it's unnecessary — I'm not interested in your blabber anyway.

Tracbac had a roguish, sad smile when he said in Swedish,

Well, little Siv, I'm not so sure about that.

Not wanting to get involved in their squabble, Benbé stood outside the open door. Still in Swedish, the clown turned to him,

Whatever. I am anxious to talk to you, and I assume that you're interested. Our conversation yesterday gave me a lot to ponder. I tried to make sense out of what you told me last night. Especially that strange controversy between the two Längsälls whether she met me or not made me wonder. Just for the record, he was wrong.

Tracbac stopped, got lost in thought, then continued,

This is how we met. I got a telegram telling me that Grandma was ill and dying. I left on that very day, which may sound quite touching. To be honest, I didn't go for Grandma's sake. I felt terribly listless and weary at the time, about the way I feel right now. So Grandma's illness came as a good excuse to run away from it all. Pure pretense. I always need fate to give me a deciding push to make up my mind. Then I had much more freedom to move about, without all this damn supervision. Nowadays they call a medic when I as much as give a sneeze during my morning bath.

Well — so I went, but arrived too late — exactly one day after she died. Probably just as well. Grandma wouldn't have recognized me anyway. Too, it would have been hard for me to watch her die. Of course, once there, I stayed for the funeral. Relatives came from all over. The house filled with crying, sobbing, sighing Borckses and friends, shaking hands, drying wet noses and kissing one another. I didn't recognize a soul. And I found their behavior peculiar. Was it so sad to see an eighty-six year old woman leave this world? A woman who had been rather senile during her last years? I considered her death a normal event. At least we knew where the old lady was and no one could hurt her any longer. Right — I may have looked like a good candidate to commit suicide. Nervous, depressed, that's exactly what I was. But hardly for Grandma's sake. Sure enough, my relatives got worried about my deep sorrow. They looked at me on the sly, petted my arms to comfort me, and for the rest continued to feed their tears more coffee and wine to make them last a while longer. I looked droopier than ever before.

Suddenly the clown leaped up. Standing on tiptoes, he raised one index finger like an exclamation mark on either side of his narrow face. His speech quickened as he continued,

Then it happened. Something special. A slender, young woman of about twenty looked me square in the face, her eyes flashing utter contempt. Then

91

she turned away with a shrug, as if saying, your pretense to sorrow is disgusting, you clown. You can imagine my confusion.

I don't want to say much about my relatives and their soggy-eyed reaction. They had the old lady until the very end, so her death may have hit them harder than me. To live far away from the people you love may have certain advantages. Whether Grandma lived in Wadköping or with Our Lord made no difference to me. I always converse with her, wherever she is. To me at least their grief looked a pure clown's act, though I was the real clown. But I get paid well for my clowning — and it's entertaining, or so they say.

Now, see, this little person was anything but clowning. I didn't get her full name when we were introduced, but her first name was Lillemor — little mother. That fit. She took care of all the necessary arrangements for the funeral and it ran smoothly, thanks to her. She neither cried nor sighed. Not that she sang out loud exactly, no, but she gave the impression of quietly humming inside — a sort of workhorse-hum. I pray that whoever buries me one day will do it just as efficiently.

The clown continued,

Thank goodness, the mourning finally came to an end. I stayed a few more days and in a sentimental flush I decided to ship some of Grandma's furniture to California, her fixture Axelsson included. What for? Well, no harm done. They might as well stand here as anywhere else. Who knows, a researcher may one day rest his fame on chronicling how they got here.

The shipping taken care of, I intended to drive to Göteborg and take the next boat to England. Now, I had just driven past Södertull when I got this silly notion to make a detour around Sanna, the old Borck estate where I used to spend my summers as a child. I just felt like seeing the place again. So, I turned —

He interrupted himself, smiled and shook his head.

Yes. Benjamin, do you know what it means to turn back once you've started on your way?

Bad luck! Benbé declared with deep conviction.

Tracbac smiled,

Right. Only it's hard to say what is good luck and what is bad luck. I turned, headed north . . . and right into the worst snow slush. The entire trip turned into an unforeseen adventure, really. All I knew was that Anton Borck, your uncle, had been forced to sell the estate. I didn't know who bought it but figured that if they're decent people they'd let me stay over for a day or two. In case they weren't, there's an inn about half a mile down the road. Well, I happened to arrive on March thirteenth —

Aghast, Benbé blurted,

Good grief, the thirteenth of March, another unlucky day.

The clown nodded,

92

True. I means bad luck. But it also means the following day is March fourteenth, moving day in the country, as you know. So, when at long last I had sloshed my way through Sanna lane, I found a moving van in the driveway, unloading. That took care of my intention to stay overnight. But I did want to meet the new owner and asked the movers. Längsäll, they said, Mr. Längsäll from Johannisberg. He's abroad right now so the little wife takes care of the move. So just like a woman, she wants to move on the thirteenth rather than wait for the fourteenth. Crazy remains crazy, always, the men commented. I sat there, hands on the steering wheel, my foot on the gas pedal, wondering whether I dare ask her for permission to take a quick look at the rooms I remembered so well. And then — then — as I sit there — she steps out on the porch, at the top of the stairs —

Stretching his arms wide, he stared wide-eyed at Benbé. Siv gave a snort and said,

There's this stupid look again. Don't look so confused, Jac!

The clown snorted back in anger,

So what? As if Frederick the Great couldn't have been bewildered occasionally. He had a long and eventful life! I told you to mind your own business.

He went on,

So there she stood on top of the stairs, Lillemor Längsäll, neé Borck. Well, you know more about the family tree than I do. I stepped out of the car, just to say hello. Under the circumstances, staying overnight was out of the question. Now, she made it also very plain that I was not the least bit welcome. She hardly shook my hand. Well, not surprising, busy as she was, in the middle of moving, snowflakes whizzing about her furniture . . . and I appearing out of nowhere, friend and stranger both. No wonder she was upset. That didn't make me any happier either. She really resented my coming, I learned later. Seemed I ogled her as passionately as a cat a canary during the funeral dinner. She thought it outrageous my pursuing her like that.

He chuckled, padded his head and said,

Oh, my dearest Lillemor, it wasn't any nerve on my part at all — fate was outrageous perhaps, but not me — oh, no — not at all —

So there we were, unfriendly both — I shy, she angry. You know what that little shrew told me to do? Kindly wait in your car until we've unpacked these five loads. Once it's comfortable inside you may come in for a good cup of coffee. That's the way she ordered me about. Really.

The clown's face was full of mawkish bewilderment. He turned away to circumvent another reprimand from Siv. Benbé announced, not without pride,

Oh, sure. Aunt Längsäll can be quite sarcastic when she wants to.

The clown frowned and scratched his ear. Something about Benbé's reply seemed to bother him. He waved as if to beg off and said,

Dear Benjamin. Do me a favor and don't call her aunt Längsäll. It makes her sound old. She was so young at the time —

Benbé winced, ashamed. The clown's request had put an alienating wall between them — the inexorable dividing line between two generations. Old versus young. No matter how many times the boundaries are ignored, the end result was the same regardless of who trespassed. A young person trying to sound mature, experienced and wise looks ridiculous. And an old person trying to be youthful, naive and lively embarrasses those around him. But Tracbac never tried to look younger — rather the opposite. He only wanted to keep his memories young. With an apologetic smile the clown declared,

That short scene at the top of the stairs was so absurd — I wanted to keep it untouched. There we were, she and I, trying to handle an embarrassing situation without being rude to each other and not knowing how to go about it. Large, watery snowflakes fizzled about us. The scene reminded me of a toy we used to buy at Wadköping Fair long, long ago — a glass ball filled with water and sawdust. On the bottom stood a young couple, holding hands on one side, brooms in hands on the other. Turning the glass ball upside down started a heavy snowstorm of white sawdust. On the pedestal underneath were the words: *Groom And Bride Went To Town To Shovel Snow,/ Groom And Bride Walk To Town To Unearth Truth.*

Benbé laughed. Siv frowned, full of suspicion,

What's all the merriment about?

The clown told her,

Really, my dear, it was about something utterly childish.

Well, here we were like inside one of those toys, wondering what we should do while the movers stared at us. I tried to behave as well as I could, given the circumstances. I wanted to spend a day or two at the inn, I told her. I was not about to inconvenience her, absolutely not, though I would like to come back and visit the grounds and see old Anton Borck's strange machines by the waterfall — all childhood memories. She consented, more or less reluctantly, and I drove off to the inn. I stayed a full three weeks — from the thirteenth of March to the third of April.

Yes. Three weeks. I can still smell the cozy mustiness of the inn. A combination of lavender, fresh linens and cheese. Being a good clown and as cunning as a snake, I faked too. I bought some surveyors' paraphernalia, leveling instruments and such, and lugged them around each time I drove to Sanna. The joke was on the people, not her. I never even showed her my gadgets because she would never condone such schemes. She wasn't the type. Meanwhile winter turned bitterly cold. We took a few rides. No, not in my car. We took the sleigh. The snow was foot deep. A fine white glaze covered the tree branches. Then, on the twenty-ninth of March a mighty storm blew in rain squalls and cleaned house. When we woke up on the first of April the snow was as good as gone and at noon we had sixteen degrees Celsius in the shade. Like an April Fool's joke. But the weather remained stable. The wild anemones appeared and the trees sprouted their delicate network of tiny light green leaves. Oh, it was all so very beautiful, so real mild and soft and light. I left on the fourth.

You left? Benbé repeated, almost disappointed.

The clown nodded,

I left and there's actually nothing more to tell. So, why am I telling you all this? Dear fellow, I've never told a soul, not a word all these twenty years since that snow melted and the leaves burst out. I carried that spring buried deep inside me all these twenty years.

He hesitated momentarily before he went on,

All right, let me tell you why this sudden blabber gush. It's because you need to know. The day before I left she asked me for a present, a memento. I refused. I could not, would not, dared not leave anything behind. She said, well, then I'm going to give you something. She gave me one glove of a pair she had worn before Grandma's death. She said, I wonder whether they'll ever meet again? There is nothing more meaningless than a lonely glove — except, perhaps, a lonely human being —

Benbé interrupted him quietly,

But she isn't alone —

The clown nodded and smiled,

No, thank goodness, she isn't lonely. But now you see the reason for my brooding. Why did the girl give you that glove? Why not she herself — if she wanted to give me a sign, a message? I may never find out. We have never written and we never will. I am simply too much of a coward. Not for my sake, mind you, but for hers. Still — I'm about to reverse twenty years of cowardice.

His hands pushed against his knees, his face upward bent, he stared blindly into space, lost in thought. Siv said,

That's an excellent expression, Jac. Try to stay that way as long as you can. You look as if you were about ready to jump —

Tracbac said,

Now, Benjamin, I want you to return home. Go to Sanna, to Lillemor — then, if you can do it delicately, without hurting them — without hurting them too much — bring the girl back here, I mean Sanna — you call her Sanna-Sanna — the girl I've never seen — except on an occasional snapshot, at different ages — up to the time she was fourteen — then Lillemor stopped sending her photos altogether. I never could figure out why. She might have wanted me to forget, or thought that I had forgotten. That

95

would probably have been best for all concerned. Certainly for those two, Lillemor and the girl. But I can't take it any longer. It's an obsession by now. She's mine and I want her here. I need her here. Granted, it may be just a fixed idea, but she's my daughter, and — and I don't want to be without her any longer —

All three were silent as the minutes ticked on. Tracbac sat perfectly still, trying to retain his pose for the painter. Siv remained absorbed in her work. Benbé twirled his thumbs with studied indifference to mask his surprise and confusion, his mind a literal blank about his predicament. In flashbacks he tried to conjure up mental pictures of Sanna, the estate and its people. Someone was pushing him back into this small, familiar circle to break it apart. It made no sense.

The clown said,

I suppose you think it's impossible. Well, as I said, there's just a chance in a thousand to bring it off. That chance depends on you. I can't go there. Even if I managed to wangle myself in without creating too much havoc, I would still be a huge question mark on the Sanna estate. Also, I can't keep my visit a secret. The syndicate and the mass media would spread the news across the world, if for no other reason than to intimidate and gall me. I can't write either. We haven't in twenty years — how can I now start writing to these people — I mean to him, telling him: Hi, I heard that you have a daughter, would you please send her to me? You see — that's like telling him: She's my daughter; I want her. Not even a wealthy American can be that boorish.

Ever more pensive, he went on,

No. You are the only person who could possibly intervene. It came to me when you played that dumb joke with the cat. And then, seeing that glove, I knew for sure —

Hitting his palms against his forehead, Benbé questioned,

And how do you think I should manage the whole thing?

Siv interrupted again, frowning,

Stop bothering Jac. He's getting tired.

The clown went on,

It's really very simple. You go home, visit your relatives, tell them about your visit here. And mention me. A lot about me, of course — how I am, what I do, etc. Tell them that I'm very lonely — and that is certainly no lie. Tell them that you'll return here, then just mention casually that Sanna could come along with you, you're certain she'll be welcome. Absolutely certain. Well, you'll see how the girl reacts, whether she would even want to come here. It isn't so utterly impossible, is it? Not totally impossible, right? A young girl wants to get out, see the world, doesn't she? I'm sure she would!

Well, at least it's possible. You tell them Uncle Jonathan would be delighted, you're sure —

He bent forward, managed a tired smile, shook his head and repeated,

Yes. Uncle Jonathan will be absolutely delighted. — There may be a few fibs that go with your assignment, Benjamin. But there's a lot of truth that goes with it.

Siv voiced again her disapproval,

Don't you see that you're exhausting Jac? Why do you let him talk so much? Can't you take over for a while?

But the clown objected with a shrewish wink,

Wouldn't you know, I awed the young fellow with my one hundred and one love affairs. He's speechless, trying to figure out how to become a Don Juan like me. His gender's pride!

Turning to Benbé, Tracbac continued,

Of course, of course, and again of course, all that hinges on Lillemor's approval. Now, why shouldn't she agree? She must understand that I'll do everything I possibly can for the girl. Everything! And do tell her — well, you've seen for yourself that we don't live a loose life around here. Don't forget to mention that! You've seen yourself. Well, why shouldn't she agree? Think again — why else would she send the glove if she didn't want something from me? Right?

Strange, I've told him twice already that she didn't. But he keeps insisting that the mother sent him the glove. Is he stupid? Or doesn't he want to hear what I'm saying? And why doesn't he?

Siv put her chalk down and got up. Quietly, but decisively, she announced,

No. That's enough. I don't know what you're talking about. But Jac is tired. — Just look, look at him, she cried out, frightened. She ran toward Tracbac. His head reeling, his eyelids flopping, he looked suddenly like a tired child. She caught his head between her hands to steady it. Slowly the clown's drooping mouth revived in a wily grin. He said,

Let go of my head, girl. It's securely anchored where it sits. The boys of the press questioned my health, so I wanted to let the world know that Jac Tracbac is neither senile nor anything of the kind. That's why I got up early this morning and went horseback riding in the park. Longfellow asked them why they thought I'm ill and advised them to watch me. No, no one is going to report that I'm sick! My record is clear. I showed them how healthy I am. Just feel here, feel this!

He put his arms around Siv's supple waist and shook her until she laughed out loud and fell into his lap, both her arms around his neck. Benbé left, feeling out of place. No one called him back.

He lay down on his bed, lit a cigarette and reflected on what he had heard. Consciously or not, he brushed aside the essence of the story, the clown's relationship to Lillemor. He was young and naive and felt ill at ease about the entire, painful affair. It confused him. It's not my business, he told himself. I'm going to forget about it; put it out of my mind.

Never mind. Traveling, to return and invite Sanna-Sanna to visit uncle Jonathan, the famous entertainer, was a different matter entirely. As far as he could judge, the girl would be delighted about such a trip. How long she wanted to stay with her uncle was a later question and not his concern. As for him — he was only too happy about both trips. He was homesick enough to go back. He was sure that Tracbac or Rush would help him find a job on his return. Besides, being the girl's protector on the return trip presented a fascinating opportunity to show off before a woman — any young man's greatest dream! Indeed, plenty of reasons to welcome Tracbac's errand. He conjured up the most lively, fascinating scenes with every smoke puff he exhaled.

But his smoky ringlets, along with his excitement, slowly dissolved. He put down his cigarette. His hands on his back, his head bent forward, he started pacing the room in growing exasperation.

Siv called at six to ask him to dinner in the dining room. Tracbac, Siv and Rush were already seated when he arrived. Engaged in a lively discussion, the two gentlemen hardly noted his presence. Abel Rush shrugged spasmodically and gesticulated wildly, complaining,

I don't know whether to laugh or cry. Yesterday all the contracts were to be canceled. Today they are to be renewed. May I ask what's on tomorrow's agenda, day after tomorrow, in a week, a month? You're impossible to deal with. What do you think the news media will say next time you delay? You'll look ridiculous.

Contrary to his usual demeanor, the young Jew was lively, shouting and waving his hands trying to mask his happiness over the clown's welcome words,

Mr. Secretary. I'm starting November first. So now you know.

They set a date. The clown needed this fixed date as an anchor on which to chain his tendency not to comply. Shouting his secretary down, the clown screamed,

Damn it — November first — second — third — fourth — what do I know? Who are you anyway? The circus manager? You? For crying out loud. You know better than anyone else about the idiosyncrasies of stars! What would they be without them? Mediocre, nothing but, I tell you. Their salary likewise — pitiful. The crazier they are, the higher their fees. You know that very well, you crabpot! Should I faint one day, or week, or month, by all means throw in an extra number, damn it. Get married, take center stage, with her over there, that divorcée! Wedding, cannons, firecrackers, the

98

works, anything you want, as long as you keep the crowd preoccupied while I'm getting ready to play clown —

Seeing Benbé's heartbroken, sullen face on the other side of the table, the clown suddenly stopped his torrent. He stared, surprised at first, then frightened, got up and motioned the young man to follow him to the next room. Tracbac asked,

What's wrong, Benjamin? You haven't changed your mind?

Benbé answered quietly,

I'm afraid I have. You see, I can't forget how nice the Längsälls treated me. Like their own child. I can't possibly go through with your plan.

He stopped momentarily, chewing his lips, before he continued,

You understand, I couldn't bear the thought that she — Mrs. Lillemor — that she would ever find out, or even suspect — that you told me —

The clown listened, nodding repeatedly. There was a hushed silence, the clown lost in tense meditation. The hint of a sneer slid across one corner of his mouth when he said,

Listen, my boy. Don't ever say anything to Lillemor. Never ever. Talk about me, only me, as I told you. Tell her how lonely I am. If Lillemor won't come to you and tell you her side, whatever she may tell you — then — oh well —

He held his right hand horizontally to his mouth and blew at it softly,

— oh well — then, my boy, then all this was a mere piece of fluff, a thought fluff — fluff from a withering, decaying thistle. Then — just forget the whole thing.

12: A Fellow And Two Oxen

AFTER A HARD winter and an unusually wet March, spring tillage on Sanna was late. At the end of the month patron Längsäll himself had to jump in and man one of his four plows. It all happened like this. He had just hired this young, twenty-year old farm hand who hailed from noble, old hussar stock, for the season. His name was Per Lans, or Pellans for short. The problem arose when Master Längsäll could not decide on when to break in Fingal, his two-year old, wild, hot-tempered stallion. It was a dangerous job only a cavalry captain or champion horseman could manage. He had also a girl known as Sanna-Sanna on his estate. Already the Bible tells of woman inciting many men to daring blunders. So Sanna-Sanna came to Pellans and whispered into his ear,

Seems that Pellans is afraid of riding Fingal. For shame. What a disgrace.

His butter-yellow face in deep-set wrinkles, Pellans mulled this over for an entire day. When he met miss Sanna on her daily rounds through barns and stables the next day he whispered to her,

I most certainly can ride Fingal. But the boss forbids it.

Like Eva in Paradise, Sanna counseled,

When he sees how well you tame Fingal, he'll think you're terrific.

That settled it. The boy mounted the stallion and within half an hour he had three broken ribs, various strains, sprains and bruises which landed him in the hospital. The girl came off scot-free. But in passing Längsäll told Lillemor,

I wonder whether Sanna shouldn't get out into the world for a while. She's developing strange habits staying here. Be a pity for the girl, I'm afraid.

Lillemor folded her hands in mute reflection. She agreed,

Of course you're right.

One person's smart makes the other person's heart. The farm hand's accident became his master's happiest spring in decades. He was all set to hire a substitute when he received the news that the boy's wounds would heal in a matter of weeks. It was only prudent to push the fourth plow himself until then. Feeling it quiver in his hands was a thrill he had missed ever since he had left his inspector job in Ultuna some thirty years ago. Now he tuned in again on his soil, playing his plow like a master musician his many-stringed, responsive instrument. Set in his old-fashioned ways, Längsäll preferred oxen to pull his plow. Horses were quicker, but their pull was jerky and weaker for regular loads. They kept the plower on constant alert. The slower oxen trotted more evenly and required less supervision, which left the plowman free to tune in on his plow. Working it, he could feel the soothing caress of the black soil, the firm marl, the hard sand. He could respond to the jerky pull in the firm blue clay, to the steady suction of the loam in the pasture. How could a farmer get to feel his soil riding a tractor? This disgusting machine was bound to drive oxen, horse and plower into oblivion. Chemical analyses would never replace this tacit communication between hand, plow and soil.

Father Längsäll luxuriated in his spring tasks. His mighty chest doubled in size as he walked his earth with the deliberate tread of a dancer secure in his work. His straight, plump furrows turned into shimmering bloodclods in the evening haze. At the end of the day he left his fields, his plow patiently waiting for the next sunrise. He lumbered the way not behind, but between his two beloved animals, his long, muscled arms draped around their necks like a friendly yoke — a tacit testimony of his love for his work. All three returned to stall and supper, satisfied with a job well done.

While the father of the house took the greatest pleasure in his work and enjoyed it to the fullest, the women were equally content with theirs. Everything ran in an established, peaceful, regular routine. These days Benbé's adventures provided yet another interesting topic to discuss during leisure hours. Only Sanna-Sanna's failing health began to cause a measure of anxiety. It had definitely worsened during the winter months. The family members had not noticed it until some distant neighbors, various peddlers, old friends and wool merchants mentioned it and offered well-meaning advice,

Oh my, Miss Sanna has gotten so skinny lately! She doesn't look well! Perhaps some iron and arsenic might help; she ought to see some wonder doctor; or another healer; she ought to do this; or that —

Alarmed, the family took a closer look at Sanna-Sanna. She had indeed lost weight and looked decidedly ill. The youthful glow of her skin during Benbé's visit six months ago was gone. It looked unhealthy, patchy, full of pimples and bumps and stretched taut across her cheeks. Her temperament gave reason for concern too. It had been mercurial and odd ever since her teens, so no one had taken her recent outbursts very seriously. But her mood swings became increasingly worse. Unpredictable, they ranged between tearful melancholy, fretfulness and high-spirited excess.

Lately cousin Benbé had become a daily topic of conversation in the small Sanna family — their crossword puzzle so to speak. They knew him well enough to be concerned about his health, his job search successes and failures, and tried to establish his American horoscope. On his part, the young man hated to have nothing to report but failures. Nevertheless, irresponsible though he was, he took his promise to write seriously. His benefactors, seeing his infrequent and disheartening correspondence, imagined Benbé slowly "going to the dogs" and voiced their concerns in letters they had to reroute time and again because the young man kept on changing his addresses while hunting for a job. Hopeless and desperate, he finally stopped writing altogether when he reached California. Therefore Benbé's telegram from New York in the middle of March hit Sanna like a veritable bombshell, *coming to Sweden for short stay. want to meet loved ones on sanna on important matters. return to states thereafter.*

Ominous news! What did it mean? The Sannaites were having their afternoon coffee break when it arrived. Its contents puzzled them. Since his nephew's last letter came from Chicago and this telegram from New York Father Längsäll argued that Benbé had never made it to California and had therefore never met their famous relative. He hardly concealed his satisfaction about this detail and Lillemor seemed to share this feeling. Only Sanna-Sanna began noisily stirring in her coffee to express her utter displeasure.

As the sole male in the family, Father Längsäll considered it his obligation to do the logical thinking in the household. He determined that Benjamin Borck's versatile education had finally landed him a profitable job. Why else would he want to return after but a short visit? He must have a job, and a very good one at that, to afford a round trip ticket across the Atlantic Ocean just to visit his dear relatives.

The phrase *on important matters* was even more puzzling. What did it mean? It sounded very romantic. No one dared broach the subject during the coffee break. But later that night, while getting out of his smelly barnyard clothes and clay-muddied boots and pulling his nightshirt with the red embroidery over his solid, hoary frame, Father Längsäll told his wife,

It's pretty clear. The boy has found a good job. He now comes home to get the girl.

Her beautiful, lively, cherry-colored eyes wide open, Lillemor echoed,

Get the girl? What do you mean? Which girl?

Längsäll's deep sigh of surprise resembled his oxen's puffing,

Which one? Caroline, of course. You must've been blind last fall not to see how he felt about her.

Caroline? How would you know? Lillemor wondered.

Father Längsäll gave an arrogant chuckle,

Hock, hock, hock. Those who have eyes can see; 'course, dames rarely can. Especially mothers. Fathers have certain obligations and they can see. I well remember when I tried to teach those young blockheads the basics of lobster fishing last fall. D'you think they listened? The hell they did. Were busy ogling each other, sort of pecked behind my back among the reeds. Thought I couldn't see them. So that's how things are, Mama. The boy has, or thinks he has a decent job. So now he wants to get married before starting to work in earnest. Well, Mama, what are we going to do? I recommend saying as little as possible, prepare the wedding and give our parental blessings.

Huffing and puffing like his oxen, Father Längsäll settled into his bed. Relaxed, tired and satisfied after his day's work in the fields, he pulled his blanket up to his nose, mumbling,

Good night, Lillemor.

The prospect of losing Caroline bothered him more than he cared to admit. She radiated her father's robust health and even-tempered cheerfulness along with a softness she had inherited from her mother. She looked like a young buttercup in spring. No matter how greasy or heavy the food, or what it contained, the heaping platefuls she ate never interfered with her appetite or digestion. With secret admiration he watched her once putting away half a tureen of cabbage soup, a corresponding amount of pickled pork's knuckles and finally a huge piece of butter cake and then jumping up from the table as easily and gracefully as ever. He was convinced that no dish of dynamite stewed in hydrocyanic acid would bother her stomach. Hardly cause a burp.

Längsäll's affection for the sturdy girl ran indescribably deep. She shared his healthy outlook on life. No scissors had ever touched her thick, gold-red braids. To compensate for this excess of fatherly affection he paid more attention to Sanna-Sanna. Caroline was never jealous. Her parents' seeming preference for her finicky, fretful sister never bothered her. But secretly Lillemor resented it, muttering darkly about fairness and injustice. Unconscious of his fatherly arrogance, the good squire would then say,

Justice! Caroline damn well needs no justice. She'll manage just fine, regardless! —

Her complaints may not always have been justified, but "real justice" mattered greatly to Sanna. The girl was goodhearted. Her frequent temper tantrums made life hard for those around her. Her even-tempered sister found them unbearable. Even though, complaints about Sanna-Sanna were rare. If they happened, Father Längsäll would assume the airs of a worthy patriarch and declare,

Well, well, that may be. But in all fairness to Sanna-Sanna we have to admit that she . . . , then most ingeniously list all the girl's real and invented virtues.

Healthy and sound himself, he found it only natural to protect the sickly and weak. This habit may often be considered a dangerous weakness. But nothing is further from the truth, in theory or fact. Morals separate man from animal. Courageously protecting the weak means promoting, honoring and strengthening his own health. And the most laudable of man's courageous efforts is generosity. It is one of humankind's most valued jewels — a salutary, blessed gem.

103

No one mentioned father Längsäll's theory for Benjamin's new errand on Sanna again, not even the two partners. The two sisters said nothing about those strange *important matters* either, at least not until Sanna made her surprising confession on the morning of Benbé's scheduled arrival. Standing before the mirror, curling her ash-blond hair and scrutinizing her pale, pimply reflection closely, she suddenly blurted out with a tone of satisfaction,

I know why Benjamin is coming. He wants to meet Mama. Nothing else but —

Caroline blushed. She was nursing some secret fantasies of a different kind in connection with her cousin's visit and the *important matter*. Rather glumly she said,

Of course he wants to meet Mama and Papa. But us too, —

Sanna-Sanna pressed her nose and sniffed loudly to emphasize her great superiority and pity. She declared,

Oh, that's pretty silly, my dear. What makes you think he's coming for your sake? Oh well, it's possible. Good luck to you then. But mainly he's coming to bring Mama greetings from Jonathan Borck. I know.

How on earth — what kind of nonsense are you dishing up? the sister called, dropping her sponge into the washbasin in utter surprise. She forgot to dry her face which was still wet and red from her facial scrub. Sanna went on to explain, as if it were the most natural thing in the world.

How do I know? Because I arranged it. I gave Ben a small package and asked him to give it to Jonathan. He's returning with some answer or present, or whatever . . . for Mama — because the package was from her. I found it in Mama's desk.

You're out of your mind! Caroline mumbled, her expectations suddenly crushed. You took a package out of Mama's desk? What made you think it was for him?

It was addressed to him. "For Jonathan Borck after my death." Pretty stupid, wouldn't you say? If she wanted him to have it, why wait until after her death? Makes no sense. He might die before she does. People ought to stick to the truth, or leave things alone. I have a feeling that things'll change around here soon. Sort of a hunch Jonathan's going to invite us to his place. We could live there like princesses — he can afford it. I'm just afraid that Papa won't want us to leave. In that case I'll stay with him, poor Dad. I can't bear the thought of leaving him alone. Just don't think Benbé is coming here just for your sake.

Sanna-Sanna's voice had an undertone of satisfaction when she told her sister off. Suddenly the ramifications of her guile overwhelmed her. Just imagine Papa all alone on Sanna! She jumped up, leaving the rest of her hair straight. Running through the house as if it meant her life, she called for her father. She found him in the shed with his carpenter and painting tools. Disregarding his stained work clothes, she threw herself into his arms and cried,

I'll never leave you, Papa, never — never — never —

Längsäll held her at arm's length and said good-naturedly,

Well, well, what on earth? Who's asked you to leave us? Any young man asked you to marry him?

The girl answered loftily,

Ash, that's silly. No, but I have this strange feeling something critical is about to happen. If for example Benbé asks Caroline to marry him and takes her back to the United States, this idiot could ask all of us to follow. Surely you're not going?

Dismissing her fears as an overly sensitive girl's foolishly fertile figment of imagination, he declared peevishly,

You can be sure I won't.

Papa, listen — I've filched something from Mama again. I found it in her inner drawer and gave it to him. Quite a while ago, really. I suddenly remembered, today. If she finds out what I've done I'll be in terrible trouble. Then what'll I do when she gets angry? Tell her that I didn't take it?

Father Längsäll drew a deep, troubled sigh and said, weary and full of anguish,

But Sanna, child, what do you mean? Are you asking me in earnest to approve your lying to your mother? What have you taken?

The girl shrugged her shoulders,

Ash, Papa, really, it was such a minor thing. You don't think that I'd take something valuable? Really!!

Oh well then, we won't talk about your nonsense. I'm ready for my coffee break.

He felt that her mother ought to get the facts of this latest caprice. She was much better at getting to the bottom of the girl's crazy pranks. If she deserved punishment, she would get it. Easing his conscience with this argument, he took off his apron and washed his hands. Together they walked back to the house, the girl hanging on his arm.

Afternoon coffee was patron Längsäll's favorite meal. Methodically he would chew his way through heaps of huge rolls and biscuits. Ever since he again plowed his fields, he rose earlier than usual, which gave him a good excuse to extend his afternoon coffee to "give the lazybones time for a decent recovery," as he put it. This afternoon he lingered quietly at the table, absentmindedly playing with his spoon. Both girls had left the room. Finally alone with his wife, he wondered how best to approach the subject of Sanna's tale. Eventually he said nothing. He did not want to be bothered.

Lillemor sat across the table from him, busy with her sewing. She glanced at him repeatedly, curious as to what to make of his ruminations. She saw him smile and smiled back,

You're so lost in thoughts. Wonder what you're thinking?

His smile deepened. He said,

Well, guess what! I'm speculating on what I'd like to be before I die.

He hesitated a few seconds as if he had difficulties explaining his innermost longings, but he continued,

I'd like to be a real religious person.

Lillemor dropped her work in utter surprise. She glanced at him, somewhat melancholy and with a measure of irony. Finally she said,

Indeed, what a thought! And that coming from a person who's been so lacking in faith all his life.

Shaking his huge head, he said,

No, indeed, Lillemor. I've never been without faith. My parents, my grandparents on both sides, in fact my entire family have always been God-fearing Pietists. I used to rebel against all this religion when I was young. I don't know what happened, but the rebellion slowly petered out. I've come to the point where I want to be just like them. We had an old painter in our family. My father's uncle. Sort of an odd funny person who drew funny faces of the family members. Not just of those he had met, but also of those he only knew from hearsay. I don't know where all these sketches are today, perhaps at my sister's. Well, some were fatter than others, or taller, and their clothes were different, but they all had these codfish eyes and all stared into space as if they could see nothing worthwhile on this earth. And each one held a large Bible, or sermon book, or psalm book in his hand. No, ungodly I've certainly never been, but neither have I been anything else. Now I want to be like those old fellows — having nothing else in my simpleminded head but Heaven's greatness, and holding nothing but the Lord's holy words and promises in my arms. Not a single thing.

He smiled down at his hand as he fidgeted with the spoon. Lillemor's face turned a shade paler and for an instant she resembled her famous cousin whenever he was tired. There was a long silence. Finally Lillemor rose slowly from her chair. Her one hand holding on to the tabletop, she walked over to her husband and patted his mighty head. She tried to joke, but there was an undertone of hidden tears when she said,

Oh, nothing in your arms but the Bible, nothing else? Where does that leave me?

He made light of it in turn, but without the tears,

Sure, there's some space for you too. I'm quite certain. See, I'm a big fellow — with a broad chest. Nonetheless, I want to be like one of those fel-

106

lows, my forefathers. I've been feeling pretty exhausted lately, and they seem so much at peace.

He interrupted his train of thoughts and gulped the contents of his second cup. Then he said,

No. Get going, lazybones. Get something done before sundown. My animals are much wiser than I — howling by the gate. Moooo — I'm coming.

He got up and strode off, heavy, cocky. He had hardly disappeared when Sanna's small face emerged in the dark entrance hall, whispering,

Mama, has Papa told you anything?

Told me what? Mrs. Längsäll wondered. What should he have told me?

Something about me, the girl whispered briskly.

The mother frowned. Gruffly, cuttingly, she said,

My dear little Sanna, do you think that Papa and I have nothing better to talk about but you?

Well, then you didn't? the girl said, quite surprised.

Lillemor cut in sharply,

No. I can assure you we didn't, my little doll. You are not that important. Your father and I have to discuss many things, and far nicer ones than you. You are twenty years old, my child. It's time that you outgrow this childish notion that the whole world revolves around nothing but Sanna-Sanna. Do you really think that you're so special?

The girl's answer and her hopeless, disheartened voice struck bitterly at her mother's heart,

Strange. Some people are important because they are good and capable, like father and you. Others are sweet and nice like Caroline. And then there are difficult and troublesome individuals like me. Can I help thinking that you complain as soon as I turn my back?

Sanna! the mother burst out in despair. But the girl turned brusquely and ran away.

Lillemor sighed and shook her head. Rubbing her hands, she walked slowly to the window and watched her husband coming from the barn between his two beloved oxen. Looking up, he waved to her and she answered his greeting. His arms loosely cradling the animals' necks, he trudged slowly through the gate toward the glistening, fatty, almost meat-colored fields. Lillemor watched the trio — a dark, sharply outlined silhouette against the late afternoon sun.

She had seen her husband trudge in close fellowship with his animals these past weeks. But this afternoon he looked more tired, hung heavier than usual between his steady, confident, reliable creatures.

13: The Lucky Theft On Sanna

THE EXPECTED VISIT of their rich nephew from America, as Längsäll jokingly called his young relative, stirred up a fierce controversy among the good Sannaites. The longer they waited the more they differed. Some looked forward to his coming, others dreaded it. They drove themselves crazy with ever-changing suggestions. The massive patron concocted the most outlandish schemes. Both girls supported him to the fullest. Politely, but emphatically Mother Lillemor vetoed them all. She found practical jokes frightening. The longer their wait, the greater their excitement. But the climax never came.

Instead, a short note from Göteborg informed the good people that Benjamin Borck needed a few more weeks to settle some personal plans. Nothing could have soured their spirit more than yet another postponement. The news had the same devastating effect on the grown children on Sanna as the tidings on Christmas Eve that Christmas morning was delayed a week or two would have on small fry. Squashed like a pancake, their festive exhilaration turned into a dour, sullen wait. They even doubted Benbé's good intentions. Not openly, of course. One week or two, what's the difference? they said, hiding their disappointment under a detached demeanor. They were simple people whose innocent self esteem was badly shaken when they realized that they were not the only, and certainly not the most important people on their young relative's itinerary. Father Längsäll covered his feelings with a belabored joke,

There you see, my dears, we're not as important as we thought. People don't rush to see the Längsälls.

But that was not all! Her father's harmless joke hit Caroline especially hard. She blushed deeply, her eyes filled with tears and her cheeks twitched suspiciously. That Benbé was in no hurry to see her hurt her deeper than she wanted to let on! She left her perch in the window bay and ran out of the room. Once outside, she staggered to the birch grove where the trees were about to sprout new leaves. Inside, Sanna bent her slim neck and muttered,

How utterly strange. I wonder what Uncle Jonathan is going to say about Benbé's behavior?.

Like Sanna, the clown found his nephew's conduct troubling and worrisome.

Yet Benbé had valid, solid reasons for the delay. Traveling first class across the Atlantic had given him the chance to rub elbows with the "upper crust."

Among others, he met an industrial tycoon, a respected middle- aged, vigorous, energetic businessman from Göteborg, the capital city on the West coast. Among the gentleman's many enterprises was a partnership in the largest newspaper corporation on the West coast. During a golf game on deck the naive, egocentric youth found ample opportunity to tell his new friend about his adventures in America. He did not fail to mention other details of his life — his studies, his background, his hopes and plans for the future, including his wish to return and work for a newspaper in the States. As far as getting across the big hump of landing the first job, he was confident that proper connections would provide the necessary push. The alert, lively young man made quite an impression on the businessman, who thought that his paper could surely use an American correspondent with a versatile background like young Mr. Borck's.

He invited Benbé to his estate a few miles outside of Göteborg to discuss the young man's future in more detail. Several business colleagues dropped by to join them. The gentlemen were impressed by Benbé's youthful optimism, drive and common sense and suggested a managerial position for Benbé. They wanted to see him handle a few important transactions first. Benbé was delighted. He tried his best to dampen his enthusiasm and keep a professional decorum. If Venus was uppermost on the young man's mind, Vulcan rated a close second, especially now that these established businessmen treated him like an equal.

Was Benbé failing his famous uncle in California? Not at all! He intended to discharge his previous obligations in good time. The Bible had taught him the wisdom of not putting his sole trust in monarchs. Benbé had ample reasons to be wary. Would King Clown, a mere circus king, be more reliable than his crowned colleagues? He preferred to trust himself rather than put his faith in the clown's temperamental whims — or whimsical temperament.

For the time being Benbé let practical concerns take precedence over his passions. The clown had taken him by surprise with his mission and he hated to carry it out. It made him feel like a caterpillar in a vegetable patch, knowing that he would have to hurt the simple people on Sanna in the process. His distaste mounted with the daily increasing distance that further removed him from the clown's maze and brought him closer to Sanna. Caught between a rock and a hard place, he tried to put the matter out of his mind for the time being. He could always change his given promise.

So, Benbé delayed his visit for as long as possible. This caused not only a minor catastrophe on the farm in the Swedish province of Bergslagen, but it also set the stage for the destruction of a famous clown on the West Coast of the United States.

A minor tragicomic episode preceded events. An unexpected suitor for Sanna materialized suddenly which further aggravated some serious delusions. Bewitched by Caroline's unusual, stunning hairdo, a young, newly hired teacher substitute in Ekersta fell head over heels in love with her — rather than with Sanna. Unlike most modern women, the beautiful, friendly, quiet girl did not bob her hair just to please others. The bob was the current style for teenagers or women bachelors. But the shy, insecure, substitute dared not show his desire for the grand-haired girl. A whispered rumor that Caroline was secretly engaged was probably an added reason for him to find her sister — though less good-looking and a mite unpredictable — good-hearted and honest and a good mate. Thus he courted her instead. And proposed.

The proposal upset Sanna-Sanna enormously. In her excitement she ran through the house, up and down the stairs, arms flapping, crying out,

Mama, Mama, I have to get married — how perfectly awful — I have to get married —

Lillemor was shocked,

What are you saying? Stop this nonsense! Why would you have to get married?

Sanna explained,

Folke proposed to me. Yucky Folke. He can't live without me — ·

Father Längsäll came by and declared gruffly,

Why all this bawling just because a boy wants you to marry him? He's free to ask, isn't he? If you don't like him, well, give him the brush, pure and simple.

The girl sobbed,

But I do like him, well, sort of. But how can I fall in love, considering his ugly, flat face?. Sure, he's quite nice. Well, yes, I do like him. But I had other plans —

Längsäll countered,

Now, no nonsense, please. Are you too batty to give the timid boy the message, well I'll do it, hear —

Sanna stiffened in hurt pride. Drying her tears, she gave her father a dignified look and said,

So you think I have the right to make a person forever unhappy just for selfish reasons?

Immature, self-absorbed, yet fiercely compassionate, she suddenly looked very much like a certain person on the other side of the Atlantic. Father Längsäll sadly bowed his large head. Choking a melancholy smile, he thought,

If I were the intelligent, straightforward man I ought to be, I'd say, My poor little girl, you'd do the boy a favor by sending him off.

But he was nowhere near the intelligent, straightforward man he should be. He left the decision entirely to his little wife who discharged the matter with her usual, soft-spoken, level-headed resolve. She doubted the young suitor's professed despair over losing Sanna-Sanna. Since he had only proposed to Sanna to be near his adored Caroline, his hasty proposal now backfired. Sanna insisted on exchanging engagement rings. He found it unfortunate because it forced him to hock his good suit to pay for it. They further agreed not to wear them openly, but on a necklace — for the time being, perhaps forever. Sanna kissed her ring when she got it and said,

See, it's good to have someone special to think of when the rest of the world is against you.

Responding to her naive, self-centered sigh, the good-natured boy pressed a daring first kiss on his "secret girlfriend's" tightly closed lips. It would be his last.

Sanna-Sanna's emotional confusion eased slowly. But she remained irritable which worried her parents. Längsäll remarked to his wife,

Well, I'm sure she'll settle down in time, now that we've gotten over this silly incident. To be honest, I'm glad our good Benjamin gives us the cold shoulder. Lord only knows how ruffled her feathers would've been had he been here. This way at least she has time to calm down. —

Lillemor added a deep, heartfelt sigh, as if saved from a great danger,

Thank Goodness he didn't come!

At about this time Benbé was arguing with himself,

No, this ought to be enough. Staying here too long won't do. I remember my good, strict mother teaching me a thing or two. I've been here for two weeks. I mustn't wear out my welcome. Like it or not, it's time to face the music in Sanna.

He took the train to Wadköping and called the estate to announce his arrival. Längsäll answered the telephone. Benbé felt miserable and said stiffly,

Yes, my dear uncle, I'm here, finally. If you can have me, I'd like to come tomorrow for a day or two.

Patron Längsäll's answer was just as stiff and dry,

Of course you're welcome, my dear Benjamin. I'm glad you've come to visit us.

Benbé answered,

I wouldn't dream of not coming. There's also the loan I need to settle with you. I can pay up now.

In sharp contrast to their friendly correspondence this past winter, the two relatives couched their mutual esteem in polite, cold words. Benbé found it a matter of course to reimburse his uncle the three thousand crowns he owed him, especially now that King Clown provided his ambassador with a huge credit account. To patron Längsäll this short discussion on money was "especially gratifying."

Great! he said to his wife, rubbing his huge, frozen, plow-calloused fingers. The boy has the decency to pay his debt. I hardly expected it. Might've been embarrassing to remind my own nephew.

He stalked about, a broad smile on his face while rubbing his hands. He repeatedly declared his immense pleasure with the well-known, irrefutable truism that three thousand crowns are nothing to sneeze at. On a sudden impulse and a sly glint in his eyes, he finally posted himself before Lillemor and growled,

D'you think he'll pay the interest for the six months?

Lillemor groaned softly,

Now really, my dear, you ought to be satisfied with the principal. It's between relatives, you know. You don't have to be a stickler —

With a cannibalistic grin, Längsäll imitated,

Stickler, my foot. I hope, indeed I pray, that he remembers his interest. Then we'll wine and dine him like you've never seen in this neck of the woods.

Murderously pleased with this puzzling statement, he clomped out of the room, leaving Lillemor sighing and mumbling,

Oh, it'd be nice to have this Benjamin visit over and done with. There's a foreboding atmosphere here that's unsettling.

It grew worse as time went on and notions of festive receptions fell quietly by the wayside. The prospective guest's mood fared no better as he rattled in a rented old Ford on the spring-ravaged trails from Wadköping toward Sanna. In contrast to the road, the weather was terrific. Still, dreading the impending meeting, Benbé remained in a foul, resentful mood. But when the Ford finally stopped in front of the Sanna entrance it contained only a chauffeur and some luggage. Benbé had valid reasons to step out of the vehicle on the road to Sanna.

Earlier that morning Caroline had reviewed her situation. She was caught in a predicament. Practical as ever, she began reasoning,

Ben may not care much for me. But whether he does or not, I love him. Whatever others may decide, I want to please myself and be nice to him.

With that resolve, she went to the meadow and gathered all the anemones and coltsfoots she could find. Then she posted herself under the birches by the roadside to the Sanna estate. Holding her huge bunch of yellow and blue flowers, the young woman with the golden, stunning hair that had inflamed the little substitute's heart, looked like the symbol of Sweden. She waited, soulfully and patiently. Passing by, Benbé stopped politely and sent the car ahead with the chauffeur. The two young people decided to walk the rest of the way.

112

It was spring and the road was not just long, but rough and soggy as well. Walking was difficult. The pair arrived home two hours after the car.

Their late appearance affected the father in a strange way. Psychologically this was hard to explain. First he waited impatiently, then he began to sing, then, on an impulse, he proceeded to build an arc of triumph to welcome the two. Everyone helped to get it up in time — no one expected the way-farers to take as long as they did. Meanwhile, Lillemor made countless trips between kitchen and entrance, worried about her festive dinner. Where on earth were the two youngsters — could they have gotten stuck in some ditch?

Father Längsäll snapped,

Control yourself, old girl. It's not your fiancé you're expecting. They'll arrive when they're good and ready.

His temperamental outbursts remained largely unexplained. Perhaps the beautiful spring weather prompted them. Caroline's logic and her heroic decision may also have infected the others. At any rate, Benbé's reception became a grand affair — far better than he deserved.

During the dinner Benbé answered their many questions. He talked about his adventures, especially those connected with his detour to Göteborg. Like most young people, he loved to speak of his future, painting it with great verve. Knowing some of Benbé's new friends, others by hearsay, Längsäll thundered his congratulations to the young man's fortunate encounter. He shouted happily,

I must say, things look far different now than when you left last fall — without support and fixed goals.

He was excited and kept rubbing his hands. Suddenly he grew silent. Putting his hands on the table, he hemmed and hawed,

Well, listen — so, what about our relative — that famous clown — did you ever get to meet him?

Busily playing with Benbé's fingers under the table, Caroline was the only person at the table not anxiously waiting for an answer. The young man himself was so absorbed in her play that he missed the relevance of the question. Surprised, he answered,

Yes, I did indeed. I spent three weeks on his fabulous estate. I told you in my letter, didn't I?

Lillemor was quick to confirm,

Yes, you did indeed. But you only mentioned it in passing. Your uncle must have overlooked it.

Suddenly his mission with all its dread and misgivings reverberated through Benbé's mind like a dark haze. He glanced secretively at Sanna. Her eyes wide open, she stared back at him. But the little hand playing with his under the tablecloth soothed his sudden discomfort and strengthened his re-

113

solve that nothing in this world would make him act on his commission. Under this delusion he began a lively and elaborate description of Tracbac and his surroundings. Everyone listened with interest — especially father Längsäll who enjoyed hearing Benbé's woes and difficulties in trying to contact the famous man. Benbé told his hosts how kindly the clown eventually received him, not just like any dear old relative, but like a prince in a bakery shop. Soon they all relaxed and had a good time, especially when they heard about good old Axelsson acting like an old Wadköping ghost in the strange, faraway land. They remembered him well, as they did old grandmother's furniture and other things. For a while the fidgety, restless clown was — or seemed to be — a pleasant, innocent topic of conversation at a happy family reunion.

But Längsäll goaded on,

Now, when you return — are you going to visit him again?

Benbé's answer was enthusiastic and quick,

Of course! Goes without saying! Uncle, as a reporter it's in my own interest to cultivate the relationship with my famous relative as much as I possibly can. Besides, it's thanks to Tracbac's generosity that I'm visiting here. He paid for the ticket, round-trip.

He caught his breath, frightened, and dropped the small hand under the table. What if Längsäll asked why the clown had paid for the trip? What if he caught on to his special errand? What should he say?

But his fears proved groundless. Längsäll had no further questions. Laughing, winking knowingly and pulling funny faces, he said jovially,

Yeah, a multimillionaire like him, of course. I can imagine he is more generous than I, or farm rats like me in good old Sweden who pass some measly two or three thousand shekels to their relatives . . .

They left the dinner table in a warm, congenial mood. Benbé and Caroline made themselves comfortable on the love seat in the corner of the living room, the proper place for engaged couples. Mother Lillemor sat by the table nearby, as always busy with her sewing. Father Längsäll paced back and forth, his thumbs stuck in the armholes of his vest and humming under his breath as if loath to discard his present musical frame of mind. Seizing his opportunity, Benbé forged ahead about his various exploits, spicing each one with a good measure of extra bluster.

Happiest among the happy was Sanna-Sanna. "Blissful" might better describe her attitude. Her long, uncertain waiting for Benbé had been discouraging, and she had already seen her hopes for something great and wonderful to happen miserably dashed. The timid substitute's proposal had seemed yet another heaven-sent confirmation that all the lofty dream-castles she had built in the golden land of the West would come to nothing. Her father's bad humor, her mother's and Caroline's despondence had further traumatized her. Benbé's belated visit was now like a sign that her dreams might come true after all. She was certain that Benbé had come with an invitation from Tracbac. Time would tell.

Like her father, she paced the floor, quietly listening to her cousin's tales. Tears rolling down her cheeks and hands folded tightly against her smiling face, she would certainly have aroused concern — if someone had cared to look at her. When eventually she entered the living room, her arms stretched out, palms up, her head thrown backward, her eyes half-closed, the pitifully scrawny, sickly face beaming and her entire body in rapture, the family members sat aghast. Längsäll stopped short.

Oh, I'm so happy — I'm so happy — I feel happy to see all of you happy — Sanna-Sanna said.

Längsäll muttered surlily,

That's very honorable. It speaks well for you.

Turning toward him, she continued,

You know, Papa, I'm convinced that I'm largely responsible for this. Right, Benjamin? Uncle Jonathan welcomed you after you gave him that little package? And this package made him send you back here to us — perhaps to get all of us to come to him? Isn't it so?

What is that she's saying? Längsäll muttered.

Turning to her mother, Sanna-Sanna continued,

I have a confession to make, Mama dear. I took that little package from your chest and sent it to Uncle Jonathan. I had this feeling you wanted him to know that you hadn't forgotten him — so why not tell him before your death? Waiting any longer wouldn't have made any sense. Don't you agree, Papa?

An eternity of silence followed. Eventually Längsäll raised his forefinger and shook it at her,

Pushy show-off, as always. What a terrible, unmannerly habit, my dear child, I must say. Today the important person around here is your cousin Benbé. After that it's Caroline's turn — there's an engagement-like something between the two — or so I think. You, my little girl, may nicely stand back for a while. Your turn will come some other time.

Upset and disturbed, Benbé glanced at Mother Lillemor. Her head bent over her work and her hand persisting automatically in its ups and downs, she seemed absorbed in her sewing. But Benbé could see how her mouth opened halfway, saw her chin sagging the way chins do on very old and sick people.

14: Lillemor And Father

CHILDREN WHOREACT poorly to punishment are difficult to raise. Yet that is nothing compared to raising those responding too well. Compared with her two year older sister, nineteen year old Sanna-Sanna was a literal child, a sickly child at that. Despite her excitable fantasy and strange whims, she listened readily to reprimands from her elders. Father Längsäll had always taken an easygoing approach toward her. When he did scold even mildly, he regretted it soon. Mother Lillemor was less softhearted about rebukes than her strong, husky husband.

The frightened girl took her father's mild, good-natured criticism that afternoon to heart. She appeared happier, less temperamental, much more helpful, saner and easier to approach than before. She became a veritable smiling, friendly little angel. An intelligent father could not have hoped for better results. But Längsäll was not too bright and he was by no means satisfied. He joked with his "angelic girl," teased her with the pastor's substitute who had left Ekersta by now, but still wrote faithfully and punctually to his secret love every week as if it were a Sunday sermon. Usually irritable, she now took her father's taunts and sarcasms — "our true little Sanna-Sanna who is truly true" — quite calmly and with a slightly bemused and mildly indulgent smile — all to Father Längsäll's great consternation. Later a minor incident made him suspect that something far deeper and possibly more harmful might be behind her altered behavior and he muttered,

Well, her mild manners may look good, but they're frostbitten, that's what they are.

As if having to worry about one girl were not enough, the other's insolence began to bother him too. Indeed, that was the word he used, although he might have used a milder term if he had given it more thought. Miss Caroline and Mister Benbé had slowly reached that stage of semi-secret engagement which sorely grates on other people's nerves. Proclaiming he had never understood love's heavenly secrecy, Father Längsäll hollered,

These two youngsters do nothing but coo, flirt and neck, that's obvious to everyone. Wonder why they run as if antbitten as soon as someone gets close.

Not enough that his memory played tricks on him, he suffered a good measure of fatherly envy to boot, a sort of middle-age mental measles, a most innocent, but inescapable kind of envy. He wanted to take "other measures,"

116

he declared, but left unclear what exactly he had in mind. Resolved — his appetite great, his motions deliberate — he growled more than ever before.

Without specifying whether good or bad, Sanna-Sanna had a name for it: Dear Papa in one of his moods!

Simply said — his mood!

Mother Lillemor was the first to react to the "brazen thickheadedness" the couple displayed. The two were at breakfast, planning their various projects for the day, solo or together. Abruptly she interrupted them rather harshly,

Not that I intend to throw Ben out of the house — certainly not — but we must still bear in mind that he can't stay here forever. That's why you two should gradually prepare for the bitter separation. Papa's trip to town today is an excellent opportunity.

Deeply hurt, Benbé blushed and said,

It'll be a great pleasure to join him.

But Mother Lillemor answered dryly,

I can well imagine. But it won't be Mylord going to town. Caroline is going with Papa to buy yarn for me. That, I think, is more than a gentleman can do.

Längsäll agreed readily,

Yes. Sure. Our honored guest will have to make do with Sanna-Sanna.

Mother Lillemor sniffed,

Well, there's still another lady around. Though she doesn't care much for flattery, I'll have you know.

Teasing his wife with his pity, Längsäll rumbled,

So, now you know your fate and duties for the day, Ben.

His joke was more to the point than he realized. Benbé knew that his uncle was unwittingly correct with his tease. Being alone with Mother Lillemor was the one thing he had been trying to avoid all along. It had become inevitable, whether he liked it or not. Sanna-Sanna had confessed to giving him the small packet and he had to give an account. So, when father and daughter drove off and Sanna-Sanna returned to her rooms, Benbé remained in the hall. Depressed and nervous, he prepared to face the issue. Luckily, Mother Lillemor thought along the same lines. She said,

Come, let's sit down by the table and face each other. I'm going to cross-examine you, so to speak. Please, don't consider my feelings or some such nonsense. All I want is facts. Then I may want some advice — if there's one to give.

She cleared the huge, round table and sat down, a heap of various-colored remnants that needed to be scored for rag-rugs before her. Smiling, she pushed a big heap over to Benbé, her winks exhorting him to make himself useful. Benbé remembered the clown's tale that she had been the only dry-eyed, clear-headed member in the family at dear Grandmother's funeral. He mused,

Whatever, she sure has a lot of inner strength. If there's trouble ahead, heaven forbid, she won't be the one to flinch.

Lillemor cut into his thoughts,

Well, Ben, let's get right down to business and start with the most important item. Tell me, has Jonathan Borck sent me a message — something that you might find difficult to deliver?

Having staked his course, Benbé answered automatically and conscientiously like a witness at a trial,

Yes. He gave me a terribly tricky job. He wants Sanna to come to him — I assume for good, or at least for some time.

Mother Lillemor nodded quietly to indicate that she understood. Again Benbé watched her mouth going limp, just like before when the girl in her excitement admitted to mooching the package. She said,

Sure. Just about the most difficult assignment possible. Not to mention my part in it. Well, I must say he hasn't changed much. I had a hunch when you elaborated on his sallow skin and loneliness. Then the girl's story of the glove. I hadn't forgotten that package. It's just that I haven't opened that drawer for years, so Sanna's confession came as a complete surprise. I had no idea the package was gone, much less that it had reached its destination.

She kept silent for a while. Then she continued just as softly as before, wondering with obvious curiosity,

What did he say when he got it?

Benbé blushed, mulling over his answer carefully before he said,

At first he said nothing. But when he thought up this idea with Sanna he needed of course to tell me enough so — well, so that I'd understand the connection —

Picking up a new piece of cloth to score, Mother Lillemor mumbled,

Of course. The connection may be pretty hard to understand. No one knows that better than I myself. Attraction between two people may sometimes take strange turns.

Her amused smile almost frightened Benbé when she interrupted herself,

Oh well, I'm not talking about the kind between you and Caroline — thank goodness, that's easy enough to understand. But there are others. I've had plenty of time to reflect on the subject. For example, I don't think women are in any danger when admiring a man. No, we just need to keep our hero at a distance; our adoration would vanish if we didn't. But a case of two-thirds pity and one-third pure contempt is a dangerous mixture that causes many sickly and deficient children to be born into this world.

Sanna flickered through Benbé's mind. He reeled under the icy calm of her voice when she continued,

118

Yes, my dear Ben, that's the way it was at any rate. Two parts pity and one part contempt. Don't misinterpret what I mean by contempt. Despite all his idiosyncrasies, Jonathan was, and surely still is, a wonderful, good human being. It's not his intelligence, it's his emotional faculties that I find contemptible. Now, this may sound un-Christian, I can't help that, but a healthy person like me feels a natural contempt for sickly people. And I — I'm not even Christian, I'm an atheist, have been a plain atheist for as long as I can remember. I can't fight with my God the way Längsäll does. All I can fight with is myself — and that is far worse.

That's how I loathe Jonathan. His profession might have made him worse. Petty bourgeois that I am, I don't appreciate his sophistication. Längsäll pulling his oxen — that's a man for me. Artists and such — sure they're interesting, perhaps special and entertaining, but that's all. My behavior may be hard to understand. But it's as I said — we women find a man we both despise and pity hard to resist. It's a dirty trick played on our female pride. A fellow needing us — gee, it smells pride from far away. Healthy, strong men do likewise. They don't need to push their good points to attract females. Look how small they become courting us — can't live without us, just we give them our small, beautiful hand so they can stumble along on life's terrible path. Gosh! Bunk all of it! Längsäll's proposal was far better. That buffalo said, Now, don't rush it, Lillemor, because I can take care of myself, without you, I assure you —

She threw her head backward and burst into pealing laughter, contagious enough to rub off on a depressed Benbé.

She laughed until her tears came. Wiping them away with her silken kerchief she resumed,

Oh, well, I'm no expert on humble suitors — for all I know they may laugh behind our backs and it'd serve us right if they did. Still, humble fellows with valid reasons for humility are most dangerous for guarded and unguarded hearts. I should know. All right, Ben, you're not an inexperienced little girl. I don't need to tell you all the secret thoughts of a mature woman. Although that's hardly what I'm doing here. Sooner or later everyone does what I'm doing — grope for reasons why I did what I did. It's not easy, for sure, but it's essential if you value your life. One should be able to brush aside and forget a little embarrassing mistake, as the saying goes. But that's dead wrong. The blunder will never leave you. I would like to open a preschool and teach all youngsters, Do whatever you feel like doing, but remember that whatever you've done is done. It will backfire. Make you suspicious and be on guard. So be careful. There's no forgiveness. But so be it. As long as it isn't cowardice. No account gets written off, neither on earth nor in heaven. Not even the Good Lord, Längsäll's confidant, much less we ourselves can cancel debts. The poet recommending self-forgiveness and martyrdom is dead wrong. The very thought is cowardly and meaningless hogwash. I know.

Her two final words I know were like whips — soft-spoken, energetic blows, spoken like a chairman of the club finalizing an indisputable fact.

With only a slight shift in her voice, she continued,

To return to the issue, I must admit I have difficulty seeing my way clearly. What is right and what is wrong? I mean, what can I do, how cause the least possible damage — hardly daring to consider it the greatest possible good? And, whether it's cynical or not, we need to think of the economic ramifications too. Längsäll and I won't leave much to our children and poor Sanna, with her sickly idiosyncrasies, will hardly be able to take care of herself, much less have someone supporting her. Over there she'll be wealthy. Knowing Jonathan as well as I do, I'm sure he'll be good to her. The danger is more in that he might spoil her. Or that the people in her new environment might play her a fool.

She contemplated for a while, then continued with a chuckle,

You must admit, Ben, this world is neither just nor reasonable. Both he and she are peculiar and, judging from what you've told us, these two are quite similar. Only, his oddity has allowed him to become a genius, if only a circus artist. Anyway, it made him famous and extremely wealthy. But now this poor thing — what's in her future once we're gone? People aren't nice to her — probably can't be. That's the way of the world — the sick chick gets pecked to death. I tell you that it's pretty difficult at times to prevent thoughtless, nasty people from making a fool of her. It gets more difficult as years go by. As long as she was a child, her idiosyncrasies could be shrugged off as cute or entertaining. Nowadays they're painful to watch. No, justice and sanity are scarce, for sure. Längsäll puts his trust in heaven, believing everything here on earth is for the best. But poor me believes neither in heaven nor finds her way on earth. Just my tough luck.

She hesitated, then went on,

Well, there's another thing in favor of my letting her go. Blood is supposedly thicker than water — call it the voice of the blood or some such thing. To be honest, I don't believe it. But I'm far from all-knowing and perhaps there's some truth to it. I reason differently: two people, loners by nature, might slowly get to like each other for the mutual benefit of both. See, this I think is the crucial argument. Who else besides those closest to her care about Sanna? No one. And the great Jac Tracbac may forgive my questioning who essentially cares about him? True, I really don't know, but I have my suspicions. So, all things considered, my maxim is: Whatever God has joined let no man tear asunder.

Her body rocking slowly back and forth, her face utterly sad, she mumbled,

Well, if only I knew — who knows, who knows what is right in the long run — ?

Her last words reminded Benbé that she had not even mentioned the most difficult part of the problem. Overcoming his shyness, he wondered,

Tell me — above all, how would you explain Sanna's trip to Uncle Längsäll? Tracbac worried about it greatly. He told me that we'll have to drop the matter altogether if it proves impossible. Lillemor will have to decide, he said.

She smiled and said,

Yes, it's easy enough, isn't it, to let Lillemor decide. —

She hesitated for a second, then she continued with a heavy, tired firmness in her voice,

Well, well, my boy, it's going to be difficult, difficult for him and for me. But, you see, that is our problem — and it has nothing to do with her.

Her voice returning to normal, she resumed,

Good, my dear Ben. We've talked about the main issues. Now I know at least how things stand. I need a few days to think things through and you'll have to grant me these. If you don't, well, you can always devote them to Caroline. By the way, now that I have the pleasure of being alone with you, you might as well tell me a little more about Jonathan, or rather about his surroundings and life style. What kind of people does he associate with? Are they decent enough?

Remembering Tracbac's special request, he reassured her that Tracbac led a very decent and quiet life. At first Lillemor listened closely. But then something else crossed her mind. Smiling and slightly self-conscious, she interrupted him

Say, did Jonathan tell you something about me?

Benbé told her the little he remembered about the funeral, the furniture his uncle had shipped over and other such details. Smiling, he added,

Well, yes, one more thing. He hated to hear me call you aunt. It wasn't appropriate. It made you sound too old. She was so young, he said —

Oh, he said that?

Now Lillemor smiled too. Her bright, reflective gaze stared into the void and tears began to roll down her cheeks.

Frightened and rather absurd, Benbé wondered,

What is it? Have I said something to — ?

She shook her head and closed her eyes. Then her head dropped slowly down to the table, her face buried in the heap of many-colored rags.

When Längsäll and his daughter returned home that evening Caroline reported on her errands to her mother. Her father, bored with the debate on yarns and yard goods, paced the floor. Upset, he stopped abruptly in front of his surprised, innocent daughter. His hands in his sides, he stuck his tongue out and growled,

Do me a favor and scram! I'm tired of listening to all this gab about yarns and other nonsense all day. Good bye, young lady!

Her nose stuck into the air like an insulted hen, Caroline stalked out of the room.

Lillemor burst out,

Now, what's the matter with you? Have you all gone mad around here?

Längsäll growled morosely,

Yeah, you should talk. All you do is sit here all day, drinking coffee and nothing more to think about but your dinner. Look at me! I'm supposed to be happy and cheery despite all my worries. Do you know why I went to town? Just so I could think in peace and quiet about important matters. And I've been thinking, mind you, thinking all day long. And now I'm tired and sad.

He resumed his pacing and continued,

Oh, well, I'm done thinking, at least for myself. So, now I want you to listen without fainting or some such stupid habits. Whenever Benjamin returns to America he may take your daughter along. What do you say to that?

She said nothing, but continued knotting her remnants as if she had heard nothing. Only her face, showing the first, tiny spider nets of aging, turned dark yellow. Längsäll watched her anxiously, surprised, wondering why she did not answer. She did not look up and it took quite a while before she regained enough composure to answer. There was a slight tremor in her voice,

Well, Längsäll — you mean — I assume — you're thinking of Caroline?

Dammit, who else should I've been thinking of?

Längsäll seemed angry over his wife's unusually slow comprehension. But he quickly calmed down, continuing in a serious tone without losing a certain inner annoyance,

Well, as I said, I've been mulling it over. Also, through friends and friends' friends I've been able to substantiate that the things Benjamin told us about his future plans are not just immature, boyish fantasies, though they're still rather vague. But you have to take risks in this world. So, that leads to the question when the wedding is going to be. For all we can see — they're engaged and there's nothing we can do to change that — anyway, neither you nor I have anything against the boy. So, the question is not whether, but when? Of course, they could easily wait for a year or two, but what good would that do? To have the girl mooning around, longing, waiting — thanks, but no thanks, as far as I'm concerned.

He stopped short. Stretching his heavy body, he exclaimed with serious dignity,

All right, my friend, I've told you my opinion regarding the girl. Now it's your turn. Let's hear your objections.

Mother Lillemor let go of her remnants. Her head at an angle, she squinted into the evening sun streaming through the window. Eventually she said softly,

Oh, I really don't have so many objections. I'm sure you're right —

With forced triumph in his voice Längsäll interrupted her,

You're damn right I'm right. Doing it this way we'll get the honeymoon trip and other stupid things for free, so to speak. Benjamin can stay with us for a few months. I assume he'll need to go to Göteborg for some further consultations with his bosses. That'll get you some extra time to prepare, bride's dress, trousseau, housecleaning and other such things. Well, it's sure going to be nice here! Anyway, we can have the wedding between Whitsun and Midsummer, before we start on the hay. It's as if it were all pre-arranged. My friend, you may accuse patron Längsäll of whatever your featherbrain may think of — but see, you can't say that he's impractical. Because then you'll hit a brick wall!

Pacing the floor, he continued to brag noisily on the tremendous advantages of this wedding, though secretly it lay very heavy on his heart. Lillemor sat staring into space, her fingers idly clasped together, her head slightly backward bent. She looked like an old woman sitting in her church pew, absentmindedly listening to the preacher's sermon. Suddenly she shook her head as if waking up from a daze. Glancing diffidently and quickly around, she straightened her back and resumed her work. She said,

You know, there's something else, Längsäll, something that might make the two of us still more lonely. It's not impossible that Sanna might want to join them on the trip.

Längsäll stopped, inquiring,

Impossible? What do you mean not impossible? Of course, it could be both. Question is whether she wants to go?

Impatient, Mother Lillemor explained,

Well, that's just what I meant. I can't say anything before having talked to her.

Highly surprised, Längsäll goaded,

You're only guessing? Could someone else have talked to her? Benjamin perhaps?

Mother Lillemor was quick to emphasize,

No, no, Längsäll. No one has talked to her. And I promise you, no one is going to talk to her without your consent.

Längsäll mumbled,

My consent? My consent?

Mother Lillemor's face hardened. She needed to be hard now, hard on herself and hard on him she loved. She said,

The thing is that Jonathan has asked Benjamin to deliver a message — to ask you and me and of course Sanna whether she would like to come and possibly stay there. He feels very lonely.

Father Längsäll resumed his wanderings, pacing the floor rather quietly now. Both husband and wife were silent until finally he slowed down and came to a stop. Staring at the floor, he mumbled,

He feels so lonely — he feels so lonely —

Raising his head, he uttered dryly,

Well, you see — that's really a decision only Sanna can make. As far as I'm concerned, I'm not going to say either yes or no —

He stood for a long time, as quiet and immovable as she. Her gaze was fastened on her work. But she finally forced herself to face him during this discussion. Their eyes met and she saw Father Längsäll's smile — a hard, defiant, nasty smile — a smile she had never before seen him smile. It was her turn to mumble,

What are you smiling at?

With a strong voice, but otherwise very calm, he answered,

Am I smiling? I didn't realize. I was just thinking how right I was when I wished to become a really, really religious man. It would mean so much to me — so much — so very much.

He dragged his words, especially the last ones.

They fell silent for a long while. Eventually she stammered,

I understand — it's just that for us it comes — for you it comes — comes for us —

He gave her a deep look. Her usually calm, intelligent eyes spun, reeling in their sockets. She looked almost idiotic. Her chin drooped as if she had difficulty breathing —

He walked quickly over to her and stroked her cheeks with the back of his hand. As if afraid that his words would choke her, he said hurriedly,

You mean that this comes as a surprise?

She nodded and closed her mouth. He stepped over to the windowsill and remained there, silently, his forehead pressed against the post. With his coarse pointer he wrote one word: Lillemor.

Without turning, he finally said calmly,

To be truthful — Lillemor — it came — that's what you really mean — no — no, it really did not come as a surprise.

Eventually he added,

Well — this is — in turn — my confession.

He returned to her. Her eyes were misty and lethargic. He sat down at the table. His large, coarse hands dived into the heap of remnants and let the slinky silk slowly glide through his fingers. He said,

Yes, Lillemor — you see, in the end we're — we're going to be poor — real, real poor —

15: The Fall Of The Clown

Rumors about Jac Tracbac, famous and celebrated artist, began to circulate all across the United States.

According to some short newspaper articles, the great clown was about to return to the public arena after a two year retirement. These rumors were immediately denied. No, Jac Tracbac had not the least desire to perform. After discrediting Jac's willingness to a come-back, the reporters began to elaborate on his tour. New York was to be his starting point. Half a dozen playwrights were listed as possible scriptwriters for his act. Then followed a retraction of everything the newspapers had said. The latest news flash was that Tracbac, having suffered a heart attack, needed to take a rest. He was to recuperate for several months in the European spa Bad Nauheim.

Rumors continued until the following announcement appeared on April first: *Jac Tracbac will perform in the capitol of (the city's name) Wednesday November 1. Tickets will go on sale October 31. No advance reservations.*

Underneath this news item a life insurance company had managed to slip in the following advertisement:

Insure your life before getting in line to buy tickets for JAC TRACBAC's performances. Avoid taking risks since you stand a good chance to die, either of exhaustion or of laughing at his antics. Consider your family — they may want to see Jac's act several times.

The members of the syndicate were outraged. They found the ads "indecent." Mr. Adam and the religious organization he chaired, their fear mitigating their anger, considered them a bad joke. Mr. Cow worried,

If Jac sees this, he'll think we're behind all this and refuse to perform. Then what are we to do?

The others agreed. Taking the bull by the horns, Abel Rush held the article under Jac's nose, saying,

Look, Jac. They're making fun of you and advertising in your behalf — all at the same time.

Tracbac studied the notice carefully. Finally he laughed out loud,

No! Just look at these jokers! I must say, that's a heck of going about their business. Really. It's like an ad I might have pushed when I was a producer. Rush, you ought to insure me too. Let the little orphans inherit after me.

He frightened his secretary when he ended his tirade with the joke,

Abel! Abel, I think the syndicate would be wiser to get life insurance for me rather than for the audience. It might come due much sooner than they think. That, my boy, will make a fortune for all of you.

The remark might have passed him by had not Jac Tracbac's health deteriorated these past few months. He stayed in bed for days on end. Then he quarreled endlessly with Longfellow, who was barely allowed to leave his room, except to get food for his boss. Longfellow suffered his master's moods with true Christian forbearance and took the torrents of abuse with a quiet,

Well, Sir, you ought to know me best, you're my master. Sure, a weak-brained fellow needs to stay in bed and be mean. You may need it. Go on, Sir. Go ahead! Don't mind me. I forgive you.

Tracbac continued screaming,

Get out of here, you moor!

With a smirk on his face, Longfellow countered,

All right, Sir, all right! —

Rush had a term for these moods: self indulgence. The clown's physician O'Henny voiced his own opinion,

Never mind. We're all slightly crazy. Why should the clown be an exception?

The clown had ample reasons for his mood swings or illness or whatever his behavior was called. The date for his first performance had been advertised in all twenty cities — before he ever had a chance to draw an outline for his comic act. His ideas now greatly clashed with those of the syndicate's complicated proposals. He wanted to feature a plain, absentminded professor on an expedition in North Africa. Sleeping in his tent, this good professor is dreaming of his beloved wife back home when suddenly a lion enters his tent — these wild beasts are dangerous in the wild, but they can be tamed if necessary — so, entering his tent, the lion lies down on the sleeping professor's chest. About two years old and well trained, the wild beast starts licking the man's face who now dreams that the lion's mane is his wife's hair. He begins stroking the mane. Slowly awakening, he realizes his mistake. Here the real Jac Tracbac specialty kicks in by honing in on the clown's terror.

The clown considered his plot "funny enough to bring the house down in stitches." But the gentlemen of the syndicate declared the suggestion the most stupid and childish they had ever heard. The clown was beside himself and screamed,

Childish! My foot! These are children who want to be entertained. Remember that.

Then, in a change of heart, he added mildly,

Just think! Imagine these kids screaming when they see me smooching the lion's nose, thinking it's my wife. I can just picture them die laughing in

127

their seats. I guarantee you, they'll howl so hard you'll have to call the ambulance!

O'Henny said,

All right, that's for the kids. But there are adults too. You can't include anything sleazy or obscene in a scene with a lion. People will find it dull without pornography!

That's when the clown blew his top again. He had no use for pornography!

What do you think I am? A buffoon?

Well now, what do you think you *are*? O'Henny said with his customary insolence. Jac pulled his ear, screaming,

Oh? Wait till I show you what I am! It'll frighten you out of your wits, I promise!

The clown walked out on his terrace, shook his fist at the ducks and preached at the top of his lungs,

Bear in mind, corn must be kneaded, the husk be burned, where will you find your share? All is consumed. Where is your gain?

Frightened more by the bamboo stick than the enigmatic threat, the ducks quacked a noisy answer and flapped their wings. Meanwhile, O'Henny had a conference with Siv,

This behavior is all very well. But these emotional outbursts make me want to take a closer look. Is there something else on his mind beside this upcoming tour?

Her beautiful forehead in angry frowns, Siv said morosely,

Well, he's expecting his daughter!

Surprised, O'Henny repeated,

What's that? His daughter? He has a daughter? What's wrong with her?

Siv said,

I don't know a thing. I never even knew about her until he told me the other day,

Well, right. Perhaps I ought to have told you before we were married that I have a daughter. She's coming here soon. Which should be all the same with you now — we're divorced anyway.

The doctor's smirk bothered Siv, but she continued,

Well, according to Jac, this daughter is a marvel of beauty and wisdom and she counts the days to get here. But then, I'm not even sure she's coming. She may send her regrets.

O'Henny had good reasons to worry about the clown. His behavior grew stranger by the day. The worries for the tour with its complications were enough already, though that was nothing compared to his growing anxiety about his daughter. The realization of suddenly getting another person "as a present," so to speak, haunted him. Lacking in normal development, his emotions were stunted. He felt completely off-balance and his behavior became ludicrous. He taunted beautiful Siv,

It'll be nice to get a sweet, good-looking girl into the house for a change. You'll finally get to see what beautiful is, you amber-eyed darkie.

His taunts made her angry. It was foolish enough to tell a gorgeous person like Siv that she is ugly. But to brag about a beautiful daughter he had never even seen was outright absurd. Sad, Siv could not refrain from asking,

What do you know about her or her looks? You've only seen her on pictures taken when she was small.

The clown was angry,

Well now, I've seen her mother, haven't I?

Siv smiled and said,

Regardless, you ought to be careful. The mother may be perfectly gorgeous, but you can hardly brag about your looks, my poor Jac.

My looks?

Shocked, the clown went to consult the mirror in Siv's bedroom and studied his reflection. Reassured, he muttered,

There's nothing wrong with this face. It might be on the skinny side, but the features are noble, I dare say.

Siv laughed and agreed,

Well, then everything should be all right.

It was lucky that not many strangers dropped by these days to visit the clown whose mounting narcissism made him garrulous. He gave in to a sudden urge to confide in Longfellow. Pretending to be on his way out, he stopped by the gatekeeper's lodge where the Negro was leisurely minding his chores and announced,

Longfellow, did you know we're getting company? A young, good-looking lady.

The news left the Negro cold.

Oh, really? Well, she'll always be welcome — just so she's not so pretty to make my old lady jealous. I won't kiss or bite her. So, I'm no danger to her.

Upset by such indifference Tracbac said morosely,

Longfellow, bet you can't guess who that young lady is?

I've no talent for guessing, the Negro told him nonchalantly. Dissatisfied with the response, Tracbac walked out on the road. Suddenly he turned and called,

Well, idiot, you could at least ask!

Longfellow was quick to answer,

All right, all right. Who's this dame coming here so all of a sudden?

Tracbac stretched his body to its full length, deeply blushing and pointing at his chest, he declared,

It's my daughter.

What? the Negro said.

My daughter, Tracbac repeated.

His mouth gaping foolishly, the Negro said,

Your daughter? How come?

Not knowing whether to be angry or amused, the clown shouted,

You nut. I'm telling you that I have a daughter and you wonder, How come? Don't just stand there, smirking, you toothpaste ad. Wait till I tell Siv about your crazy answer! Yeah, how come people have kids. Honestly! Brains!

He started running up the driveway to tell Siv, but he soon regretted acting so impulsively. He blushed. On second thought he found it wiser to keep Longfellow's stupid remark to himself.

This interval of happy self-delusion did not last long. Slowly but surely his happiness waned — somewhat like an oil lamp running out of oil. His anxiety increased. Siv actually preferred him this way — anything was better than his overbearing demeanor. Still, there was no news from Sanna. Eventually even Siv began to wonder when the girl would finally arrive.

With a sour, weary face Tracbac said,

How would I know when?

You ought to write, or wire a telegram to find out, Siv advised. But that he refused to do.

Oh no. She comes whenever she feels ready to come. Rushing her would only compound problems. Not until the middle of June did he finally agree to send a telegram.

Benbé's answer had a light tone,

Patience. Wedding takes precedence above other matters.

The answer dumbfounded Tracbac and hardly improved his mood. Wedding? About to get married? The news was neither good nor bad. Of course they could get married. But it made no sense doing it right away! He had hardly begun the impossible task of getting the only person he could possibly claim as his own before someone else claimed her. Time and again he needed to remind himself,

Great. Of course they can get married if they want to. But I'll be darned if it makes sense —

All his thoughts revolved around his daughter Sanna-Sanna. He hardly remembered the existence of another girl — never even thought of her. But for Benbé it seemed baroque to consider anyone else but Caroline as his bride. The possibility of a mix-up never occurred to him.

The mistaken identity about his daughter had one advantage — Tracbac finally took time to plan his tour. He was ready for discussing it with the gentlemen of the syndicate. Even though he had not yet finalized the program, he appeared more amenable to some of their suggestions. Abel Rush assured his friend O'Henny,

Our little funnyman is definitely smarter and more considerate than all of us together.

Agreeing in general, O'Henny shook his head with a warning,

Perhaps. But it's better he's somewhat off his noodle — crazy in small doses, so to speak. Not everybody is normally normal. I have a hunch we're in for an unpleasant surprise.

The clown did eventually surprise them, though not the way the doctor had imagined. No crazy stunt; just a regular accident. Tracbac used to work out daily on the high trapeze in his gym, if only for a few minutes. A very grateful audience of urchins of varying sizes and skin tones — black, yellow, white — would usually come and watch him. But this morning the clown shooed them out, claiming that he was not about to perform anything special. No one minded, except his favorite black boy Hiawatha who climbed a tree from where he could easily see into the gym. He watched Tracbac doing warm-ups, then raise the trapeze all the way to its highest setting. Fearing an accident, he scampered from his perch and ran home, calling,

Dad, dad, he's all the way up there without the safety net. There's no one with him.

So? He's done this before, his father shouted and gave the boy a box on his ear. But he worried about his master and ran to the gym where he found Tracbac on the floor in a thick layer of sawdust, unconscious, blood running down his nose. The large Negro picked him up, carried him upstairs and put him on Siv's bed. With a feeling of utter helplessness he began to cry, mumbling,

He did it on purpose. I know he did.

Tracbac suffered no further damage than a broken shinbone. Siv sat beside him when he regained consciousness. He lay quiet for a long while, lost in thoughts. Then he said,

You must be wondering why I didn't use the safety net. Rush is suspicious too. Do you think I did it on purpose? That I want to break my neck to cause you trouble? No, believe me, it's no fun to upset folk. It was an accident.

Skeptical, Siv inquired gruffly,

Sending the children away and forgetting to call Longfellow, was that accidental too?

The clown was impatient,

The children! The children! Do you think I want to expose them to the risk of my landing on their skulls? And Longfellow — stupid fellow wondering how come I have a daughter! I hate safety nets. My glorious debut as a clown was hanging a man in the safety net. Shall I make my exit hanging myself? Great start, great finish, wonderful profession. All right, I had no business going up there all alone, I admit. I was tired, I was nervous, I hadn't slept well. To top it off, as I was standing way up there I suddenly remembered that fool I hanged — like a flash through my brain. That must have made me dizzy. I saw him falling. I rushed forward and — booms, there I was, lying prone at the bottom. Such tricks can happen to the best of us. Do me a favor — forget your ugly suspicions. I'm going to perform. It's in my contract — accidents may not keep me from performing. If the bone isn't healed, well, I'll be as great and as first-rate as always, even sitting down. I have experience. I know the tricks of the trade.

Then at least explain to me what made you so nervous and why you couldn't sleep? Siv said, her voice as strict as a mother's when questioning her mischievous son. Tracbac stared quietly at the ceiling. Eventually he said softly,

Why I was tired? Well, dear Siv, I could tell you. But I don't want to.

He closed his eyes to let her know that he wanted to be left alone. Later that day Siv told Rush of their conversation. Worried, Abel Rush tried his own analysis,

It could very well be my fault. He got a letter yesterday afternoon. I recognized the sender's name on the envelope. She once meant a lot to him and I thought it tactless to open it. So, I gave it to him and asked later whether he wanted to respond. No, he didn't. It was a very personal letter, he said.

Was it Mrs. Längsäll who sent the letter? Siv inquired. Rush shrugged without answering her question.

While Tracbac's bone healed well, his weariness, impatience and anxiety increased. Siv suggested,

Read something. Don't just lie there all day, staring at the ceiling.

He did not want to read. After a week or so he began taking notes. Siv was curious and wondered about his newfound interest,

What are you writing?

The clown grinned craftily,

Well, wouldn't you like to know, you little hag? It's a sort of catechism. Hardly something Father Luther would have written, though.

A clown catechism? Siv suggested.

Tracbac was all dignity,

That's it. A clown catechism. Nothing for worthy colleagues or other contemporaries.

Can't I get to see it? Siv asked.

Certainly not. I'll read it in due time. I'm an outstanding reader, outstanding, I'll have you know, the clown assured her with exaggerated dignity. Siv had to be satisfied with his answer.

While his minor accident kept Tracbac confined and his mobility limited to occasionally jotting down notes, his European representative wasted his time in pursuing his own pleasures. Benjamin Borck and Caroline had become inseparable. Her father considered this "preoccupation Caroline" insulting and offensive. As usual, Längsäll was extremely busy. His spring preparations out of the way, he devoted his time to the important task of "shoe-ing both people and dames" on his shoemaker's last.

His wife was no less busy preparing Caroline's bridal chest, a job that seemed endless. In truth, this "bottomless trousseau" and the repeated "wedding date delays" were Mother Lillemor's desperate, selfish reasons for keeping her girls at home as long as possible. It's unnecessary to defend her schemes of endlessly postponing wedding and following separation.

One of the travelers, Sanna-Sanna never objected to these repeated delays. Throughout the summer she remained calm and even-keeled, though unusually silent, "feeling" more than "knowing" the facts. Cousin Benbé "sensed things" too — but, in contrast, was wrong more often than not.

When do you think we'll be off on our trip, Sanna?

I don't know, Benbé, but I have a feeling —

Do you think that you'll like it over there?

I don't know, Benbé, but I have a feeling —

Well, then, what is your feeling telling you?

It's foolish to confide in others. People only make fun of you later.

Initially the wedding date was set for the week before Midsummer. Then it was moved to the middle of August. Father Längsäll abandoned his shoe last and his wonderful creations to manage the produce of his fields. But in spite of Mother Lillemor's constant rescheduling the wedding was finally set for the end of July. Then a small, painful incident seemed to stop all traveling plans. The young priestly novice Folke, who admired Caroline so much that he proposed marriage to Sanna-Sanna, returned to Ekersta. He and Sanna-Sanna were still wearing their engagement rings and he felt free to renew his proposal.

Sanna became upset all over again. But this time there was a slight twist. The young man might have improved during his absence, or Sanna was infected by Caroline's wedding fever. Whatever the reason, this time Sanna found his proposal quite appealing. She urged him to wait under the shade trees. She was going to discuss it with her mother in the weaving room. To avoid the many servants nearby, they went to the living room, its doors open to the adjoining office where Längsäll sat adding up his accounts.

Informing her mother of the latest news, the girl expressed her inclination to accept. Mother Lillemor became angry,

What is that now? In the spring you gave him the brush-off. And now, after having at long last finalized your trip, you want to get engaged? If you want to stay with Jonathan Borck for a short time only, well that's all right with me. But it's certainly pretty irresponsible to change your mind so easily on as important a matter as that.

Sanna-Sanna looked at her mother. There was something sly and nasty in the girl's usually so mild eyes when she said,

I can't believe that you consider it irresponsible to follow the voice of your heart?

Längsäll heard the two angry voices. His thoughts still on his accounts, he rose to find out what all this was about. Mother Lillemor heard him and added quickly,

There's a difference between the heart's voice and the heart's whim. Now we'll stop this drivel. If you don't want to go, you stay. But your unpredictable behavior frightens me. All summer long you were looking forward to this trip —

Changes again? Längsäll muttered, sighing as he stopped short in the door. Sanna-Sanna pretended not to notice him. Turning to her mother, she reflected,

Yes. Sure. You are right. I did look forward to the trip. But the more I think about it, the more I doubt my decision. Remember, I'm going to be the fifth wheel — or third, to be precise. These two newlywedded turtledoves won't have much time for me — and you can hardly expect that either. That leaves me completely alone with that strange uncle. I don't know him. Who knows whether he'll like me?

Oh, he's going to be nice — nice — nice — , Längsäll tried to calm her down.

Sanna, still not acknowledging his presence, continued,

Actually, what sort of demands can I make on his goodwill? Or, look at it from the opposite side — what rights does he have over me? Really, he sends his regards and wants me there. What gives him the right?

Lillemor's face turned yellowish brown as it had during her recent serious discussion with her husband — a mark of her fatal illness. Softly, but very emphatically, she said,

My dear child, neither he, nor I, nor Längsäll has rights over you. Well, yes. You owe Längsäll your gratitude for feeding and dressing you all these years.

Now well, but that was no more than his duty, the girl mumbled.

Mother Lillemor stamped the floor and almost shouted,

Be quiet. He has no obligations toward you. What you got was pure goodness on his part —

Suddenly she paced back and forth through the room, her eyes wide open, her brows in folds and her hands raised as if she were about to hit. All of a sudden she slapped her own face, hard and mercilessly. Then, just as

134

suddenly she stopped her pathological outburst. Her innate willpower took over. Panting, she said softly,

I don't know, but what is all this talk about rights and duties? The only person who has any rights over you is yourself. Längsäll and I hope that you use these rights to your advantage and our happiness.

Unmoved by her mother's violent outburst, Sanna-Sanna reflected for a while. Then she said, as softly as her mother,

All right. Then I'll just have to go back to the fellow again and talk some more.

She left to "talk to the fellow" — the suitor who sat patiently waiting under the huge shade trees. Leaning against the door, his head bowed, Father Längsäll had quietly watched the episode. The two women ignored his presence, and he did not interfere. When Sanna left he returned to his office without another word.

Sanna returned soon, flinging her arms and legs carelessly about in girlish abandon, and told her mother,

Okay. I've given him brush number two. He was rather surprised, but did not take it too hard. No, it's best that I leave as planned. Who knows, I might even get rich enough and then people won't consider my whims freakish. They'll call them creative brainstorms. Who knows, I might even marry this rich uncle Jonathan. I can't see anything against it — if there's the desire. What do you think, Mama?

Her mother looked up and gazed thoughtfully at her girl's cocky face,

Oh well, if nothing else, there's still the age difference between you. He's old enough to be your father.

Imagine, I had the feeling, Sanna-Sanna countered. I mean, that he's old enough to be my father.

The painful interlude was over. That afternoon Mother Lillemor wrote the letter which Abel Rush handed Jac Tracbac, unopened.

135

16: A Man May Die, But His Deeds Live On

JAC TRACBAC, THE former Jonathan Borck, received Lillemor's letter
on the day before he had his accident in the gym. These were its contents,

Jonathan!

*Following your request, I am sending Sanna to live with you, probably in a
month or so, depending on the date of the wedding.*

*My decision to let her go has nothing to do with your complaints. I have no
sympathy because I find your feeling sorry for yourself disgusting. As famous as
you are, you must have plenty of admirers to keep you company. Sanna may go
because you are wealthy enough to provide a better future for her than I can. I
am sure you will treat her well — about the only good thing I can say about
you.*

*I need to add a few things about her character and how to handle her.
Please, understand that she is not the average person, but very impulsive.
Though alert and friendly in general, she is often depressed and can be quite
nasty, especially about minor things. Then be kind, but firm with her. Kind-
ness, I believe, is essential. Längsäll agrees — and he seems to understand her
much better than I do. He thinks the girl behaves awkwardly because she lacks
self-confidence. Sometimes she sounds conceited, or something like that. That,
according to Längsäll, shows her desire to compensate for her inferiority complex. Her defiance and egoism cover up her low self-esteem. Well, I think
Längsäll's argument is correct. But if you treat her gently she'll respond like a
little angel. You may need some self-discipline, patience and consideration. It's
important that you keep that in mind. Treat people with respect for their indi-
viduality — Längsäll says, and he is right.*

*She is very suspicious, which adds to the problems. She often thinks people
look down on her and make fun of her. Be very careful about jokes. Be gentle so
as not to offend her. She may often claim: I knew that beforehand. That's her
mistrust, you may be sure. Laugh it off with: How foolish, what made you say
so? — or some such thing. Längsäll does this, and quite successfully. She will
readily admit her distrust. Tease them out of her if they are ridiculous, or reason kindly with her. It is like loosening a tight knot, but she'll be pliable and soft
in response.*

*Well, it's late and the mail leaves early in the morning. I have given you
some hints on her character. There's much more to tell, but you'll see yourself
when you get to know the girl. Underneath it all, you are not nasty, and you
may show some measure of responsibility toward her.*

*This much about Sanna-Sanna. I have given Benbé detailed instructions
about her health, which is precarious. In fact, I have written a real catechism, a*

health catechism so to speak. Please, study it carefully. An old landed lady like me had ample opportunity to collect a storehouse of knowledge over the years.

Finally a few lines about us.

I was dumbfounded when Benjamin brought your regards concerning the girl. What egoism, what nerve, what baseness! So, the gentleman feels lonely and nothing else matters. I can't believe your shabbiness. Well, that may be as it is. I had to weigh what was best for the girl — and leave it at that. You have not been much in my thoughts all these years and you ought to find that quite natural. Your actions have now forced me to reflect on what you meant and mean to me. Opening these secret wells has been quite a revelation. You are like a boil on my body, a loathing in my heart, a disgust in my soul, a shame, a stain on my honor in life and to my memory in death. Help yourself — we share and share alike.

I once expressed remorse and you told me to believe in God. I did not then, but I've learned to believe.

I believe in the God of revenge because I've seen him, heard him, felt him. One thing — and with the mark of death in my sick body I confess: I don't believe in heaven, I don't believe in mercy, but I believe in eternal punishment. Now that my days are numbered, I know that I shall live forever.

Signed, Lillemor Borck.

He had quickly scanned the letter, anxious to find news about the children and their planned trip. He read and reread it several times that afternoon. It did not say much, and what it said reinforced his misunderstanding. Sanna was the bride. Caroline was not even mentioned. He studied the letter carefully a second time around. The advice and suggestions concerning the girl's character pleased him. His impending responsibilities filled him with tenderness and pride. Pacing the floor in "grandmother's rooms," he repeated time and again,

Oh, my dearest Lillemor, trust me. I understand as much as Längsäll — I'm not stupid — depend on me, my dearest little Lillemor.

His endearments seemed odd, considering her bitter remarks. Even after the second reading, her deep-seated hatred had not fully filtered down his consciousness. He seemed deaf and blind to her charges. But he marveled at her odd signature. Lillemor Borck. It used to be Lillemor Längsäll. That should be her name still. So why sign Borck? It remained an issue he would brood over for the rest of his life. The simple answer was that her conscience forbade her to use her husband's name, though she mentioned him repeatedly as if thereby wanting to emphasize his unquestioned authority. Her Borck signature also meant that both writer and receiver were Borcks. They shared in the credit of what they had done.

Eventually the gist of her words hit him full force. She blamed him — no, both of them. As if trying to brush it out of his mind, he took the letter to wipe the perspiration off his forehead and mumbled,

The real problem is that she's ill. She meditates on death, pain, her short life span. Wonder what's wrong with her? How can I find out? But even if I knew, what good could I do? How inconsiderate to get me all upset, knowing I can't help her.

Quickly he corrected himself,

I don't mean inconsiderate, I mean ill-considered. Of Lillemor.

Her words pierced the armor of excuses behind which he had tried to hide. It had delayed, but hardly neutralized the blow. He vaulted, arms pressed against his chest, and crouched down. The sudden physical reaction subsided as quickly as it had surfaced. He looked at the letter, shook his head ponderously and said,

It's dangerous, to write a letter like this — simply disastrous.

He threw the letter on the desk he had used during his childhood and which still spotlighted Grandma's grossly misspelled praise. He paced the rooms as if reluctant to leave before deciding what to do about the letter. He kept looking at it, fingering it, mumbling,

It spells disaster. Especially for those who do stunts.

He meant himself and his work as clown. People who later called the famous Tracbac a mental case should have heard his soliloquy in reaction to this frightening, sickening letter. He said,

What shall I do? Reread the letter, memorize what she said about the girl and then burn it — now that I think I've gotten over the initial shock? Or forget it in some drawer — with the chance to suddenly stumble upon it — who knows how I'll react then to all its venom? Imagine finding it when I'm especially depressed or excited — it could wreck my nerves. Or imagine finding it before a performance? That could be fatal, considering my emotional instability. No, I have to burn it now! That's safest all around.

The fact that he acknowledged his emotional instability showed that he knew very well what ailed him. One seemed to cancel out the other. But it also prevented him from making a final decision. He prepared to burn the letter. Then he decided not to do it, arguing,

No. I'm taking all this too hard. I can't bury my head in the sand like an ostrich. Meet danger head-on. I may forget the contents of the letter, but I'll never forget the hurt and shame on reading it. Destroying it will only increase my suffering because I'll keep on brooding over its contents. How did she say it? What expressions did she use? Perhaps she didn't mean it the way I thought? No. I'll have to hide the letter. As painful as it is, it is a document about my life. End of discussion.

Tracbac set out to find a good hiding place. His unused old desk drawer with its single lock was close by and therefore best. He put the letter in, locked it and put the key in his vest pocket. That done, he felt the kind of mock serenity one may find after a funeral. It's done and over with.

Nonetheless, he and those around him knew that his equilibrium was disturbed. When Abel Rush later offered to answer the letter, Jac answered calmly,

That letter concerns only me.

Rush scrutinized the clown's face carefully then said with studied unconcern,

There's a mark on your forehead.

Jac pulled a mirror out of his pocket and checked his face, repeating absentmindedly,

A mark on my forehead?

It took him a few minutes to realize that he had used the letter to wipe his perspiration. It had left some ink stains on his forehead. His own and Lillemor's dread had fused. A drastic change came over the clown when he saw the sign of his and Lillemor's combined dread. The change shocked Rush, who could not understand the reason. But the clown cut a funny grimace, walked to his secretary and whispered,

Beware of big brother, little Abel. Don't you recognize this infamous symbol? It's the Mark of Cain.

Rush could make no sense of his words. But in Tracbac's mind the letter leaving a mark on his forehead was a macabre omen that made perfect sense. The episode further underlined Tracbac's emotional distress. It showed that people know very little about one another. They should never criticize or judge too harshly. This may be a difficult art to practice, but its absolutely necessary.

Tracbac's friends had their doubts about his repeated assurances that his fall from the trapeze was a mere accident. Again, what defines "a mere accident"? Though it may look like a convergence of "unfortunate coincidences," psychological reasons must not be overlooked. The chain of events leading to Jac Tracbac's accident is a good case in point. Lillemor's letter had hurt him more than he cared to admit. All night long he had brooded over whether her cruel condemnation was justified. Then, jittery after a sleepless night, he had performed his normal morning exercises in an abnormal frame of mind. Like an immature little boy he felt defiant and dejected and protested her harsh judgment. He wanted "to show a stiff upper lip, regardless" (at least to himself). If, "contrary to expectations" an accident happened — well, blame a certain person who'll never have redress for her mistake. Cranking the trapeze to its highest point without regard for safety precautions was spiteful and totally unnecessary for the regular work-out. Not to permit the children to watch with the feeble excuse of not wanting to crush their skulls showed his mindset for a serious accident.

Events leading to the letter and from there to Tracbac's "tough luck accident" were easy to trace. The drama began the day young Jonathan Borck

139

met Lillemor Längsäll on Sanna. A consequential act never dies. It reverberates throughout a person's life and survives him.

Yet another point in Tracbac's explanation deserves attention — his flashback vision of "that man I hanged" he claimed had made him dizzy. Here are the details:

Though less illustrious and celebrated, Jac Tracbac had been a top-notch acrobat-clown some twenty-five years ago, performing in an itinerary circus with a partner, Mac Tracbac. They worked as a team of "twin brothers," calling their act "Mactracjacbac" — a funny tongue-twister acronym of their names. Since Mac was the better acrobat and Jac the more resourceful comedian, Mac did the stunts. Jac kept the audience laughing with his jokes. Their professional excellence notwithstanding, their personal relationship was strained from the start. Both were smart enough to know that it was in their own interest to get along. But eventually their relationship soured so much that they decided to separate the following year, thus dissolving their "brotherly act."

Daring, agile and stubborn, Mac used to insist on performing without safety device even at the most dangerous top level. Jac on the other hand, nervous, sickly, fearful, found it difficult to watch his companion dare his life. He insisted on his using a safeguard and even designed a strong steel springboard to this end. Mac refused to use it. At first they argued among themselves, then with the director who could not make up his mind between the two. Finally Mac accused Jac of trying to ruin his partner by making him use this device in order to make himself popular.

Furious about this unfair accusation Jac informed the local police chief that Mac's act was potentially dangerous without the device. The chief immediately ordered Mac to use it. Jac had won. He personally supervised the installation of the device with an especially sturdy steel spring. But Mac was furious.

The accident happened a few days later, before the safety rope had been seriously tested. Mac's act included a jump with two or three somersaults between two swinging trapeze. During Mac's first somersault the rope pulled too far out, the slack looping around the acrobat's neck during the second somersault. He never completed the third somersault. In a straight fall, he remained dangling in midair, his neck broken. Then the rope broke at the winch under the roof and the man fell to the ground, dead. Had the steel spring been more flexible and less rigid, the outcome might have been less severe.

The audience screamed as circus attendants quickly removed the body. People jumped out of their seats. The noise became unbearable. Suddenly the shouts leveled off, the crowd wondering. What was the other clown doing in the arena? He stood there, his head thrown back, his face up, his mouth wide open, his arms thrown up as if trying to catch his partner in midair. Then, stooping forward, he walked slowly to the spot where the body had left a deep hole in the sawdust. Staring at it, he moved his hands hesitantly, as if searching for his comrade. Was this the continuation of the act? Had there been an accident or not? Was this one more of the tricks circus artists contrive to titillate the nerves of their audience?

Aware that an overly upset audience may easily run amok, the circus director had watched anxiously. In the sudden calm he saw the other clown's continued performance as a maneuver to reverse the potential mob action. Thus he approached the clown, who kept looking for his fallen partner in the sawdust pile, patted him on his shoulder and told him good-naturedly,

Hi, Jac, what are you waiting for? It's your turn to show what you can do! In a whisper he added, Turn somersault! Do anything you want! Laugh! Shout! Anything!

For a few seconds the clown stared a him, dumbfounded. He would never know whether he knew what had happened or not. When told to continue, he was confused enough to imagine a minor accident. With a tremendous scream, a grotesque clown's howl, a blend of heartfelt subconscious terror and the belly laugh expected of him, he somersaulted and cartwheeled, rolled back and forth across the arena, climbed the trapeze and, a death cry on his lips, he took a leap far more dangerous than the one that had killed his comrade. His overstimulated brain had given his body an agility he had never had before.

It was then that suddenly the entire scope of what had happened hit him full force. His head bent, he walked toward the exit. But the director pushed him back, hit him, screaming,

More, more, lazy Jac!

The audience roared, convinced of watching a spine-tingling, exceptionally well-done horror scene at the end of which the two partners would reemerge together again. Encouraged by the public's shouts, Jac continued his act. He bounced on his knees across the arena and along the barrier, chomping and raving like a crazy ape, screaming,

Quiet you idiots, for goodness sake! Why don't you shut up, you miserable creatures! A man has died! Don't you understand? A man has died!

But the people heard nothing beyond their own roaring laughter, their excitement, their shouts. They saw the clown taking a sudden leap and falling prone on his back. That convinced the audience. This was an exciting, funny piece of entertainment.

The director ordered his stagehands to carry Jac out as quickly as his partner before him. The audience, surprised, turned restless again, unhappy that the two clowns failed to return and acknowledge their stormy applause. People whistled and booed. Some began to stamp their feet in a frenzy.

Stepping out in cold blood and facing the mob, the director saved the situation again. He bowed elegantly in the ensuing hush and declared,

Ladies and gentlemen! Your applause touches us deeply. We regret that one brother is too exhausted to receive your esteemed applause. The other thinks it's unfair to appear without his partner. We are sorry.

Miffed at the strange reason given, the audience wondered who of the two was too weak. But they liked this brotherly love act and received the director's news with cheers and shouts. The next act was announced.

The truth was that none of the brothers could come out. One lay on an old shag sofa, the other sat beside him, occasionally stroking gently across his cheek, or shaking his head off and on as if to say,

Well, ladies and gentlemen, this can really happen if fate wills it. Who is to blame?

A doctor appeared to confirm the death. That done, he checked the other clown. Worried about his emotional stress, he gave Jac a strong morphine injection. Jac never noticed. He was half-asleep when attendants carried him back to his quarters.

Tracbac's nerves were totally shot. He sought treatment in a private nursing home. After a few months he was well enough to continue his recuperation in Florida. The circus director visited him to discuss a new contract. He told the clown,

You were fabulous that awful night. I had a hard time to keep my hands still.

Jac Tracbac answered morosely,

Well, I might have been. But I can do this only when feeling threatened and desperate.

The director tried a joke,

All right. Then we'll frighten you.

This joke eventually generated the famous Jac Tracbac repertory which played on variations of terror.

They did the first show in the same city where it had happened to see whether people remembered Jac's performance following the accident as an "admirable presence of mind," or as "despicably callous." It was neither the one nor the other. Public opinion is hard to predict.

He was well received. Consequently the fateful city became the cradle of Tracbac's fame. Twenty years later, confined to the couch with his leg in a cast and scribbling on what Siv thought were his memoirs, Tracbac still agonized over his partner's death and the details surrounding it. Still, the elimination of his former comrade and adversary had paved not only the way to his own success. It had done more than that — it had provided the very source on which Jac Tracbac's fame rested now. A few years after his triumphant comeback the people nicknamed him "Clown Terror." Despite all this, in his own mind Jac remained the dead man's partner, as he explained,

Poor Mac never had a chance to dissolve the partnership. I prevented him.

He searched for close relatives, but found only an old aunt whom he gave a decent pension. She later turned out to be an impostor and nowhere near related to Mac. Tracbac shrugged it off,

Can I help it the poor fellow left nothing but a swindler? Continue the pension. Dishonesty is no fun; poor thing needs some consolation. Decency has its own reward.

The hounded syndicate continued to agonize. One nice day the gentlemen convened and wanted to know specifics. Jac waved his little notebook cockily about and told them,

Look here, I almost finished the skit.

The answer left the gentlemen still guessing. Mr. Adam felt oafish asking,

I don't want to aggravate you — but how many partners do you need?

The clown tried to sound cute,

As many as the premises permit.

That worried Mr. Judah who sighed and mumbled,

As many as the premises will hold?

The clown grinned,

More than that. As many as the lines allow. The audience is going to be my partner. On stage I'll be solo.

The gentlemen cheered, still bewildered. Eventually Mr. Adam got up enough courage to comment,

But Jac. Your skits tend to revolve around this moment of fear, the famous Tracbac terror. How are you going to manage that — ?

You mean who's going to frighten the clown? Silly question — my partner of course. The audience will do that. Don't you think they can?

Seeing the gentlemen's nonplussed smiles, he mocked,

Good and cheap, right? A partner who pays his own way. Long live the audience clown!

17: Somersault

THE POOR GENTLEMEN of the syndicate were in for more disappoint-ments. The aggravation of not knowing the skit's contents soon over-shadowed their happiness about Jac's completing the draft. Frustrated, they probed until Jac Tracbac finally told his secretary to reveal that this time his extraordinary act involved a conversation between him and the audience. He, Jac, would explore some general thoughts on his profession to stimulate and challenge the good people. In short, he intended to tell people certain truths.

Tell people the truth? After some quick, intense deliberations, Mr. Adam declared,

This has to be stopped. In Tracbac's own interest. Tell the audience the truth? Our friend Denny ought to look into this. He's the psychologist. Let him decide.

They called a meeting and requested O'Henny's attendance. Instead of meeting as usual in the gatekeeper's lodge near the clown's home, they rented a conference room at the Hotel Ambassador for the purpose.

O'Henny arrived totally ignorant of the topic under discussion. His ha-bitual aloofness contrasted sharply with the agitated atmosphere around him. Abel Rush looked nervous and insecure when Mr. Adams with trembling voice and hands read Tracbac's message to the group. O'Henny grinned,

Really, this idea of telling people the truth sounds rather feeble-minded. The gentlemen agreed wholeheartedly,

That's right. Absolutely correct!

O'Henny continued,

Still, it's an interesting thought. But, whatever it is, I'm not going to get involved in this. The tour might turn out to be a flop and both you and Tracbac stand to lose a lot of money. I won't, because I'm not stupid enough to invest my money in a clown. So, I really don't care.

Judah snapped his stubby fingers, whining,

But my dear friend, my dear friend! Couldn't you help us out? He mustn't perform unless he changes his program.

The doctor became impatient,

So, what shall I do about that?

You could help us. Talk him out of it!

Indeed. Of course, I could do that. Let me call him right now, O'Henny said.

O'Henny called. Tracbac answered the telephone. O'Henny said,

Jac, it's about your tour. I'm here with your gentlemen and they're asking you to delay until you come up with another program. Now, don't blow your top, your excellency.

But Tracbac remained furious. Gasping for breath, he screamed,

How dare they? They've been after me for six months. They've bothered me no end —

The doctor said gently,

Please, don't scream, your excellency, you're cracking your phone.

Somewhat calmer the clown said,

Denny-Henny. My regards to the gentlemen; tell them to kiss me.

I shall, your majesty, the doctor said and hung up. He relayed the message.

The gentlemen received it in silence, pacing the floor and glumly pondering their predicament. O'Henny sat down by the desk, lit a cigarette and offered one to Abel Rush. After a long while the honorable senator Mr. Adam stopped in front of the doctor and said,

Denny, my boy, I've always appreciated your input. I want you to do us a favor. Considering the circumstances, we have to call the tour off, not just for our sake. Tracbac needs it even more. You've suggested your nursing home as a good place to treat our mutual friend on numerous occasions.

That's right, the doctor readily agreed.

The senator continued weightily,

Good. I think this is the time to start. Lately our friend's idiosyncrasies have taken on alarming proportions. For example —

He cited half a dozen incidents. Talking all at once, the other gentlemen added at least as many. Finally the doctor asked,

All right, what is it you want? That I lock Jac up in my nursing home until he comes to his senses?

As simpleminded as agitated, the others shouted agreement,

That's right! That's right!

O'Henny said,

All right, that shouldn't be impossible. Only question I have is: who'll then be running the nursing home? I or my patient Tracbac? I have a strong feeling that Jac wants to run his own affairs. I may be able to run the home, but I can't run Jac Tracbac. Vice versa, he can't run my nursing home. But he is capable of running his own business — better than anyone else can. What you propose is sheer nonsense. Leave me alone!

Their zeal blinded them. They did not leave him alone. With his most resonant senatorial voice, Mr. Adam coaxed,

Denny, you ought to remember your duty as a physician. Tracbac needs help. Badly.

The young man stood rigid, breathing heavily, his legs wide apart, his head lowered between his solid shoulders. His handsome eyes glittered rapaciously as he sniffed,

My duty? You're getting on my nerves. If I were to do my duty I would lock you up, gentlemen. Only I wouldn't send you to a hospital. Heck no, you don't need medical treatment. I'd have *you* locked up in Sing-Sing. And I might do just that!

The three men were outraged. Mr. Adam screamed, Mr. Cow bellowed, Mr. Peck squeaked,

What? What? What?

Tiny Mr. Judah stuck his plump hands nervously into the air and said,

Sing-Sing? Why? What have I done?

O'Henny told him off, cutting scorn in his voice,

What you and the others have done? Frankly, I don't care what you've done. But you're not stupid enough not to know. You know also that I'd have no difficulty getting you there, all of you. It might be a costly enterprise, but pretty efficient.

He turned to leave. Swallowing heavily, the three gentlemen did not answer. They knew the young man's incredible ruthlessness. They knew also his pull with a fabulously wealthy millionaire. For a while they were silent. Then they whined and bleated like small, frightened lambs,

What's this? How come you're losing your temper? What a most cruel misunderstanding!

O'Henny rang the bell for the maître d'. When he arrived O'Henny told him calmly,

Please, see these gentlemen out. They're disgusting. Don't you agree?

Knowing O'Henny too well to be surprised, he ushered them out. Like frightened dogs, the three gentlemen left without another word. If the good gentlemen thought their exit miserable, they had yet another surprise coming: their gold-brimmed Tracbac syndicate was doomed.

Facing his friend alone, Abel Rush complained bitterly,

Those jerks deserved the thrashing. But with your control of the whip that wasn't difficult to accomplish. Now let me remind you that as a physician you need to consider Tracbac's mental health now. I'm beginning to wonder . . .

He touched his forehead with his index finger and reported several recent incidents, among them the clown calling an ink stain on his forehead his Mark of Cain. The physician listened carefully. Then he ordered lunch for both. They ate in utter silence. After the meal O'Henny said finally,

Let's drive out to his place. His mention of the Cain's Mark means that something else is on his mind. Occasionally even smart people brood, though I wouldn't call it smart doing that. Now the gentlemen have thrown him further off balance. We'll have to cheer him up.

They drove to the clown's estate. By the gate they encountered Mr. Cow, the syndicate's trusted lawyer. As if oblivious to O'Henny's Sing-Sing threat, Cow greeted his antagonist with outstretched hands. A broad smile on his wrinkled lips, he said,

Dear O'Henny. Let's never misjudge each other again.

Ignoring the hands, the physician said morosely,

Trust is fine as long as it can last.

When Mr. Cow turned, O'Henny shook his forefinger at Mr. Cow's broad back, turned to Longfellow and said gruffly,

I forbid you to let this customer inside without special permission from me or your boss.

The Negro rolled his eyes and said heatedly,

My boss' permission? He sent for him.

The two young men exchanged looks of surprise. Now what? They had believed themselves to be experts on the human psyche. Tracbac conferring with Mr. Cow, a man clearly on his way out and now smiling all over his face did not make sense! They entered the mansion and found the owner waiting for them in the hall, feigning sympathy with Rush,

My poor boy. It's my sad duty to inform you that you lost your job. But you may stay on as my personal secretary. Your salary will be the same — with an added bonus for good behavior.

An ungrateful Abel Rush still wanted to know,

That doesn't explain fickleness. Who's given me the boot? Mr. Cow?

The clown answered softly,

Not at all. The syndicate no longer needs your services for the simple reason that I dissolved it. From now on just one person makes the decisions around here. The syndicate served one function — to negotiate the contracts between me, the movie companies and the twenty cities. That automatically reverts to me. I'll settle it in a jiffy.

Visibly nervous, Rush told him,

Sir, I have certainly no reason to praise the syndicate, but I was hired to work for them. I want no part of your shenanigans. The whole thing stinks.

Tracbac rubbed his hands and grinned,

Did you say stinks? That's putting it mildly. Doesn't do justice to my slick maneuvers at all. Let me add, I have not the slightest intention to involve a sucker like you in our affairs. Remember, my boy, one schemer needs another schemer to concoct successful schemes, or he's out of luck. Now, Mr. Cow has the proper qualifications — a traitor to the core. He was the legal soul of the syndicate. He's the only one familiar with its legal entanglements. He's therefore the right man to break it up. Might cost me a few extra dollars, but so what? I earn enough. Remember, the enemy needs to be attacked from inside. That cuts war expenses by fifty percent.

Hobbling on his crutches, the small man gave the two men before him a conceited, airy glance and Abel a patronizing slap on the shoulder.

O'Henny said,

The scheme isn't bad and you'll pull it off all right, Tracbac. You should've been a great potentate, or a great crook, which actually amounts to the same anyway.

Tracbac was insulted. He considered himself linked to royalty, so he snorted,

It's hardly the same. As for myself, I took the golden mean between king and crook — the great buffoon.

With that he hobbled over to Siv. Grinning and rubbing his hands, he called,

The stupid ass keeps braying about his meager pasture while his peasant master keeps reaping the fat harvest.

Humiliated, Rush shook his head, muttering,

Well, I'm not so sure he's in his right mind. But wily he sure is.

Denny laughed,

I think that quite the opposite is true. He's not wily, but very clever, for sure.

Outside Siv's door the clown stopped short. His face covered with a deep, crimson blush and suddenly he looked neither smart nor wily. Biting his lower lip and pulling his earlobes, he stared cross-eyed at the floor, lost in thought. His complicated errand with Siv overwhelmed him more than he could muster. Sanna had become a big problem.

Admittedly, the problem preoccupied Siv too. The arrival of a daughter she had never known existed pained her. She felt suddenly superfluous. Sure, Jac would continue to like her, as much as he was capable of liking at all. But in Siv's eyes the girl was "the intruder." From now on this stranger would replace her — literally push her aside. The little melancholy gypsy could not help being jealous. To be divorced from Jac was one thing. That even had its advantages. But to be replaced and lose him completely — well, that was something else entirely. Knowing that Jac could not do without her in the long run made the situation worse, though that, in fact, was her only comfort. Whenever she worked in New York Jac would soon send a letter telling her, in several variations,

My dear Siv, it's been surprisingly long since your art was discussed in the newspapers, or been on exhibition. You know that I'm not given to flattery, but I consider it a crime to see your talent wasted. Convinced that your social obligations in New York undermine your work habits, I strongly suggest that you find a quiet place where you can work in peace.

Siv's answer would be short,

If there's such a place it must exist somewhere in the Pacific Ocean. All right, my egoist, I'm packing my gear and head back —

Her "giving in to Jac's egoism" became routine in their relationship. But this time around things were different. Siv felt suddenly "free," absolutely free for furtive crying sessions into her pillow. Outwardly she remained calm, trying to find the best solution for both of them. She told him,

If now Benbé and his wife (calling her "Benbé's wife" was much easier than saying "your daughter") come here this fall they'll arrive just in time for your opening night. Benbé was always interested in what you did. Send them a telegram, Jac, just to make sure!

Although hurt by the "young'un's lack of interest," Jac finally sent them a wire. Benbé wired back at once. Their boat was scheduled to arrive a few days before the event. A second telegram followed, announcing their arrival on the very day of his premiere.

Holding the first of the two telegrams, Jac entered Siv's room. She read it and announced, using Jac's own words,

Excellent. That's just excellent.

Her private ruminations took a different turn,

It's unpleasant to meet this intruder. Of course, I can't leave Jac before making sure he's at ease with her. I'll also need to advise her on his moods and habits. I owe him that much.

Having thus made up her mind, she calmly resumed her work and said,

It'll be nice to meet the girl. Once opening night is over, I'll return with her to let her settle in. That done, I won't be visiting as often and be less involved than before.

She smiled, adding,

After all, we are legally divorced. It's not proper that I live with you — I think it's even against the law —

The clown's blush deepened. His eyes expressed relief as if a burden had been lifted from his heart. Unaware of how foolish and clumsy he looked, he stammered,

So, it's really been on your mind too, Siv? What a relief! You're so right and I agree wholeheartedly — it isn't proper, really. It was different when it was just between the two of us, and our friends. They knew us, so they never misunderstood. It's not the same when Sanna is here. What kind of impression will she get? A bad one? I'm her father, it's my duty — the poor man actually uttered the word "duty" as if he were the chief justice of the United States or the archbishop of the Anglican church — yes, it's my duty to consider such matters. Let me tell you. We Borcks are the worst kind of petty bourgeois — old-fashioned, well, yes, real bigots. I can see you smile, my girl. It's the truth. Sure, you can't say that I'm intolerant. But then, I'm just one of those whoopee artists. Sanna's mother is a Borck. She's so very strict —

He fell silent. Staring into empty space he repeated dully,

She's strict, extremely strict — with herself and others —

Siv continued painting in silence. He awakened. Resolute, he continued,

Her — her stepfather is an utterly decent fellow. But I understand the Längsälls are Pietists, a sort of Quakers, you know. So, the girl grew up in a provincial home with strict rules. I've thought about this a great deal, believe me. You may really pity me — it's caused me a lot of anguish trying to decide whether I should talk to you or not. I don't want you to misunderstand me. Now, you've given it some thought too. You've brooded perhaps as much as I did. And come up with the same result. Talk about two hearts — one soul! You're phenomenal, amber-eyes. You're grand, simply, outright grand!

Siv said,

Don't touch me — I'm painting —

Rationalizing his sentiments further, the clown resumed happily,

You've always preferred to live in New York. Your art, elegant and refined, thrives in the glitter of city life. It's bound to wither in this dark, gloomy place. Your art must come first, ahead of other concerns. You mustn't waste or neglect your talent— ever. Come to think of it, you shouldn't even return with Sanna after opening night. She must think it odd to see you here, acting like the hostess, knowing you and I have been divorced for years — wouldn't you say?

Interrupting his pretentious gush, he lapsed into a naively sanctimonious tone. He sounded suddenly like Sanna's little pastor's adjunct,

Don't misunderstand me now. You must know, yes you do know that I never considered our relationship questionable. To the contrary. Oh, you know very well what you've meant to me. One doesn't talk about such things. One shouldn't. It's too delicate, too brittle to put into words — they're too clumsy. But now we must consider my daughter — that's our responsibility —

Siv interrupted him with a soothing smile,

But, dear Jac. Why waste so many words on the subject? We both agree that my presence here is absolutely improper under the present circumstances —

The clown corrected her with the mien of a schoolmaster,

Under the approaching circumstances. So far it hasn't been wrong — to the contrary — absolutely, the opposite is true.

Siv smiled,

Thanks. But now leave me in peace. I'll have to finish your portrait before I leave for New York. I'm not going to lug it along —

With an air of importance the clown advised her,

You ought to exhibit it in the foyer during opening night. You're so impractical, really, my child. Wonder who's going to think for you when I'll stop doing it?

Utterly calm, she contradicted him as she waved him goodbye,

Well, there'll always be a solution.

He threw her a kiss and left the room, his heart eased, his problem solved. He wouldn't bring his daughter into a milieu that he knew her strict mother Lillemor would consider unsuited for her. The thought of being without Siv occurred to him, faintly, in the secret recesses of his heart. But his pride in playing the good father and sacrificing himself for his child took precedence and mooted the thought of losing her for the time being. With her angelic goodness, Siv had immediately understood his concerns and eased his conscience!

He threw bread crumbs at the ducks and watched them flutter about as they screeched and fought for the morsels. Singing in treble above the din, he meditated,

Angels in charge of heaven tell us to tread lightly into heaven's gates. Rejoice, they say, but beware of clumsily trampling on the holy abode.

The ducks were unmoved. They continued their spats. He screamed,

All right. Skim the best for yourself first, but don't grudge your friend some decent leftovers. Nasty ducks. Nasty characters.

Siv sat perfectly still, the brush hanging in her limp hand. Listless and tired, she listened to Jac's harsh, shrill voice. She knew the tune, but not the words. From the easel before her "Clown Terror" grinned at her with an immense mouth and spasmodic, crinkled lips. It gave her the feeling that the tune issued from there.

A few days later, maintaining he needed to investigate the theater and its stage, talk to the management, etc., etc. Jac Tracbac drove to the city where he was scheduled to start his tour. Since all this had already been settled, this trip was unnecessary. But Tracbac felt compelled to check that everything was all right. With a weighty mien he pinched his earlobes and walked the circumference of the colossal circus building, the Capitolium. For want of anything better to do, he stuck his head through the receptionist cubicle, inquiring how many people this circus could seat. Delighted with the answer he said,

Blazes. That'll be plenty of dough!

That done, he went to the best hotel in the city, the nearby Auditorium Annex and reserved with painstaking care one room for himself and one for his daughter and conjectured son-in-law Benbé. Unable to think of anything else that needed to be done, he returned home.

Hiawatha opened the gate to let his car pass. Running alongside and rolling his eyes like a seasoned actor in a tragedy, the boy announced gravely,

Sir. Your wife has cleared out!

Tracbac was shocked.

What is it you're saying?

The boy bared his white teeth, feeling wickedly elated like all young bearers of important, even sad news. He tried hard to hide his grin when he repeated,

Sir, your wife has split!

Longfellow came running. Pushing the boy aside, he explained,

It's just a joke, Sir. When Mrs. Siv left she gave this pup a ten dollar bill, saying she's running away, never to return. The boy took her words for real along with the money, Sir.

Longfellow grinned, proud of his pun.

Oh, that's what it is, Tracbac mumbled as he drove up to his black entrance door. The vestibule with its barbaric, colorful chests and collection of Indian objects felt suddenly uncannily empty. It felt like an abandoned heathen temple. DeGrazy came to welcome him, embarrassing Tracbac who felt like a husband suddenly having to admit his wife's philandering to an outsider. Morosely he said,

I hear that Siv has left. Did she leave any message?

DeGrazy answered,

Of course. She asked me to relay her regards. Nothing more, actually. She said that you knew about her departure.

Tracbac mumbled,

Yes. Sure. Certainly. I knew that. I just thought she might have left a special message. Well, all right. It's all right.

The clown drifted through his maze, switching all the lights on as he passed in a new mania for illumination. When he saw a Negro servant in one room turning them off behind him, he bellowed,

Turn it on again, you idiot! You turn off just one more light here and I'll lock you in with the garbage.

Frightened, the Negro switched the lights on again, then ran to warn his buddies in the servants' quarters. The servants knew Tracbac as a good-hearted man and liked him. But they knew also how impossible he could be at times, outright underhanded and as sly as an ape when angry. Limping on his crutches and cutting faces, he resembled an ape as he mumbled under his breath,

Sure. To think, no sooner than my back is turned. As if she couldn't have waited the three weeks until Sanna arrives. No, not the least consideration for me. Plain as day. New York calling. It's dull here. She wants to dance — tra-lala —

He attempted a few pirouettes in his illuminated loneliness, grimacing with the pain his bad leg caused him. Eventually he came to "grandmother's room." Lighting up, he stopped before his desk. Lillemor's letter was in its drawer, locked away, out of sight. He had lost the key, misplaced it somewhere. But he knew that the letter existed. Its physical intangibility would never diminish the devastation it had caused. His fist came down hard on the desktop three times. Bitter, he said,

You are hard, Lillemor. Yes, you are. Hard. Triple hard. Now you've made me sacrifice even Siv for your sake. Sure. Right. You're giving me Sanna instead. Excellent. We share. We share. Yes. But hard you are. As hard as a rock. Excellent. Excellent.

As if protesting her toughness and wishing to shame her, he turned the lights off in the room. They might burn everywhere else. But not here. The letter must be left in darkness.

His feather duster waving in his hand, Axelsson came shuffling through the hall, driveling,

Nathan, you're a dog. You filched from the Jew, you stole from your own grandmother. You were a perpetual liar. My dog had to die because of you. Say that you are not a dog, Nathan! You can't deny that, can you?

The old fellow smelled whisky for miles around. Making a wide circle around him, Tracbac snorted,

Oh, for crying out loud.

The old man's babble depressed him even more and he sought refuge in Siv's room. Trembling, hoping against all hope, he wanted to find some consolation, some note she might have left on her desk. Something. Anything. Carefully, like a detective, he searched the small apartment. But he found nothing. Eventually he gazed at his portrait. "Clown Terror." It made him ill at ease. But suddenly he cheered up. The painting was far from finished. He could easily see that. With a chuckle he clapped his hands, calling,

Oh no, my little Siv. You can't fool me. You wouldn't leave this masterpiece incomplete! No. You'll be back, for sure, won't you?.

A few weeks later Tracbac and Abel Rush stood side by side on the railroad platform in the city where the tour was about to begin. They were waiting for Jac's daughter to arrive. Tracbac was nervous. His breathing came heavy, in spurts. Rush was hardly less nervous. The train was five hours late. Mindful that Jac's performance was due to start in half an hour, Rush kept pulling the clown's arm. But Jac sputtered with rage and stuck his cane at the secretary's legs. The scene resembled one of his spontaneous circus skits. Rush reminded him,

Remember — you're just going to say "hello." No more. Afterward she'll be all yours.

Tracbac promised.

Finally the express came rolling in. Tracbac detected Benbé's round, happy face in a window right away. He called and waved his hat while the train came to a stop. Benbé shouted back. Tracbac ran forward to meet them and saw a young, smiling woman jumping off and greeting him with outstretched arms,

Well, here we are —

Tracbac stared at her. This beautiful, smiling, red-cheeked, healthy, beaming girl was his daughter? He broke into sudden sobs. His hands shook as he embraced the girl, stammering,

Child, my dear child.

He did not dare to kiss her but threw himself into Rush's arms, mumbling,

I've seen her. Let's hurry. Tell her that we'll meet her after the performance.

Anxious to get going, Rush turned his head and relayed Jac's regards, adding,

We're in an awful hurry.

They had hardly turned their backs when a lanky, skinny, sickly looking, pimple-faced girl followed behind the two. Surprised and disappointed, she looked around, wondering,

My father? Didn't my father come to meet me?

Benbé hissed,

Why, yes. But he was in an awful hurry. What kept you dawdling so long?

The girl defended herself, subdued,

Oh, I just put some color on my cheeks. It's customary in this country. I so want to make a good impression.

Then her sad face lighted up. Stepping out on the platform, she opened her arms wide and mumbled with a blissful smile,

My father, I'm here. In a few minutes I'll see my famous father and he'll meet his Sanna.

People turned their heads as they rushed past, staring at the strange creature. Caroline blushed and took her sister's arm. She was embarrassed. And ashamed for feeling embarrassed.

18: From A Clown's Catechism I

ANNOUNCER: Hello! Hello! Jac Tracbac's first performance from the Capitolium will start in seven minutes. My glass cubicle up here on the gallery allows me a grand view on the park below. The weather is not the best — but despite the November mists rolling in from the sea, I can see the bright stream of cars coming down the ramp off the highway. The chief of the mounted police is in charge. Everything under control. Jac has arrived, though he forgot to shake hands with me. A king's punctuality gauges the civility of the performer and in that respect our Jac is king. He hates to wait and does not want others to wait for him. His promptness assures that his audience appears on time. I asked the cashier whether the performance was sold out and she told me,

No, not quite. Only 9000 of our 4800 seats. Joker, that kid. 4800 at $20.00 per seat makes a grand total of $9600.00 per performance. Not bad. Now, Jac donated 40% of the gross profits to the needy. He does not consider it charity. Most of my ideas come from the poor, he tells me. They are my colleagues. I guess you know that Jac's suing the Tracbac syndicate. Manipulations, he claims. He's dissolved the syndicate. No trial date set yet. It's hard to see now — looks as though the car line down Lake Avenue is abating. A crowd is gathering in the park to catch a glimpse of Jac. The press got our friend Pech for an interview — you know: Pech is Pech and nothing but Pech. We asked him whether the rumor of Jac's long-lost daughter being found was true. No, not a daughter, but his mother-in-law, Pech said. He's been able to dodge her for twenty years. Now, cars have stopped arriving. The police chief stands at attention on the stairs for the governor's party. I'll have to leave this place and crawl into the other glass booth. Ladies and gentlemen — I'll be back in two minutes.

JAC. Abel, why do you keep staring at the clock? You look extremely annoyed.

ABEL. We're two minutes late.

JAC.	Ash, that's your imagination. We came here directly from the station and got dressed — well, I didn't have to dress up exactly. Do I look all right, Abel? I do? Great. Did you see her? What a pretty girl she is! Sure, it really shouldn't matter. And did you see how healthy she looked? After a long trip like that? Apple-cheeked and happy. Why did her mother say she's sickly? I can't help wondering —
ABEL.	Sorry, Jac — but we're always on time —
JAC.	Yes, indeed. I've always been. That's why it won't hurt to be a few minutes late for a change. Why always be the same? Always on the dot. Frightfully dull, don't you think? — No, Abel, there's nothing wrong with the girl. Thank goodness. One less worry. What? What about the clock? Ah well, all right, hand me the catechism. And the rattle. Now then, we're ready. My pants properly zipped up? Listen, that's nothing to laugh about! Damn it, it's most important for a guy who's about to perform in public. Give me an aspirin, please. I have a headache —
ANNOUNCER.	Now then. I'm in my new glass cubicle, sitting sort of like a diver in his bell jar on the bottom of the sea. Sea of people! This soundproof double glass wall muffles the deafening applause for Jac outside. That leaves us free to talk. My only chance, actually, at getting in a word edgewise. Next to this cubicle outside stand a table and a chair — Jac's only props this afternoon. My aide Johnny is outside too. He'll hand me the latest gossip in the hall through a flap in my glass wall. I see all kinds of acrobat props hanging from the rooftop. Now, let's look at the audience. The color of fashion this fall seems to be mole gray, supposedly Jac's favorite. I nice compliment to our dear Jac. The governor and his wife are now taking their seats in the center box. She looks stunning, as always. There's no time to present other famous folk. Oh yes! There's our great senator Adams, film magnate Judah next to him. Both members of the recently dissolved syndicate. They mustn't feel overly offended. Ah! Something special here. My neighbor in the box next to my cubicle is the most beautiful gypsy in the United States — Siva Yala, dancer, artist, Jac's wife — ex wife that is. Her dress, well what's her dress like — brown suède. Why? Perhaps it's current gypsy-fashion. Her escort is no less famous — eminent neurosurgeon Dr. O'Henny — brother of oil-O'Henny. What a good-looking pair! Wonder what old Jac thinks of

156

that . . . . Oh dear, it's two minutes past time. Imagine 4,800 of us filing in on time and the sugar lump on his table still shines in all its loneliness. Sugar lump — it's the electrical wire box connecting all the microphones running through the walls of this enclosure. Ah! There's a stir outside! Oh! Great! This soundproof booth has its advantages. The audience is applauding wildly — the screams must be deafening. Everyone is rising to his feet. Jac's coming up the walkway. But why — why on earth aren't they lifting the boom? Oh, he's jumping across, clown style. Wonder what that'll do to his injured leg. Well, oh no, well, yes. He made it, but just by a hair. Almost took a nose dive. The audience got frightened. A young lady not far from where I'm sitting flings her arms about, screaming something. People around her are trying to calm her down. Jac notices. He's waving at her. Now, he's coming this way, his leg dragging slightly. Oh, yes (suppressing his excitement) Hi, glad to see you, Jac.

JAC. (in the same manner) Hi yourself. How're you doing?

ANNOUNCER. Hm, hm. Fancy that. Jac himself opening the cubicle door to shake hands with me. Won't wash it for a week. He's wearing coat tails of brown suede — yes, same as Siv — scarlet vest with gold embroidery, white pants with immense ruby buckle, white medium-high boots with ruby buttons. In his right hand is a long silver rattle, about a foot long, with a golden clapper and a large red spinel at the top. It's a present from the State of Missouri for his help during the flood a few years ago. He carries a small notebook in his other hand — presumably containing his clown catechism. Now what's he putting on the table? — Gee whiz! Yes, a pair of small brown suede ladies gloves. Smoothes them down with his long, slim fingers. Must be some souvenir, mascot perhaps. The audience is going wild, though he hasn't even said Hello. He's returning to the barrier — oh, he's taking a walk around the arena to greet people in good old clown fashion. He's rattling as he marches along, rattling and bowing to the audience like a decent old fellow. Flowers come floating down. Kisses are thrown — good grief, just getting a third of that . . . . Some daring lady throws her arms around his neck. Poor Jac, she's seventy, at least. He walks on, trying to move away from the barrier, stops before the governor's box and bows — governor's wife throws him a rose. He picks it up and fastens it in his buttonhole. Walks on, rattling as he

157

walks. A quick handshake with Adam and Judah — obviously no hard feelings there. He stops again — oh yes, right below Siva Yala's box. My goodness, what a bow! His hand over his heart, almost down to the floor — another bow — well, won't she throw him a flower? Noooo, oh well. She looks real shy, literally shy. And I thought there aren't any shy ladies left on this earth. Modest yes, but shy? Now. He's steering directly to his table, rattling ever wilder and wilder. Probably to get the people to quiet down. They're settling down. Time for me to be quiet.

JAC.   (in sing-song)

> *Rattle, clown, rattle.*
> *Tremble, heart, tremble.*

Ladies and gentlemen, I'm happy to welcome you here this afternoon. I'm very happy indeed, as happy as a clown can be who's been able to rally so many wonderful, kind, intelligent people. We have a full house. Now, I have advertised this performance for adults only. No children allowed. Despite that, I'm going to ask you to act like children: naive, impulsive, spoiled, willful — as children are these days. So go ahead. No restrains.

I shall read selected chapters from my catechism. I got the idea from a mother who wrote a health catechism for her daughter. Her efforts were totally unnecessary. I've seen the girl and never have I seen a healthier, sounder girl. So, that little mother — her gloves lie here before me — must have exaggerated. But that's the way mothers are, and we must put up with them. Nevertheless, the idea to write a catechism for clowns I got from her. I have known quite a few clowns in my life, myself included. We aren't always healthy and need a few pills here and there — as well as good advice.

Well, ladies and gentlemen, so that you may profit from these "pills," I'm asking you to pretend. Be clowns while I'm talking to you and you'll get full value for your dollar. Am I asking too much? First I want you to be children; now it's clowns. It's not as hard as you may think. It simply means being yourself, nothing else.

Now, what is a clown? Above all, he is a human being — a human being wearing funny gear. Look at me. I look like a better toady. And that's what I am. A clown is a toady. Always ready to serve his master — the people. They expect

158

him to flatter — tell lies, or, better yet, tell the truth dressed out as jokes; make people think: the fellow is joking, he's exaggerating — because it's not me — (in off-key sing-song) no, that's not the way I am — Oh, noooooooo! No? No? Oh yes, you are. Yes. YES INDEED.

Therefore, ladies and gentlemen, it should be easy for you to play the toady — so, by all means, let yourself go. Leoncavallo's harlequin declares that his heart and his other organs are human. No one denies that. The worst scoundrel is a human being. And what is a human being? My clown's rattle for the correct answer.

ANNOUNCER. It took a minute, but the public is getting the drift. There's a flood of answers — they're all screaming at once, drowning each other out. The clown is holding his ears. No telling whether they're any good. The clown sounds his rattle, asks for silence.

JAC. Ha. I fooled you there and I keep my rattle. I had the one and only right answer. I kept quiet. You see, silence is the only right answer to a stupid question. Dear sisters and brothers, dear toady souls, never ask this question. I'd feel sorry for you if you did. It's the end of stupidity to ask what a human being is. No, just go ahead and be yourself. Be human because that's what you are — no more, no less.

About the clown — a human being in funny garb. Now, we mustn't judge people by their clothes. If I see a decent-looking woman, how can I be sure that she is decent? Take the other extreme — a woman, scantily dressed, everything hanging out for all to see. Do I know she's a whore? See, I don't. Again, I can't be sure whether a man in tails and tall hat is or is not an honest blue-collar worker — he might be a diplomat or banker, or something like that. Sure, a man in jeans could be a laborer. But I can't be certain, can I? He could be a politician. To sum it up, dear clowns and toady souls, it's darn difficult to judge. It's easier to trace how you became slaves to fashion: mass thinking, media hype. Just look at yourselves, my friends, all 4,800 of you, sitting here under one roof, a mere drop in the ocean of humanity. How can I find out about your value system? Where would I begin to search? And how? Worse yet — why would I even want to start this kind of investigation? Isn't one clown much like the other — utterly hollow? Like my rattle here — all noise and glitter on the outside, but empty inside? Tell

159

me, am I not right? What do you say? Yes? No? Oh yes. I am right. I'm sure that I am. AH YES!

ANNOUNCER. I just said that I can't get in a word edgewise unless the people applaud and stop him. Oh dear. The mood has changed. They're reacting to his insults — scream at the top of their lungs, raise their arms, threaten him. Countless whistles sparkle suddenly in the glare. The din is deafening! All hell is breaking loose! Like the roar of the Niagara Falls. Usually he is at his best when frightened. But this storm does not faze him. Funny that so many people brought whistles along. I never carry such things around. Do you? The director shouts through the intercom, but I can't make out what he's saying. Wait! There's an announcement on the screen. *Ladies and gentlemen! Smoking not allowed! No whistling! It is strictly forbidden to throw rotten eggs at the clown!* Well, it's one thing to forbid these things. It's quite another to make this raging mob listen! — What now? A sudden shift! They're applauding, laughing, waving handkerchiefs! What a reversal! I wonder why? (in a whisper to Johnny) Johnny, Johnny, has Tracbac said something? Ah. Well. Well. Mass psychosis in action. No sooner had the rules against smoking and whistling appeared on the screen, when Tracbac calmly pulled his cigarette case out, stuffed six cigarettes in his mouth and lit them. Now he sits there, arms crossed, puffing away on six weed sticks. He's challenging the rules — and the audience loves it. The fire marshal comes running in a hurry. Starts a heated argument with Jac. Shows him the ordinance. Jac reads, nods, pulls the cigarettes out of his mouth. No, I can't believe this! With a straight face he's stuffing the burning cigarettes into the marshall's front pocket. The upset young man runs off in a cloud of smoke. The audience is in stitches. Jac grabs his rattle forcefully and shakes it. I'm switching you over to Jac.

JAC. Ladies and gentlemen. You should've seen this bunch of jerks in action just now. I'd like to ask you — was it really so funny watching me ruining the poor fellow's clothes? Does that make me a hero? You really don't ask for much, do you? You don't mind seeing an innocent person abused. Of course, I'll have to pay for the suit and for playing the hero. But you would never laugh, hardly smile if I were to apologize and pay up on the spot for behaving like a cad. No, you'd yawn your heads off. Well, enough said.

160

Now, before moving on, I'd like to introduce two honorable gentlemen. One is our distinguished senator, philanthropist and religious teacher, the Honorable Mr. Adams. The other is our well-known film magnate Mr. Judah. Both used to be members of the Tracbac syndicate, which is now legally dissolved. I'd like these gentlemen to come down here to greet the audience. Oh, you don't want to? That isn't nice, gentlemen. That tall, white-haired gentleman over there is Mr. Adam, and the little, fat, dusky, blushing fellow next to him is Mr. Judah. Now, gentlemen, do tell me — how can you afford to give so many expensive, sturdy whistles to these jerks and ladies? You wouldn't be squandering public money, would you? Oh my, you're leaving already? But the program has hardly begun! All right, yes, part of the program is done. Goodbye, dear friends. Goodbye rosy dreams of forty percent. Ladies and gentlemen, please rise to cheer their exit. Applaud these agents of greed and shame. Fifteen seconds silence to mourn, if you please!

ANNOUNCER. (whispering) Johnny, listen. Try to find out why the chief of police is now in the governor's box. Hurry.

JAC. There we go. The two gentlemen have left us to our fate. Two lice less in my fur, the ape declared and continued his breakfast. Feel free to blow your whistles. This is a free country. Everyone may commit a crime. Our laws are excellent security valves whenever decency pressures rise too high. Just buy a few dollars' worth of crime from the government to raise your spirits. When laws are made for weaklings, dejection and despondency evaporate. They simply don't exist for daredevils who whistle at a clown who burns holes in an officer's shirt. So, go ahead! Be yourself! As long as you are my honored guests I'm willing to pay the fines.

Now, yes, where were we in our catechism? This is the volume for protection. Just when you tried to frighten me. Sorry that you failed. Now, let's see where my finger got stuck. Must be a hint from fate. Chapter four — "Handling Extremely Stupid Audience." My friends, let me skip this chapter. It doesn't apply to charming friends like you. Not that I ever considered you the elite. Let me not exaggerate, if you please. But I shall declare you lovable creatures, culturally and morally refined. Will that do? I'll just read the first lines so you may catch the idea before we jump this chapter. This is what I wrote, *If the audience is extremely stupid, the*

161

clown says something like: "My charming friends. Not that I considered you the elite. Let me not exaggerate, please. Let me simply declare you lovable creatures, culturally and morally refined." Now, that will do. So, having communicated your cultural and moral refinement, I can skip the rest.

ANNOUNCER. Jac has the laughers on his side again. Gold fillings glisten in red mouths from the gallery's top row to the orchestra seats down below. (Whispering) Hi, Johnny — what did you find out? Oh, they wanted to cut his performance? — Because he embarrassed these two gents? — Oh, the president wanted to confer with O'Henny first. — Gad, now that he's got the audience with him they won't dare to stop it. — He's turning pages in his book — he's reaching for his rattle — shakes it again —

JAC. As I'm leafing through these pages, my scribbles make no sense. Those ink stains on fingers, forehead, clothes were for the cat. Let's see, in this twelfth chapter here I wonder whether a clown should be as foolish as he looks, or worse? You tell me, my friends. Are we more successful when we look foolish, or when are sane and sly? Just between us clowns, I think appearance makes for success. I used to think that a cunning fox in sheep's clothing is best. But I was wrong. A foxy face fools the sheep. And foolish faces can play people for fools. People fear the fox and thus their fears make them unwitting victims. See, a roaring lion lords it over the world — until he gets whipped, because he's a coward at heart and runs.

So, my dear brothers and sisters, human clowns. Don your sly masks and expose your cherished blunders. They'll turn to gold. People love to discover that they've been fooled. Having unmasked the wily fellow, having outsmarted him makes them feel good and superior. We clowns mistakenly believe our tricks entertain others. Wrong. We only provide an opportunity for the audience to enjoy their own clownery. Every one his own clown — that's our unconscious, secret wish. The real surprise comes when recognizing this truth.

Looking further in my catechism. In my thirtieth chapter I find the question: Should a clown be a daredevil or a coward? A man or a mouse? —

ANNOUNCER. Just listen to that applause! All hell is breaking loose. Jac Tracbac wanted to know whether a clown should be a man

162

or a mouse! The noise cuts through even my soundproof walls: "Clown Terror. Clown Terror." It's not his catechism — no, they're applauding Tracbac, the Artist. His strangely clever terror-, fear- and funny cowardice combination has made Jac one of the world's most popular clowns. Underneath all his clowning he is a very daring fellow. I mentioned his bravery during the floods which earned him his precious clown scepter. I dare say, his behavior this afternoon is ample proof of his courage. He's always teased his audience — successfully most of the times. It's amazing how this small man takes on the enormous crowd filling this theater. True, it's all in fun and there's no real physical danger. But it's surely a psychological blow to have these thousands shout disapproval. Well, all is enthusiasm once again. They're throwing flowers — already, well before the finale. But Jac looks rather angry — who knows whether he's just pretending or whether he welcomes this disruption? He rattles, again and again, but in vain. If anything, the roar is getting more turbulent. I wouldn't advise our police chief to stop this performance, certainly not right now. Jac is finally standing up, to bow — no, no, wait a minute — he's limping over to Siva Yala's box — she bends down to pat him on his forehead — he — he — his shoulders are stooping forward — looks as if he's crying — but that could be part of his act — you never know with him. Well, yes, he's crying all right — Siv gets nervous, confers with Doctor O'Henny. But the doctor shrugs, calmly sits down, his arms crossed — the people are nonplussed — some are alarmed — the governor's wife has left her seat — the overwrought young girl we mentioned earlier is getting up now — Jac's turning away — oh — playacting or not, the matter can't be too earthshaking. But, yes, he's obviously upset. He's returning to his table — no, he's not sitting down. He's bending over the sugar lump — something seems wrong here — his arms stretch out backward, his hands interlock —

JAC.   Damned rabble. A man is dying and you're applauding — he's hanging there — then lying in the sawdust — and you think it's hilarious — for twenty-five years you've been cheering his death — he had to die so I could keep you amused — damned rabble —

ANNOUNCER.   I can't hear what he's saying — but he looks terribly upset — visibly shaken, the audience turns. Oh, he's finally sitting down — what a relief. That was some interlude — but now he grabs his rattle, he's rattling — good — the show finally continues —

JAC.   Ladies and gentlemen. You were kind enough to applause when I asked whether a clown ought to be a man or a mouse and it touches me deeply. But really, it's a stupid question — considering that we already agreed that all of us are clowns, more or less.

I'm afraid you'll pretty soon regret your applause — retrieve it somehow or something like that. You seem to misunderstand what I'm all about. My background and my road to fame may have led you to believe that my catechism is a tribute to clownish cowardice. But that's wrong. Yes, I've played the cowardly buffoon for twenty-five years, but found the opposite to be true. A clown needs courage, if for no other reason than that he, alone, stands for or against the crowds — it doesn't matter which. Take this afternoon — I am a singular gadfly on the mighty body of my audience. You could so easily squash me. And what about you? Oh my children, you don't realize how alone each one of us really is. Follow my advice — dare. A weak person may find a nook where he can hide. But there's no fun in hiding. The hunter is bound to spot where he's hiding, yank him out of his shelter and kill him. Remember, it's the weak person's fear that arouses the killer instinct in the mighty. It makes him powerdrunk. That's how the weak becomes an easy prey. The courageous always wins. His enemy may kill him, but he is the victor in death.

Actually, we clowns need double courage — in life and in art. And we need special courage when playing the meek. I've seen your eyes gleam with murderous lust when I running across the stage, full of honest and not just simulated fear. Cruelty and cowardice are twins of daring and compassion. A daredevil may be stupid, or a good-natured fool, but he is always healthy because he's alive. In contrast, a weakling never is. He's like a corpse that poisons the air.

Cowardice kills.

Once in my green youth I had a friend. A wonderful guy — happy, strong, agile, daring, bold — too bold for his own good. He fell and he died —

ANNOUNCER.   As if wanting to illustrate — a fellow way up on the topmost rung is bending forward, flapping his arms as if about to take

164

a dive. He's shouting something. I can't hear what he's saying, unless I open my door. Ah. Yes, he's screaming, There you see, cowardly Jac, he paid for his courage. More shouts, like Bravo — damn it — it's true, he was too daring. Jac grabs his rattle. Shakes it. He wants to talk.

JAC. You're wrong, ladies and gentlemen. He fell because I was afraid. Afraid of seeing him fall and kill himself. That's why he died. And that's not the whole story. That's how I became a famous clown. I made money on selling cowardice in small dosages — in tiny paper cups as it were, the way snuff dealers dispense their snuff. You love my routine, don't deny it. The wild beast in you gets its kick watching my terror. Now, don't tell me that I'm wrong. I have twenty-five years of experience in the cowardice department. I know precisely what I'm talking about.

I've decided to put a stop to my disgrace. No one can take it forever. I want to save face, as the Chinese say. I'll continue to entertain you, my sugar lumps, but it's going to be different from now on. The only way for me to get rid of my fear is by using my courage. I have the power to gather tens, hundreds, even thousands of clowns and toadies and tell them, I'm a coward, surely the worst coward around. That's a slap in your face because you love to see me terrified. That shows how cruel you are. You are the real cowards. Yes, my dear audience, I challenge you — stone me, kick me, hit me all you want. I promise to pay the fines. So, go ahead. Come on. Let yourself go. Act out your urges. You don't want to, my honeybunches? But you do. No? Are you sure? Of course you do! I say that you want to do just that, my dear little toady souls! Yes, indeed! You DO!

ANNOUNCER. Ay, ay, ay, things are getting out of hand again. He seems intent on getting them upset. Well, that's always been his forte, driving the audience to the brink of confusing farce with reality. This is how he's exposed himself to danger more than once. But today he's toeing the limit in an atmosphere of brewing threat. Honestly, it takes a lot of courage to calmly sit there, leaf through his notebook. He exchanges glances with Siv whose face is ashen with fear. He smiles reassuringly, as if trying to calm her down. The director comes running with his loudspeaker. Seems he wants to stop the performance — if it's not too late already. Yes, now, look at this, there's that girl getting into the act again. She's trying

165

to get away from her companions — but they're holding her back. She pulls herself free, oh — wait a minute, she must be part of the Tracbac act — yes, obviously she is — the audience thinks so too — they're quiet now — wonder where that crazy girl fits in — just look at her and Jac. He was so calm before. All of a sudden he's changed. He stares at her as if he were seeing a ghost. She walks toward him with outstretched arms — almost trance-like, unconscious of what she's doing — and he — his face is distorted — the real Clown Terror — obviously we have reached the climax — the moment of terror — he's fooled us again, good ol' Jac — farce remains his art. The girl starts talking!

GIRL.   (ecstatic) My father. My great, beloved father. Don't be afraid. Your daughter is protecting you. Your daughter is going to plead — for you —

ANNOUNCER.   It's as I thought. She's part of the act. With a ghastly smile in her face she spreads her arms to the audience as if pleading for mercy. But now — I don't understand — Dr. O'Henny has suddenly jumped out of his seat and is running over to Jac — grabs him by his shoulders, bends him backward and massages his throat — the director is there too, talking to him — there's an announcement on the screen: *The performance is ending* — wait, Jac has regained consciousness and is shaking his head — the director makes an announcement through his loudspeaker — it's flashing on the screen: *The performance is ending for now. We will continue after a short intermission.*

19: From A Clown's Catechism II

ANNOUNCER. Hello and welcome back. Our performance resumes. Extremely lively disagreements in the foyer during the intermission, mostly in favor of Jac. The young lady who interrupted his performance and who so strangely upset him is his daughter from a previous marriage. He hadn't seen her for years. Hadn't even known she was here watching him. Though I was wrong saying that she was part of the act — I apologize for the mistake. She had the lucky presence of mind to diffuse the momentary threat to her father from the audience. She looks smartly elegant in her mauve tailored suit, quite distinguished, though her face isn't exactly beautiful. Judging from her behavior, she must have inherited her father's intelligence and lively artistic spirit. The charming woman next to Miss Tracbac is her relative Mrs. Benjamin Borck. She too is wearing a mauve tailored suit. The friendly young man next to her is her husband, a well-known journalist for a large, northern European newspaper.

My little rascal of an aide has outdone himself today. Never known for his competence before, Johnny took advantage of the confusion during intermission and slunk into Jac's dressing room along with various relatives, his physician, his secretary and Siva Yala. Surprise, surprise — not the least for old Jac himself — the room was festively lit and full of flowers — Mr. Judah's brilliant idea. He bid Jac welcome and pressed a huge, gilded laurel wreath on his head. With tears in his eyes he urged Jac to publicly apologize for embarrassing him, Mr. Judah, during the performance. Jac declared that he never apologizes for insulting people. But Mr. Judah pleaded with him, insisting on reconciliation. Tracbac suggested a compromise — he asked Judah for forgiveness. Judah hugged and kissed him on both cheeks even before he had completed the sentence. Then Judah wanted Miss Tracbac to hug her father while he shook hands with Mr. and Mrs. Borck. A real maudlin act which our alert Johnny soon discovered when he heard strange noises coming from behind the flowers. There was a movie camera hidden in the wall. If Johnny is correct, we'll soon have a touching newsreel of Judah with the Tracbac family in all of Judah's movie houses. Copyrights for various press releases and singular picture postcards of these pictures should offset at least part of the loss suffered from the break-up of the syndicate.

The audience is seated again. The governor's wife must have given her stylish Ethiopian dwarf antelope fur to the wardrobe girl. Her dress is made of something fashion experts call penguin mole — whatever strange animal that now may be. Johnny might know. Her outfit aroused at least as much curiosity as Jac's new-found daughter. Both were topics for lively discussions during intermission. Here, we're ready for another session of clown catechism. It's reassuring to know that our government supports catering to people's real needs.

We are again waiting for Jac. Our stunning Siv and her escort have returned to their seats. Same for Mr. Borck and his charming young wife. There, our applause machine is cranking up again. I wonder how many horsepower the handclapping generates. Ah, there come Jac, his daughter and his secretary. Father and daughter are holding hands. *Jac and his daughter* flashes across the screen. The announcement may have its merits, but I don't think it's Jac's style. The audience seems to agree. Well, what now? Johnny, what's the uproar? Oh, I must say that's taking the bull by its horns. About thirty young ladies, representing the local women's club, have entered the arena to welcome Jac's daughter with a charming bouquet of roses. Miss Tracbac seems overwhelmed, but hardly surprised. The young ladies line up for a song. Johnny, what are they singing? Oh, it's "Home, Sweet Home." They're swaying in rhythm to the tune. Well, this huge circus arena is hardly home, but the audience loves the thought. It's a touching scene all right — Jac looks less excited, seems wanting to hide behind his secretary. He may have preferred to celebrate her welcome less publicly. My dear clown, that's part of your job. Well, well, but his daughter seems delighted. She acknowledges the ovation gracefully, definitely with more poise than her famous father. Jac takes his seat by his table. Ah yes, well, now that this sentimental interlude is over — I'll turn the broadcast over to Jac.

JAC.	(whispering) Dear little Sanna, please follow Mr. Rush up to your sister and brother-in-law —
SANNA.	Couldn't I sit here with you, Father? I could turn the pages for you —
JAC.	Thanks, my dear child, but I'd rather do it myself —
SANNA.	I would so very much like to share your happiness, just as I shared your anxiety before. The people seem to like both of us —
JAC.	Yes, we'll share our happiness, Sanna, but later, later, after the show. Now go with Mr. Rush — I beg you —
SANNA.	Well, if it means doing you a favor — of course — my Father. Mr. Rush, please take my arm —
JAC.	(sighing, then cheerfully) Ladies and gentlemen! I want to apologize for the disruption and even more for my return. But there's a reason for all this — a most happy occasion — an addition to my family — a daughter. Her weight? You wouldn't believe it if I told you. A small man like me rarely fathers as big a daughter as I did. I thank you ever so much for sharing my happiness.

Now, here is a fitting chapter. It's called "Life's Changes" — no, let's call it "Life's Clownish Pranks And Their Impact On The Clown's Art." It's a serious discussion on the shifting viewpoints in human wisdom and experience. The clown needs a certain sensitivity to the pretenses involved. Take a handsome king — he may lack both heart and intelligence, but he may govern most successfully regardless. No one need ever know his shortcomings, even after the customary historical re-evaluation. But a mediocre clown will never do. He mustn't even try. I'm not talking about brains — if he runs short of smarts, genius can be bought — prepared, with sauce and garnish on top. The audience swallows it because it's used to standardized merchandise and pre-packaged foods. Still, the clown can never fake emotion. People tolerate faked feelings, may even buy into it at times. But burn-out is a violent, self-destructive internal struggle. It spells death to the artist's art.

I had a wonderful time, way back when I pitched my small tent wherever the police seemed friendly enough. I drummed vigorously in front of the ticket booth to get some blind old woman and her deaf old mate to come in. But the tent remained empty. Only children's heads appeared, peeping across the fence — the ever present bunch of happy freeloaders. Every morning, to get my stale old bread — the healthiest fare there is — I lined up between two fellows, the one behind used to bump his knee into my rump; the one ahead trampled on my toes with iron-tipped heels — and both called me names like clod or circus bum. Now, take the word clod! Name calling pegs you, pegs anybody. Being called names keeps you humble, makes you reflect on religion, goads you on to become the world's boxing champion. One thing is sure — you'll never be indifferent to it.

Traveling the road is the artist's lifeline. Don't contradict because I've been there — I know. Makes you cope with a lot of discomfort. But it's the greatest teacher too. You dare most after watching a fight. The best and cheapest substitute for rouge is a bloody nose. Many see gold as life's salt, but it's the wrong preservative for the clown. Sure, the art world's great factories distribute quality goods elegantly packaged to millions of takers. That's all right. But real clowns are poachers. We must scour the woods for whatever we can find. Then we sneak back into town with freshly bagged game and offer our wares with innocent faces — until the sheriff gets wise to us and locks us up — or kicks us out because we can't pay the legal bribes.

ANNOUNCER. The crowd doubles over with laughter. Even Jac is surprised at the response. A fellow is shouting from the gallery. What's that? "Oh, Right on, Jac. It's touching to hear you share your poor comrade's poverty. Come on, tell us your income, poor clown!" Jac settles down to answer him.

JAC. My secretary can tell you my top fees — if you tell us your top income — if there is any. I wager the sums are about equal. One thing is true, though. Poverty has always been the patron of the arts. Probably still is. As generous as she might be to her favorites, Fortune never comes on command. Only a few at the top command wealth, while poverty is generous and free. Do you suggest that I sell my extravagant palaces, my old Ford, my luxury yacht, my beautiful wife and well-stocked bar and give the profits to the poor in order to keep my status as clown? It won't work, Sir. Life would have to do that for me — like my enemies ruining me, or my friends cheating me. To give away all you have — that's for saints, or the insane. No, Sir. A clown is not crazy, much less a saint. It would be nice to perform in Heaven, but there's no interested audience up there. And there's no heaven for the clown without an audience. Anyway, what do you want from me? Stop attacking me! There's always another day for all of us, you know. I'm quite willing to hire you for my tour, all the way. Then, while I listen to the applause, you may stand behind me, whispering in my ear, "Remember you're a jerk. You teach one thing, live according to another!" Keep in mind, I'm not talking about myself. I'm talking in universal terms, about all people, about my brothers. Remember too, I'm not a person! I was a syndicate and now I'm dissolved. So take note and shut up.

ANNOUNCER. Our good Jac is upset again about this stupid interruption from the gallery. Big drops of perspiration are running down his cheeks. Probably an added aggravation to his previous emotional upset. Doctor O'Henny is leaving his box, going down to the arena, talking to the secretary — the secretary is leaving now, letting the physician take his place. Jac doesn't notice the change. He's leafing through his notebook. Now he's rattling.

JAC. (lively, dark, comical) Rattle, clown, rattle. (Surprised, heatedly) What d'you want here? Where is Rush?

DOCTOR. With Siv. I thought I'd take his place for a while.

JAC. Ohhh? Does that mean I'm performing under medical supervision? Tell me! Speak up! Don't be shy!

DOCTOR. Now, don't be absurd, Jac —

JAC. Absurd? I'm as absurd as I want to be. Worse. But all right, be my guest and sit here. Sit down, sit down. What about a cigarette? — Oh, that's forbidden. Stop staring at me.

As I said, ladies and gentlemen. Many are assigned to poverty. But only few understand poverty's real blessings. I'm not — even though I was utterly poor when I started as an assistant circus boy. Extremely poor. I and a pal my age — no, not the one I hanged, no, someone else. We once dined on rats — loved it. Our circus mama had nothing else to feed us — served them in a stew, like rabbits — we didn't know what we were eating. We ate and thrived. I can't remember what they tasted like. Can't really blame her either, poor, decent woman. She could have slaughtered her three big dogs. But, see, these were trained to perform tricks. They were an act. They had to stay alive. Just like me — I do tricks, I'm an act, I may live. So far!

171

Well, another chapter here, chapter three — question: "Should the Clown Be Very Humble?" The answer is an absolute yes. Why? Because an arrogant clown loses touch with life. They say he can't be sensitive to someone he scorns. Now, what is a poor clown, the lowliest of all, if he doesn't understand his fellow man? He is spiritually ruined. In the past people tended to look down on the circus artist. Perhaps no longer nowadays. See, many so-called better people considered me socially inferior. Lice, cads. And that got me to think — you bastard, don't you understand you're short-changing yourself? You miss out on the chance to know Jac Tracbac. Well, I was "Stable-Nathan" at the time. I got the name because I took care of the animals for a circus in Topeka. I had a girl friend, name was Mary-Ann — no, we never got married. See, she was ambitious. I didn't suit her. She became a kindergarten teacher, still is — so, I thought: you bastards, how stupid you are, you'll never know the real Stable-Nathan. Pity, really. I feel sorry for the bunch —

Well, ladies and gentlemen — hear what I have to say. Always keep a fistful of compassion in your pocket. Whenever anger gets the better of you, just swallow a pinch of compassion. Leaves a pleasant, soothing taste in your mouth; your headaches vanish and your disposition clears up. Only the stupid remain angry.

Look, another question in my catechism: "Should a clown be proud? —"

Certainly. He needs his pride to remain a human being, to be a clown. And he must be proud of his profession — or leave it. No one is worse off than someone ashamed of what he's doing. He has no hope and hopelessness is the worst punishment under the sun. Life has many rewards, but none can measure up to the satisfaction derived from work performed with a happy heart. Why shouldn't the clown be proud of his work? He has every reason to be. Yes, sir. What? — What are you saying, Denny? That fellow up there is shouting again? What does he want now?

DENNY.   Oh, he wants to know whether you're proud of being a fool.

JAC.   Oh, certainly, you little cherub-seraph up there in circus heaven. Yes, because the clown controls the people's merriment with a rattle in his hand and wisdom's crown on his head.

172

ANNOUNCER. The audience loves this banter. They wonder whether it's part of the act. Johnny says it's improvised.

JAC. The same goes for the pride in being human. Well, what kind of pearl is that to be proud of, you wonder? Many a black, slimy mussel holds better contents! Two people meet, a third arrives. And the third, believe it or not, gets cocky about that! What nonsense! No one should just shout: Look, I'm a human being! Only those with compassion and courage in their hearts may say it with pride. Even the listener must earn this mark of distinction.

The misanthrope sees humanity afflicted with misery. Sure, you are so damn right — man is a wretch — no need to repeat that — you're the best example — it's part of man's deplorable state. As you sow, so you shall reap. See, the misanthrope pulls the wool over his eyes and ears and goes to sleep. Let him sleep in peace. No need to rouse him. He's a coward. His soul will never rise because his body rots first.

Now that I've told you this and you know this part, my finger stops at the chapter called "The Clown's Relationship To His Audience." My honored ladies and gents, after your crude behavior this afternoon that topic is highly controversial. I hope you kept your whistles! You did? Good, then I may safely proceed. Sometimes you are rude, outright boorish, which makes me want to leave the stage. — Yes, I hear what you're shouting from the gallery, my dear fellow. I mustn't be shy. Just leave. But, you see, I got paid for performing my act this afternoon. Don't get the bright notion I would want to shortchange you. Neither shall I return one red cent. My dear audience, you look most unpleasant at times. Are your facial expressions a reflection of mine, perhaps? Or vice versa? Never mind — if we're both unpleasant, we both share. Art experts have warned me — an artist mustn't frisk his audience. Damn it — whom else could he pick on? His associates? Of course, them too. But them only? Better perform behind locked doors, or to an empty hall. The only exception is the producer, during rehearsal. Never grovel. But keep the producer in mind, even while jumping across the barrier to sock the fellow one between the eyes. Every good clown expects a good fight, with repeats. He needs it to feel alive! No tame words here. His pulse must race; never slack off. Frisk the audience? I've done nothing

173

else all my life. I am a clown, not a monk communing with Our Lord. Choose your equals. Yes siree. My dear clowns present in this hall, I honored you by making you my equals. Here. This afternoon. When I stop and my rattle falls silent you leave, return home or to your parties. To continue playing your comic acts with other clowns.

From his stage the clown controls crowds as much as they control him. They're one unit, caught in one ship. If he rocks, they rock back. We're brought together for a time in a space that has no fourth dimension, where my fate is yours, and yours mine. Dear artist, beware of your audience. Don't surrender to their spell. Look upward — there's your god. His strong arm holds the thread of your fate.

Yes, my genuine artist, be wary — don't submit to people so they need not submit to you. A fireproof chasm exists between you two. He may talk all he wants — no one listens to him anyway. No, my dear artist, if you want to flirt with the crowd, then go ahead and flirt. Audience, if you find that tragic, then express your anger, whistle — if you want to laugh, then laugh — together — or go ahead and cry if you feel like crying. But dry your tears with a common handkerchief. Mind my advice, my flirtatious artist — frisk your audience all you want, but do it so no one catches on — let no one get wise to what you're up to —

The arena is a short-lived meeting place for people from both sides of the barrier. That's where the movie falls short. Who loves or hates a moving picture rather than a life-and-blood human being? As clever as they may be, these screen comedians remain lifeless and hollow — they're stuck in place, can't even break their necks. A movie screen is a poor substitute for real life. Sure, some men prefer hearing their mother-in-law's voice from a record player rather than hearing her in person. But what about the fiancée? Come, let's retain art as our fiancée as long as we can. She'll turn mother-in-law soon enough.

Now, let's have fun with chapter eleven: "What's the purpose and goal of clowning?" End of question. End of catechism. This page is bare but for a huge ink stain where the pen dropped out of the writer's trembling hand. The question reminded him of a trial in which the accused left the judge's questions unanswered. His silence was taken as an admission of his guilt. Ladies and gentlemen, I've come to the end of my wits. Now I'm asking you, *Why are you clowning? Why play tricks on our circus society? Is it for fun? Or do you have something special in mind? Are you clowning because you happen to work for a circus?* Oh well, everyone has his own answer to this, I included. Following my question is — an empty page, and a stain. What about a pun? Let's call this a "stained confession"?

Wait — the heavenly circus spirit inspires me again. Listen to this: *The true clown's calling is to make people feel alive.* Is that essential? Of course not, my friends. However, we are left with nothing if we limit our daily lives to the bare essentials. In my case, I limit my craft to what my manager lets me do — and I'm using it like the savage his war drum. My primary tool was, is, and remains *terror.*

ANNOUNCER. For the first time during this strange, nerve-racking afternoon I can truly say that Jac Tracbac has the audience with him all the way. But the applause is less for the author and lecturer of the catechism than for Clown Terror, our good, old Crazy Jac. And after having nonchalantly ignored all applause all this afternoon, Jac finally rises and bows to acknowledge this resounding applause with a deep clownish smile. Again he reaches for his rattle.

JAC. Clown Terror alias Jac Tracbac thanks you kindly. But, dear children, what happened to your costly whistles? Why aren't you blowing them? Don't think that clowns shun applause. Quite the contrary. Clowns love applause almost more than their life. Now that the master clown has rattled on all this time, well, the whistles sounded as if telling him that he lost touch. That he ought to bow out. Return back to obscurity. Hide and wipe his brow.

> *Rattle, clown, rattle,*
> *Tremble, heart, tremble.*

Believe me, I'm not playing the old son-of-a-bitch to frighten children and fools. That's not my game. I frighten myself to give children and fools the chance to laugh away their terror. That's my goal — to teach people to laugh at terror. Brother clowns, each one according to his ability. There's your mission!

I see another chapter worth discussing. Its title: "The Clown And Love." Well, what can a clown possibly say on that subject? Trivial? I'm sure you gentlemen can take what I

175

	have to say. But before I do, I want to give our modest, coy ladies one minute to leave. — All right, Mr. Director, may I ask how many have left — ?
DIRECTOR.	None, Jac, none.
JAC.	Thank you, little None! My dear ladies, I regret, but I won't live up to your great expectations. My text contains not one four-letter word, much less an obscenity. Sorry about that. Remember, there's none more prudish than an old, confirmed bachelor. Take me for example — What now, Denny? I offended the ladies?
DENNY.	No, it's that ruffian up there again. He wants to know how come you introduce your daughter, then call yourself a bachelor. It doesn't quite mesh, especially with the girl's singing "Home, sweet home — ."
JAC.	But that's ghastly — I honestly forgot — I can't seem to keep straight what I'm saying? So stupid of me — crude — vulgar —
DENNY.	(stern) Now Jac, no nonsense. Don't get upset! No harm done. Do go on!
JAC.	The clown's love life is like everything else about him — it's methodical, calculating — mental gymnastics. His heart must stay in shape. Precision is essential. Like shooting practice — it must respond within a tenth of a second to the instructor's sharp, hasty command, "Shoot." Call it training the heart in self-discipline — to respond instantly to its commands: "Love! Hate! Have fun! Suffer!" Mind you, it's not just his facial expression. No, the clown's heart must instantly obey to deliver love, or hate, like a well-drilled circus dog. Quite unlike the rough, untrained, childish, foolish simpleton who is happily or sadly deluded into looking for a good home for his love. Ah, my dear clowns gathered here, that is not the way *we* are! We have made love into an art. We sell it without remorse. Every new revision, every new call to love substantiates our artistic perfection. The simple soul declares, "My beloved boy," or "My beloved girl." But we hold back. We say, "My matchless partner! My artistic comrade on love's loose wire —"

Well, my dear fellow clowns, should it so happen — and unfortunately it does occasionally — that someone in our artistic circle disregards this training, or, worse yet, thinks that he's met his true love — well, then the woman suffers. She gets hurt. Her backbone gets broken. It's not her partner's fault. His artistic honor remains intact — unless, surprised, he fumbles the issue. Don't squander tears on these idiots. Love's loose wire demands a cool head and an agile heart. It's the artist's duty to know all this. In no way may she accuse him later, telling him, "You make me sick — you are loathsome, you're an abscess, a plague in my soul . . ." she should have known that I was no great artist, no loose-wired clown, when you —

ANNOUNCER. Jac's speech is getting slurred. He seems lost in ruminations as he absentmindedly fingers the petite pair of lady's gloves before him — tries to pull one over his hand — it's too small, of course . . . he throws it down — his face looks tired, spent — O'Henny watches him nervously, comes forward with some medicine —

DENNY. Jac, how do you feel? Are you getting tired?

JAC. Well — I don't know — I've lost my thread — what was it I was talking about — ?

DENNY. You were talking about love. Look here, why don't you take your medicine —

JAC (sluggish) I? Talking about love? A clown discussing love? Damn it, how disgusting —

ANNOUNCER. Jac's totally changed. For the worse. He mustn't feel well. O'Henny administers some medicine. Ay ay — he can't swallow — the water is dribbling down the sides of his mouth. His daughter comes running down to help. They're leading him out. He himself began this squabble with the audience, but it obviously upset him. The belligerent fellow in the gallery is a former circus artist — mentally unhinged they say, trying to get into his famous colleague's act. The clown left without his catechism. The rattle too is still on the table, along with one lonely glove. The other is on the floor, forlorn and lost in the sawdust. Jac's good luck charm hasn't been too lucky for him today — I'd say! Let's hope for a speedy recovery for our dear Jac. This ends our broadcast of this year's first Tracbac performance from the Capitolium. Good afternoon.

SANNA. My father — are you feeling better?

JAC. Oh yes, yes — much better — I feel fine —

SANNA.   What a pity that we had to disrupt your performance — you
          missed hearing the applause from the people — they simply
          loved you — (pining) even me, they loved me too — what a
          reception — roses — the song — "Home, sweet home" —
          home, wonderful home —

JAC.   (tired) Well. Yes, yes, my girl, let's go home — home — to
          the hotel —

20: When The Fireworks Are Dying Down

THE PERFORMANCE WAS over. Tracbac and his family and friends — Siv, Sanna, Caroline, Benbé, Denny, and Abel Rush — sat and dined in the Auditorium Annex. The clown had quickly recovered from his nervous breakdown, but he remained sullen, depressed and embarrassed, much like a schoolboy after failing his exam. His guests drank champagne, but he kept staring into his ice water. Suddenly his face lit up as if he had found the answer to a difficult problem. Turning to Abel Rush, he said with a roguish glint,

Abel, my friend, let me say that I honestly thought I confessed — well, sort of. Nothing but vanity. Pure vanity. I am and remain a clown. Now, our arrangements for tomorrow morning —

Clearly, that was an order. But it took Abel's keen intellect, some intuition and a good deal of understanding Tracbac to know what he meant. Obviously, Jac trusted his secretary implicitly. And rightly so.

Pech, the redheaded farmer boy from Kansas, had an easy job that afternoon. The syndicate was dissolved all right, but he was still the clown's liaison to the press. And he stuck more or less to the truth — as he saw it. Tracbac had suffered a neurocataleptic attack. His doctor had warned him all along not to go on tour, but Tracbac, overly conscientious as always, had disregarded his advice — and had suffered the consequences. Luckily, the doctor himself was there to supervise. His daughter was there too, and she well deserved all the attention she had gotten from the audience. As it turned out, Tracbac's infirmity had been only temporary. He was well again and would continue his tour as planned, barring some minor seasonal changes that might crop up.

The term "neurocataleptic fever" was Pech's own coinage, drawn from his extensive medical knowledge. No use trying to find it in any dictionary. Having thus swimmingly discharged his obligations, the Kansas boy devoted several nights to the filthiest, most innocent orgies, as he described it. That's when Rush caught hold of him and told him,

Listen, fellow, Tracbac has finally concurred that this catechism idea was a flop. It's your job to come up with a skit by tomorrow morning, to be rehearsed and ready to perform within a week. Write whatever you like, as long as the title remains "The Clown's Catechism."

The young man heaved a sigh,

Farewell, orgies — for the time being . . .

179

He engaged three young ladies for the night to prick pins into him each time he might doze off. In their company and fortified with plenty of coffee, he turned out a skit featuring as much cruelty as it took creating it. The plot ran something like this: After his performance the poor clown returns to his shabby home. His meek, work-weary, but loyal wife welcomes him. Contrary to his expectations, his act turned out to be an overwhelming success. Now his ego inflates and his swelled head knows no bounds. He is tired of his dismal lifestyle. Frightened, his wife tries to check his vanity. But admirers arrive with flowers, jewels, furniture, expensive gifts of all kinds. For every incoming item he throws an old one across the fence where a huge heap of cheap trash slowly builds up. His wife mourns the loss of her beloved items. His pride mounts. Several bank managers visit and leave a large sum of money. Insolence rewarded with gold. A beautiful young girl with no more to offer but her beauty enters. Torn between conjugal loyalty and carnal desire, the clown runs between his overworked wife and the beautiful girl. Finally, without looking at her, he leads his wife cautiously out and seats her on top of the junk heap, kisses her mouth, her hand, and finally her torn shoe. Then he leaps quickly back across the fence.

He kneels before the beautiful girl, beaming, kisses her silk-shod foot, tries to kiss her lips. Now what? She examines all the costly chests, cabinets and other furniture standing about. The clown opens one after the other, proudly displaying his riches. As he is about to open the next chest it suddenly explodes in a terrifying blast. Flames flare up. Stumbling backward, the clown tumbles against the next cabinet. It too explodes. One by one, the other furniture pieces keep blowing up and soon the entire arena is aflame. The girl runs away. The clown bounces back and forth, his contorted face popping up in spurts between fire and smoke. He has lost the girl. Wanting to salvage something, he jumps across the fence. Suddenly he remembers the check, screams, "My money, my money" and runs back into the raging flames.

At that point the flames die out. For a minute there is complete darkness. Gradually the light returns, bathing the arena in a soft light. Sad but unharmed, the clown sits atop his charred furniture heap and lets the ashes run through his fingers. The weary little wife slowly climbs down from her furniture perch and carefully carries each piece back to the arena. Finally she stops before her husband and looks him over. In an effort to clean him up, she pulls out her kerchief and wipes the grime off his face. Gingerly he begins digging through the ashes. She helps and finds a booklet with charred covers. Angry, the clown pulls it out of her hand, screaming,

"The check!"

He opens the booklet carefully, surprise in his face. Slowly his disillusionment gives way to a resigned humor — he has recognized his childhood's curse — his catechism. With the solemnity of a teacher he reminds his wife of the first commandment — she responds, and they exchange some profound thoughts on the futility of vanity and the lasting value of a good childhood thrashing.

The skit certainly needed no X-rating (the original, serious clown catechism was the only Tracbac act ever prohibited for children). Its simple symbolism was morally acceptable to everyone — fire and firecrackers frightened the clown. Though he knew that this stage fire was absolutely harmless, he never knew beforehand which one of the "expensive" furniture pieces were to "explode" during his act. This element of the unexpected was enough to stir his reaction to terror. O'Henny would never have permitted more.

Tracbac approved the skit without further changes. Rush and his staff, Benbé among them, made all further arrangements. In other matters, Tracbac highly appreciated Caroline's and Rush's help in persuading Sanna to leave for California. She had at first refused, believing her father needed her. Not even the prospect of greater comfort in the villa and her superior position there would sway her. She finally relented when Rush pointed out that her presence would greatly hamper her father's work.

They expected the skit to be more popular in the West than in the more sophisticated East. They were surprised by the enthusiastic reception in all the twenty cities. Spoiled children often like the simplest toys best. The powerful women's clubs especially liked the motif of the loyal wife forgiving her conscience-stricken husband and of God's word recovered from the ashes. They greatly supported Tracbac's show and soon forgot the adverse reaction to the original clown catechism.

The two sisters Caroline and Sanna were finally permitted to attend the show when the group came to a southern city. Healthy, straightforward Caroline found the plot's simple intrigue and the light effects exciting. Sanna considered the new version duller than the first. She was ever so disappointed not to be included in the performance and not being allowed to "share her famous father's fate." But that did not lessen her gentle, tender, often roguish concern for her father. As she was about to leave again, she urged him surreptitiously,

Dear father, would you mind writing a formal authorization? I would like you to tell your employees to obey my directions as if they were yours?

What for? Don't they listen to you? Tracbac wanted to know, surprised and angry.

Oh, they behave all right. It's not really mine, but Count DeGrazy's idea. (Actually, the good major was a duke, but kept it secret because he thought his title too pompous for his present job. But Sanna "had a feeling" that he was a count — so nothing could be done about that.)

181

Tracbac muttered, but signed the authorization, wondering what kind of disastrous consequences might ensue. It never did cause a major disaster, though the idea eventually turned into a shining nuisance. For the moment, Sanna bid her father another goodbye with the ominous whisper,

My dear father. Now it's little Sanna's turn to welcome you home in style.

Oh, my goodness, the clown sighed.

Tracbac was exhausted after the tour. Remembering Sanna's cryptic promise, he decided to settle in Florida. Siv and Rush kept him company. Denny O'Henny visited occasionally. Seeing the young physician court the gypsy girl with such bitter zeal exasperated the clown and he finally gasped,

Why don't you young idiots get married? Do I have to die first and make you a decent widow? Just say the word, will you!

But the gypsy sniffed back,

Marry? Me? No my dear Jac. Having been married to you has cured me for the rest of this life as well as the next. I'll never marry again. The clown smiled,

Well, Denny, I can't help you there. Excellent, just excellent.

Both girls kept faithful contact with Mama and Papa Längsäll and wrote regularly. Alert and lively, Caroline reported interesting incidents and anecdotes, but did not write much about Tracbac. Sanna did quite the opposite. Like many neurotics, she lacked prudence and tact. Quite unintentionally she often hurt her mother's feelings with her bluntness. Addressing her letters to "my dearest Mama and Papa," she would then tell them a great deal about her "beloved" or "famous" father. Her relationship to her two "fathers" was rather unsettling and difficult to handle. She tried hard to please both: Längsäll became "my dearest Papa" and Tracbac "my famous father" or something to this effect. Lillemor noted it with her usual bitter, cynical smile, thinking,

Right on! Right on — let's empty the chalice to the dregs — in small gulps — to savor fully the bitter taste.

In contrast to the detailed reports from both girls, the Längsäll news from Sanna remained scant and never mentioned what bothered them most. The young people were still at home when Lillemor's physician had diagnosed her cancer and recommended an operation, soon. Wide-eyed, Längsäll had absorbed the news, his lips tightly shut for fear that he might cry. But the little woman tapped his chest and told him, as strong-willed as ever,

There's the reason for my irritability. From now on you'll just have to grin and bear it.

Längsäll suggested to tell the children and delay their departure. But Lillemor dismissed that idea. What if she were to die during the operation?

There would be plenty of time to inform them after the fact. Lillemor had the operation and it went well. But she never regained her old strength. Her health declined progressively.

Father Längsäll had to leave the fall plowing and his beloved oxen to his farmhands. He sat in the bedroom, whittling away at some handicraft or reading to Lillemor. Staring at her small work-worn hand on the bedspread, he placed his brawny paw next to hers and teased her,

So tiny and yet so brave! You call that a hand? Look at this if you want to see the real thing. Our Good Lord was rather stingy when he carved you women. The old fellow must've worn some powerful glasses on his nose to come up with a delicate job like this —

He tried his best to keep their spirits up, hardly daring to look out at the land for fear of betraying how much his large, strong body longed to be there. But Lillemor sensed it. She meditated silently,

Just stay in here, my dear friend. You'll be alone with your beloved fields and oxen soon enough.

Sanna too was alone. Benbé went on a business trip to San Francisco for his company and Caroline went along. The newlyweds had not yet decided where in their new homeland they wanted to settle — south, north, east or west.

At first Sanna was too busy to feel lonely. Preparing a rousing welcome for her famous father once he decided to come home occupied all her time. That's why she had needed her father's power of attorney. He had hesitated at first to grant it, afraid of Sanna's often crazy whims. But eventually he relied on DeGrazy to assist her and possibly mitigate the effect of her whims. The old knight changed his strategy when she suggested to stage the greatest fireworks ever. He liked the idea and even looked for over a hundred hiding places from where the firecrackers could blast off all at once. The noisy flares in the darkness would create a stunning — if banal — effect. In all his zeal he forgot, or may not even have known of the disturbing effects such fireworks had on the clown.

The goodhearted major was good company for Sanna and would have remained that if not one day he had shown her his stamp collection and jokingly called it his only interest and fun in life. Sanna pondered the confession for a few days then queried modestly,

Count, you must feel terribly lonesome if a bunch of stamps is your only pleasure in life.

Casually and politely, he fabricated a bold untruth,

Oh, well, I miss my dear relatives.

The girl snuggled up to him and whispered,

Yes, I too am very, very lonesome.

The good major was dumbfounded. Her answer outright frightened him. Not wanting to be rude, he answered her attack with a gentlemanly,

Well, being alone is pure pleasure for a man with my past.

It may have looked that way, but Sanna was hardly in love with the man. She felt sorry for him. With a sigh of relief she smiled,

Oh, well then.

Still, the conversation shocked the major. He left in all haste, sending Tracbac a telegram that he needed to settle important business matters elsewhere.

The poor girl was now really alone. The employees were polite and respectful to the adopted daughter of their boss. Black, white, yellow or red, the children kept their distance, although she was very generous and treated them to many goodies. Hiawatha, her pageboy, acted like a little black scoundrel in shiny uniform by poking fun at her behind her back. She was embarrassed when she found out and told him to stay out of her sight. Lonely she wandered the maze of the villa and the tremendous park, occasionally meeting the befuddled Axelsson. She watched him weaving his feather duster and heard him mumbling under his breath,

Foolish girl. Poor thing, what will become of you?

When she heard what he said she pulled out the pastor adjunct's ring from around her neck, kissed it and whispered,

Folke, my Folke, are you still thinking of me?

The question remained unanswered. At long last she decided to pay her father a visit. Looking forward to the visit, she smiled,

I'm sure he'll be pleasantly surprised.

She surprised him indeed as he was relaxing one morning with Rush and Siv at the beach. Siv noticed a chic, extravagantly dressed young lady arousing the curiosity of the jaded beach crowd. Sanna had wanted to make her famous father proud of her among the style-conscious elite. Usually unconcerned about fashion and trendy clothes, she had engaged a top fashion house to advise her. Money was no object. But she had no taste and her finery was gaudy, flashy and crass.

Luckily Siv recognized her from afar. She asked Rush to warn Tracbac before she went to bid her welcome. The clown gazed tiredly at his young friend, nodded and bowed his head. He eventually did manage a friendly smile for his daughter when he heard her tender, happy greeting,

My dear father, finally —

He looked up with a smile,

Welcome, dear Sanna. It's nice of you to come.

He had no further questions. He never asked why she had come. And Sanna soon caused friction among the trio with some uncivil remarks to Siv. It might be wrong to judge Sanna too harshly. She was extremely jealous of beautiful Siv and there was no father Längsäll to make her hold the line. Despite her naive egotism, she knew that the others would tolerate her behavior. Wouldn't her famous father protect her? She clung to him with all the tenacity she could muster. Siv tried to remain calm, but her patience gave out when Sanna, with a hateful look, rudely told the gypsy,

I have a feeling the many people around my father tire him out.

Tracbac was too exhausted and never heard her biting remark. Knowing the circumstances, Siv took it in stride. However, she left the following day, reasoning,

It's probably best for Jac that I leave. Things couldn't get worse anyway.

He alone saw her off. As she was about to leave, he looked at her, bewilderment and fear in his large, pale blue eyes. She almost changed her mind when he said,

My dear Siv, little Siv, how little we really know —

Siv was wrong. Things did get worse. Poor Sanna had always felt sorely neglected. But now, the daughter of a famous father, she tried to compensate. She was loud, silly, laughed and babbled out of turn in order to draw constant attention. In contrast, the tired, depressed clown shunned the public limelight. Whether eccentric or not, people respected his reticence. But it greatly unsettled Sanna.

Abel Rush tried his best to alleviate Tracbac's misery. He took Sanna on daily excursions, enabling Tracbac to enjoy the beach by himself. Sitting under his umbrella, his head bent, and digging in the sand for hours on end, Tracbac almost looked like an idiot. But Abel's charity ended when Sanna repeated the foolish mistake she had made with DeGrazy. Only this time she was really attracted "to the young man who never left her side even for a minute and did everything to be alone with her." She would sidle up to him, whispering emotional endearments she thought coy and feminine,

Abel, I can tell that you care for me. You're just too shy to say it. Is it up to me to make the first move?

Abel's shock was even greater than DeGrazy's. He had wanted to help Tracbac. But his singular attention had created the impression that he was in love. He screamed,

I'm engaged, Sanna. I am engaged.

A deep crimson blush crossed the girl's pale, pimply face. She stood rigid, stunned. Then she said haughtily,

If that is so, it was heartless to behave as you did. I trusted you. I'm truly sorry for my father who hired you. Just don't think that I want your love. I too am engaged.

Her eyes flashing in anger, she proudly displayed her engagement ring and kissed it passionately before pushing it down her bosom again.

But every cloud has a silver lining. To be safe, Abel Rush took the first bus to San Francisco where he finalized his engagement to Ester. He had dated the girl for years and only his secret, hopeless love for Siv had somehow prevented him from marrying his sweet Jewish girl. Sanna's proposition had been a heaven-sent reminder to accept what fate had provided for him. The wedding was a few weeks later. Benbé represented Tracbac as best man and Caroline was a bridesmaid.

Jac was now alone with his daughter. Anxious to arrange her fabulous welcome party and to set off her fireworks, Sanna suggested that they return to California. But the clown dreaded the thought of being alone with his daughter in his gloomy villa. He delayed, telling her,

There's plenty of time for that. You ought to travel first and see the rest of this vast continent.

For months they criss-crossed the United States, though without staying anywhere for more than a short time. To avoid attention, Tracbac traveled incognito under his given name Jonathan Borck. But Sanna had developed a habit to attract attention to her famous father. She tried too hard to make her famous father proud of her which made it impossible for him to stay anywhere for long. The odd, unhappily wandering pair aroused enough curiosity and ridicule anyway. The slight, wispy clown with his store-bought, long, dark gray, shaggy coat, his pale, narrow face almost hidden behind his dark gray, wide-brimmed, slouchy hat contrasted sharply with Sanna who looked like a garish circus horse in her tawdry, flashy, trendy outfits.

One day the clown suggested that they visit Mary-Ann, his former sweetheart in Topeka who long ago had given poor Stable-Nathan the brush. The old lady, a few years older than Jac, welcomed both warmly. It occurred to him suddenly that it might be good for Sanna to have an older companion and he invited the retired schoolteacher to join his "family." The woman accepted immediately. Offended, Sanna argued,

Dear father, couldn't we make her my lector?

The clown liked that idea even better. He said,

Excellent! The ideal job for an old schoolmarm!

The old woman, used to handling all kinds of females, proved to have a beneficial influence on Sanna and her whims. She became an invaluable help to the same Stable-Nathan she had refused to marry in her younger days.

But other problems remained. Father and daughter were extremely charitable and generous to a fault. Crooks and flimflams soon found them gullible and trusting to boot. They gnawed, nibbled, and snacked on their generosity like rats on cheese. Worse. The rabble got Tracbac, habitually weary and inattentive, into legal trouble. Luckily the Good Lord, known to help fools like Tracbac, sent Mr. Judah to the rescue. They bumped into him on the street and Judah, wise, alert, and as always ready to forgive and forget, counseled Tracbac and Abel Rush on how to get rid of these moochers.

Loyal as ever, the secretary cut short his honeymoon. He took his wife to Topeka. Benbé and Caroline came along — young Mrs. Rush to keep Sanna company. The others discussed how to separate Sanna from the unethical company that tried to exploit her. They advised her to return to her father's estate while Tracbac visited Benbé in San Francisco for a while. Sanna was heartbroken to find that her presence irritated her father. She cried and wanted to return to her parents. They at least accepted her.

Clever as ever, Benbé knew a better solution. Since Sanna liked having a lector around, he suggested his former landlady for the job of companion. The Canadian would be an excellent choice all around. Financially not well off, she was practical and good-natured. She would not only be an excellent companion for Sanna, but her presence would improve his uncle's home life too. Sanna took the bait. A personal lector and a companion at her side plus a black servant under her command would lift her social standing to aristocratic heights. She gave Abel Rush (protected by his wife's presence) an appreciative look, musing: I might get my personal secretary too some day. — The clown's problems taken care of, the family gathering in Topeka adjourned.

Many years ago the clown had wanted to begin his tour from Topeka. His secret wish had been to visit his old flame again. The syndicate had voted against it at the time. Now she was to be his daughter's lector. A contented smile on his face, the exhausted clown took Sanna to the train station, whispering to Abel,

Remember what I said many years ago? Topeka isn't bad, I said then. Excellent.

News of events in the United States reached the two people in Sanna. But only father Längsäll read the letters; Lillemor had lost all interest. Whenever the morphine did not drug her to sleep, she stared listlessly into space. Occasionally she turned and nodded at her husband, but soon resumed her sightless stare. The painful, bitter, cynical smile around her lips bothered Father Längsäll far more than her pain. In the tradition of his forebears, he was deeply religious and would have liked to discuss religion with her. But his courage failed him there. Despite all his physical prowess, he was no match for this hard, tiny, pain-wracked human being he watched slowly disintegrating under his eyes. Once she turned to him as he sat by her bedside, brooding in helpless despair about this. With a bitter sparkle in her beautiful eyes, she said ruefully,

Yes. You with your heaven and your God. It's easy for you.

187

Her gaze, her voice, her words were like sudden stabs in his chest. He broke down. Leaning toward her, he began to cry. She managed to sit up, cradled his head between her hands, brushed her face against his and kissed his forehead and scalp. This was the last time she was able to caress her strong, gentle, patient husband.

Sanna's life in her father's villa settled into routine and improved gradually. She was proud of her "ladies" and treated them as friends and equals, mindful that it was in her own and her father's interest to do so. She liked to sit comfortably in her chair by the wayside — her lector by her side and Hiawatha in fancy uniform fanning from behind — watching the tourists Longfellow guided through the grounds. Mrs. Canadian and major DeGrazy refused to join this spectacle that looked like a parody of the *Thousand And One Nights* fairy tales. Since the valiant major's return to the estate, Mrs. Canadian shielded him the way Ester protected her husband Abel Rush,.

Tracbac returned home, well-rested after his extended visit with Benbé. A few days later Sanna staged her well-prepared picnic. She had asked DeGrazy to make up a list of guests, then invited about five hundred famous people from various walks of life who came to welcome the great clown back from his "triumphant tour through the United States." They leisurely and freely fraternized on the grounds without too much antics — "European-style" DeGrazy called it. At Sanna's request, the clown wore the same outfit he had worn at his "memorable" performance in the Capitolium. Mingling with the crowd, he looked very pleased, shook hands with everyone and smiled.

With the first fireworks at nightfall the party suddenly turned vulgar. DeGrazy called it "goût américain" — typically American. Hiawatha acted on his brilliant idea to have over a hundred hidden half-naked, bronze-colored youngsters in wild Indian costumes suddenly roar out of the shadows. With their lanterns bobbing wildly about, they scorched a good many dresses in the act. Seven concealed jazz bands added their cacophonies to the wild scene. DeGrazy's camouflaged rockets spewing one flame pillar after another into the sky did the rest. The noise was deafening, the fire dangerous, the rockets frightening. Shocked, Tracbac uttered a muffled howl, clutched his chest, and bolted homeward. The guests thought his panic attack a splendid practical joke and applauded wildly. Tracbac managed to control his terror eventually when he finally reached the safety of his black door,. Leaning stiffly against his entrance, his left hand pressed against his pounding heart, he acknowledged their ovation. Siv caught up with him and stood by his side. With a wide sweep of his arm, he snickered sardonically and whispered to her,

Home, sweet home —

More unplanned surprises followed. Intentionally or not, once unleashed, the juveniles opened the cages and let the apes run wild. The frightened animals ran amok among the screaming crowd, swung between the many trees and finally settled on the rooftop. They looked like a grotesque frieze. The clown's favorite female chimpanzee stormed up to him and threw her arms around his neck. Under his soothing grip she finally calmed down, scratched her thighs and, gripping his hand, watched the sputtering fireworks with him.

Outside the gate a large police cordon held he throng in check that had accumulated with the mounting racket. Alarmed at first, the guests soon calmed down and cheered the spectacle, their American craving for sensationalism gratified. The older ladies especially found the theatrics piquant and the younger set soon played their own games in the large, strangely lit park. The danger of exposure under a sudden fiery flare only added spice to the erotic game.

Sanna bathed in the general excitement like a fish in water. Smiling happily she eeled her slender body rhythmically through the crowd. She liked the good-looking young men and made no efforts to hide her attraction. They in turn made openly fun of her, calling her a silly goose. The older ladies liked her better. Her unconscious wantonness struck a familiar cord in their fading sensuality. Watching her with heartfelt sadness, Siv kept a happy façade and whispered to Tracbac,

Look how easily Sanna fits in.

But the clown gruffly and harshly disagreed,

She behaves like a hussy.

Suddenly Sanna spied "an extremely good-looking young man" watching her from behind the jasmine bushes. Head thrown backward and smiling blissfully, she turned toward him with outstretched arms. But on closer inspection this perfect, beautiful Greek face had eyes as cold, hard and cruel as crystals. She ran away, screaming, her arms flung over her head. The good-looking young man merely shrugged, mumbling to himself,

Poor Jac.

It was none other than doctor O'Henny, famous neurologist and specialist in mental disorders.

The party took its course, brilliant and tragic. The huge Longfellow stood by the gate, his eyes rolling wildly while shaking his fists like an angry, cursing, black sorcerer. His plants were ruined, the apes running wild, the waterfalls smashed. What was left to show his tourists? How now satisfy their curiosity and convince them of his famous master's high morals?

The clown stood in his dark entrance, his loyal ape holding his hand on one side, the world's most beautiful half-breed sitting on the other. The clown's harsh words about Sanna and his tone worried her. She whispered,

What now, Jac? Do you think that you can —

She had wanted to say "put up with it," but stopped short. The clown pondered for a while. Then he mumbled morosely,

Well. I'm a man, or try to be. What I've taken on, I'll see through. —

She waited a while. Then she said haltingly,

What if you're tired, nervous, sore — don't you think the girl will notice — ?

Again she did not complete her sentence. The clown said,

You think that I can't hide my despair?

Siv nodded. The clown meditated for a long while. He let go of his ape and it quickly disappeared. Without looking at Siv, he put both hands on her shoulders, grinned faintly and said,

Don't worry, girl — after all, I am a clown.

Siv bent forward and kissed him.

They stood together in the stark light of the fireworks. It looked like the happy ending to a well-made movie — the "happy tail" as the irreverent clown liked to call it. The audience applauded wildly.

A few days later Jac Tracbac, alias Jonathan Borck, received the news that Lillemor Längsäll had died on Sanna.